PRESIDENT LINCOLN.

THE ASSASSINATION OF PRESIDENT LINCOLN AT FORD'S THEATRE—AFTER THE ACT.

BOOTH BEING BURNT OUT OF THE BARN.

ILLUSTRATED LIFE, SERVICES, MARTYRDOM,

AND FUNERAL OF

ABRAHAM LINCOLN.

SIXTEENTH

PRESIDENT OF THE UNITED STATES.

With a Portrait of President Lincoln, and other Illustrative Engravings of the Scene of the Assassination, etc.

With a full history of his Life; Assassination; Death, and Funeral. His career as a Lawyer and Politician; his services in Congress; with his Speeches, Proclamations, Acts, and services as President of the United States, and Commander-in-Chief of the Army and Navy, from the time of his first Inauguration as President of the United States, until the night of his Assassination. Only new and complete edition, with a full history of the assassination, by distinguished eye-witnesses of it. Mr. Lincoln's Death-bed scenes, and a full account of the Funeral Ceremonies, from the time his remains were placed in the East Room at the White House, until they were finally consigued to their last resting place, in Oak Ridge Cemetery, at Springfield, Illinois; with Addresses and Sermons by the Hon. Schuyler Colfax; Hon. George Bancroft; Rev. Henry Ward Beecher; General Walbridge; Bishop Simpson, etc., with a full account of the escape, pursuit, apprehension, and death of the assassin, Booth.

Philadelphia:
T. B. PETERSON & BROTHERS,
306 CHESTNUT STREET.

CONTENTS.

LIFE AND PUBLIC SERVICES

OF

ABRAHAM LINCOLN.

HIS BIRTH AND ANCESTORS.

ABRAHAM LINCOLN, the sixteenth President of the United States, and the skilful ruler under whose wise administration the country in its hour of peril has been enabled to combat successfully with the traitors who have attempted its destruction, was born on the twelfth of February, 1809, in that part of Hardin county, Kentucky, which is now known as Larue. His father, Thomas Lincoln, and his grandfather, Abraham, were born in Rockingham county, Virginia, a section of the "Old Dominion" to which their ancestors had migrated from Berks county, Pennsylvania. In the year 1780, the grandfather removed his family to Kentucky, where, taking possession of a small tract of land in the wilderness, he erected a rude cabin, and proceeded to make his new home comfortable and productive. His daily labors were attended in their prosecution with great personal danger. There was no other resident within two or three miles, and the country was infested with Indians, who allowed no opportunity to pass to slaughter the white settlers. His gun was carried as regularly to his work as was his axe or any other implement necessary to the successful clearing of the land, and at night when he retired to the bosom of his little flock, the faithful weapon was placed in a convenient corner, where it could be quickly grasped in the event of an attack from the wily enemy.

Individuals and whole families living in the vicinity were murdered by the Indians, but Abraham Lincoln for four years escaped their bloodthirsty characteristics; but at the end of that period, while clearing a piece of land about four miles from home, he was suddenly attacked, and killed, and his scalped remains were found the next morning. The loss was a severe one to the widow, who now found herself alone in the wilderness with her three sons and two daughters, and with but little money with which to provide even the necessities of life for the young members of her household. Poverty made it necessary that the family should separate; and all the children but Thomas bade adieu to their remaining parent, and left the county, the second son removing to Indiana, and the others to other sections of Kentucky.

DESCRIPTION OF HIS PARENTS.

Thomas also left home before he was twelve years old, but subsequently returned to Kentucky, and in the year 1806, married Miss Nancy Hanks, who was also a native of Virginia; so that it will be observed nearly all of the immediate ancestors of the President were born upon Southern soil. Thomas Lincoln and his wife were a plain, unassuming couple, conscientious members of the Baptist Church, and almost entirely uneducated. Mrs. Lincoln could read, but not write, while her husband could do neither, save so far as to scribble his own name in a style of caligraphy which a few of his more intimate friends could decipher. He, however, appreciated the advantages of education, and honored and respected the superior learning of others. His kindness of heart was proverbial, and he was always industrious and persevering. His wife, although uneducated, was blessed with much natural talent, excellent judgment, and good sense, and these qualifications, with her great piety, made her a suitable partner for a man of Thomas Lincoln's attributes, and a mother whose precepts and teachings could not fail to be of vast benefit in the formation of her children's characters. This estimable couple had three children—a daughter, a son who had died in infancy, and Abraham. The sister attained the years of womanhood, and married, but subsequently died without issue.

ABE" GOES TO SCHOOL.

When Abraham, or "Abe," as he was already called at home and by his companions, was seven years of age, his name was entered for the first time on the roll of an educational institution—an academy which had but little pretension in outward appearance, and the presiding genius of which had neither ambition nor ability to impart greater instruction than that which would enable his pupils to read and write. His term of schooling was, however, to be of short duration.

THE LINCOLN FAMILY REMOVE TO INDIANA.

Mr. Lincoln, although a Southerner by birth and residence, had become early imbued with a disgust for slavery. He witnessed the evils of the "peculiar institution," and longed to be free from the disagreeable effects of a condition of society which made a poor white man even more degraded than the unfortunate negro, whose energies and labors were controlled by an unprincipled and lazy master. With these sentiments he naturally desired to change his place of residence, and early in October, 1816, finding a purchaser for his farm, he made arrangements for the transfer of the property and for his removal. The price paid by the purchaser was ten barrels of whiskey, of forty gallons each, valued at two hundred and eighty dollars, and twenty dollars in money. Mr. Lincoln was a temperate man, and acceded to the terms, not because he desired the liquor, but because such transactions in real estate were common, and recognized as perfectly proper.

The homestead was within a mile or two of the Rolling Fork river, and as soon as the sale was effected, Mr. Lincoln, with such slight assistance as little Abe could give him, hewed out a flat-boat, and launching it, filled it with his household articles and tools and the barrels of whiskey, and bidding adieu to his son who stood upon the bank, pushed off, and was soon floating down the stream on his way to Indiana, to select a new home. His journey down the Rolling Fork and into the Ohio river was successfully accomplished, but soon afterwards his boat was unfortunately upset, and its cargo thrown into the water. Some men standing on the bank witnessed the accident and saved the boat and its owner, but all the contents of the craft were lost except a few carpenter's tools, axes, three barrels of whiskey and some other articles. He again started, and proceeded to a well-known ferry on the river, from whence he was guided into the interior by a resident of the section of country in which he had landed, and to whom he had given his boat in payment for his services. After several days of difficult travelling, much of the time employed in cutting a road through the forest wide enough for a team, eighteen miles were accomplished, and Spencer county, Indiana, was reached. The site for his new home having been determined upon, Mr. Lincoln left his goods under the care of a person who lived a few miles distant, and returning to Kentucky on foot, made preparations to remove his family. In a few days the party bade farewell to their old home and slavery, Mrs. Lincoln and her daughter riding one horse, Abe another, and the father a third. After a seven days' journey through an uninhabited country, their resting-place at night being a blanket spread upon the ground, they arrived at the spot selected for their future residence, and no unnecessary delays were permitted to interfere with the immediate and successful clearing of a site for a cabin. An axe was placed in Abe's hands, and with the additional assistance of a neighbor, in two or three days Mr. Lincoln had a neat house of about eighteen feet square, the logs composing which being fastened together in the usual manner by notches, and the cracks between them filled with mud. It had only one room, but some slabs laid across logs overhead gave additional accommodations which were obtained by climbing a rough ladder in one corner. A bed, table and four stools were then made by the two settlers, father and son, and the building was ready for occupancy. The loft was Abe's bedroom, and there night after night for many years, he who now occupies the most exalted position in the gift of the American people, and who dwells in the "White House" at Washington, surrounded by all the comforts that wealth and power can give, slumbered with one coarse blanket for his mattress and another for his covering. Although busy during the ensuing winter with his axe, he did not neglect his reading and spelling, and also practised frequently with a rifle, the first evidence of his skill as a marksman being manifested, much to the delight of his parents, in the killing of a wild turkey, which had approached too near the cabin. The knowledge of the use of the rifle was indispensable in the border settlements at that time, as the greater portion of the food required for the settlers was procured by it, and the family which had not among its male members one or more who could discharge it with accuracy, was very apt to suffer from a scarcity of comestibles.

DEATH OF MRS. LINCOLN—"ABE" LEARNS TO WRITE.

A little more than a year after removing to Spencer county, Mrs. Lincoln died, an event which brought desolation to the hearts of her husband and children, but to none so much as to Abe. He had been a dutiful son, and she one of the most devoted of mothers, and to her instruction may be traced many of those traits and characteristics for which even now he is remarkable. Soon after her death, the bereaved lad had an offer which promised to afford him other employment during the long, monotonous evenings, than the reading of books, a young man who had removed into the neighborhood having offered to teach him how to write. The opportunity was too fraught with benefit to be rejected, and after a few weeks of practice under the eye of his instructor, and also out of doors with a piece of chalk or charred stick, he was able to write his name, and in less than twelve months could and did write a letter.

HIS FATHER MARRIES AGAIN—ABE FINISHES HIS EDUCATION.

During the next year Mr. Lincoln married Mrs. Sally Johnston, of Elizabethtown, Kentucky, a widow-lady with three children, and who was admirably adapted to supply the vacancy which existed in the Lincoln family; and a superior woman, between whom and Abe a most devoted attachment sprung up, which ever afterwards continued. About the same time a person named Crawford moved into the neighborhood, and understanding how to read and write and the rudiments of arithmetic, was induced to open a school, to which Abe was sent, and in which he greatly improved his knowledge of the first two branches, and soon mastered the second. His school-garb comprised a suit of dressed buckskin and a cap made from a raccoon skin. His memory was retentive, and as he took an unusual pride in his studies, his close application made him a favorite scholar with his teacher, while his superior knowledge, limited though it was, caused him to be used by the more ignorant settlers as their scribe whenever they had letters to be written. A brief period at this school, and to use a fashionable phrase, his education was finished. Six months of instruction within the walls of an insignificant school-house is all the education that Abraham Lincoln has received during a long lifetime, a greater portion of which has been spent in public positions, where ability and talent were indispensable requisites.

BECOMES A HIRED HAND ON A FLATBOAT.

For four or five years after leaving school, or until he was eighteen, he constantly labored in the woods with his axe, cutting down trees and splitting rails, and during the evenings, read such works as he could borrow from the other settlers. A year later, he was hired by a man living near by, at ten dollars a month, to go to New Orleans on a flatboat loaded with stores, which were destined for sale at the plantations on the Mississippi river, near the Crescent City, and with but one companion started on his rather dangerous journey. At night they tied up alongside of the bank, and rested upon the hard deck with a blanket for a covering, and during the hours of light, whether their lonely trip was cheered by a bright sun or made disagreeable in the extreme by violent storms, their craft floated down the stream, its helmsmen never for a moment losing their spirits, or regretting their acceptance of the positions they occupied. Nothing occurred to mar the success of the trip, nor the excitement naturally incident to a flatboat expedition of some eighteen hundred miles, save a midnight attack bv a party of negroes, who, after a severe conflict, were whipped by Abe and his comrade and compelled to flee, and after selling their goods at a handsome profit, the young merchants returned to Indiana.

THE FAMILY REMOVE TO ILLINOIS—ABE SEEKS HIS FORTUNE AMONG STRANGERS.

In March, 1830, Mr. Thomas Lincoln removed his family to Illinois, their household articles being transported thither in large wagons drawn by oxen, Abe himself driving one of the teams. Upon the journey, and while crossing the bottom lands of the Kaskaskia river, the males of the family were compelled to wade through water up to their waists. In two weeks they reached Decatur, Macon county, Illinois, near the centre of that State, and in another day were at the tract of land (ten acres) on the north side of the Sangamon river, and about ten miles west of Decatur. A log cabin was immediately erected, and Abe proceeded to split the rails for the fence with which the lot was to be enclosed. As a rail-splitter, as a tiller of the soil, or as a huntsman, to whose accuracy of aim the family depended in a great measure for their daily food, young Abraham Lincoln was active, earnest and laborious, and when in the following spring he signified his intention to leave his home to seek his fortune among strangers, the tidings were received by his parents and friends with the most profound sorrow.

Confident that a more extended field of observation and action would be more suitable to his tastes and disposition, he packed up what little clothing he possessed, and went westward into Menard county. He worked on a farm in the vicinity of Petersburg, during the ensuing summer and winter, at the same time improving himself, in read ing, writing, grammar, and arithmetic.

HE TAKES ANOTHER TRIP TO NEW ORLEANS—BECOMES MILLER AND SALESMAN.

Early in the following spring he was hired by a man named Offutt, to assist in taking a flatboat to New Orleans; and, as it was found impossible to purchase a suitable boat, Abe lent a willing and industrious hand in building one at Sangamon, from whence, when completed, it was floated into the Mississippi river. The trip was made, and his employer was so much gratified with the industry and tact of his hired hand, that he engaged him to take charge of his mill and store in the village of New Salem. In this position, "Honest Abe," as he was now called, won the respect and confidence of all with whom he had business dealings, while socially, he was much beloved by the residents—young and old—of the place. He was affable, generous, ever ready to assist the needy or to sympathize with the distressed, and never was known to be guilty of a dishonorable act.

HIS SERVICES IN THE BLACK HAWK WAR.

Early in the following year the Black Hawk War broke out, and the Governor of Illinois calling for troops, Abe determined to offer his services; and a recruiting station being opened in New Salem, he placed his name the first on the roll; and by his influence inducing many of his friends and companions to do likewise, a company was soon organized, and Abe was unanimously elected captain. The company marched to Beardstown, and from there to the seat of war; but during their term of enlistment—thirty days—were not called into active service. A new levy was then called for, and he re-enlisted as a private, and at the end of thirty days again re-enlisted, and remained with his regiment until the war ended.

IS NOMINATED FOR THE LEGISLATURE AND IS DEFEATED.

Soon after his return from this campaign, in the progress of which he proved himself an efficient and zealous soldier, although his regiment was not brought in conflict with the enemy, or as he subsequently expressed it, he "did not see any live fighting Indians, but had a good many bloody struggles with the mosquitoes," he was waited upon by several of the influential citizens of New Salem, who asked his consent to nominate him for the Legislature. He had only been a resident of the county for nine months, but as a thorough-going "Henry Clay man" was needed, he was deemed the most suitable person to run, particularly as it was believed that his popularity would ensure success in a county which had, the year before, given General Jackson a large majority for President. There were eight aspirants for the legislative position; but, although Abraham received two hundred and seventy-seven votes out of two hundred and eighty-four, cast in New Salem, he was not elected, the successful candidate leading him a few votes.

BECOMES A MERCHANT AND SURVEYOR.

Soon after his political defeat he engaged in the mercantile business, but in a few months sold out, and under the tuition of John Calhoun (in later years President of the Lecompton Constitutional Convention) became proficient in surveying, an occupation which for more than a year he found very remunerative for a novice. He was also for a time Postmaster of New Salem.

IS ELECTED TO THE LEGISLATURE—STUDIES LAW

In August, 1834, he was again nominated for the Legislature, and was elected by a large majority; and in 1836,

1838, and 1840, was re-elected. While attending the proceedings of the first session, he determined to become a lawyer, and being placed in possession of the necessary books through the kindness of the Hon. John T. Stuart, applied himself to study, and in 1836 was admitted to practice at the bar. In April, 1837, he removed to Springfield, and became a partner of Mr. Stuart.

A THRILLING INCIDENT IN HIS LEGAL CAREER.

One instance which occurred during his early legal practice is worthy of extended publication. At a camp meeting held in Menard county, a fight took place which ended in the murder of one of the participants in the quarrel. A young man named Armstrong, a son of the aged couple for whom many years before Abraham Lincoln had worked, was charged with the deed, and being arrested and examined, a true bill was found against him, and he was lodged in jail to await his trial. As soon as Mr. Lincoln received intelligence of the affair, he addressed a kind letter to Mrs. Armstrong, stating his anxiety that her son should have a fair trial, and offering in return for her kindness to him while in adverse circumstances some years before, his services gratuitously. Investigation convinced the volunteer attorney that the young man was the victim of a conspiracy, and he determined to postpone the case until the excitement had subsided. The day of trial however finally arrived, and the accuser testified positively that he saw the accused plunge the knife into the heart of the murdered man. He remembered all the circumstances perfectly; the murder was committed about half-past nine o'clock at night, and the moon was shining brightly. Mr. Lincoln reviewed all the testimony carefully, and then proved conclusively that the moon which the accuser had sworn was shining brightly, did not rise until an hour or more after the murder was committed. Other discrepancies were exposed, and in thirty minutes after the jury retired they returned with a verdict of "Not Guilty."

A PROTEST AGAINST SLAVERY.

On the third of March, 1837, a protest was presented to the House of Representatives of Illinois and signed by "Daniel Stone and Abraham Lincoln, Representatives from Sangamon county," which is the first record that we have of the sentiments of the subject of our sketch on the slavery question. It was in opposition to a series of resolutions which had been adopted, taking an extreme Southern view of slavery, for which Mr. Lincoln refused to vote, and subsequently handed in the protest.

IS A CANDIDATE FOR PRESIDENTIAL ELECTOR.

In every campaign from 1836 to 1852, he was a Whig candidate for Presidential Elector, and in 1844, he stumped the entire State of Illinois for Henry Clay; and then crossing the line into Indiana, spoke daily to immense gatherings, until the day of election. His style of speaking was pleasing to the masses of the people, and his earnest appeals were not only well received, but were productive of much benefit to his favorite candidate. Accustomed from early childhood to the habits and peculiarities of all kinds and conditions of men—the refined and the vulgar, the intelligent and the illiterate, the rich and the poor—he knew exactly what particular style of language best suited his hearers, and the result was that he was always listened to with a degree of attention and interest which few political speakers receive.

MR. LINCOLN ELECTED TO CONGRESS—HIS VOTES AND SPEECHES DURING HIS CONGRESSIONAL TERM.

In 1846, Mr. Lincoln was elected to Congress from the

Central District of Illinois, by a majority of over fifteen hundred votes, the largest ever given in that District to any candidate opposed to the Democratic party. Illinois elected seven Representatives that year; and all were Democrats but Mr. Lincoln. He took his seat on the first Monday of December, 1847, and during the exciting session that followed, cast his vote *pro* or *con* on every important question, and on more than one occasion displayed his eloquence and superior argumentative ability. One of his first votes was given on the twentieth of December in favor of the following resolution:

"*Resolved*, That if, in the judgment of Congress, it be necessary to improve the navigation of a river to expedite and render secure the movements of our army, and save from delay and loss our arms and munitions of war, that Congress has the power to improve such river.

"*Resolved*, That if it be necessary for the preservation of the lives of our seamen, repairs, safety, or maintenance of our vessels-of-war, to improve a harbor or inlet, either on our Atlantic or Lake coast, Congress has the power to make such improvement."

On the twenty-second of the same month, he voted in favor of a similar resolution, and on the same day offered the following series of resolutions, which he introduced with one of his characteristic speeches, humorous at one moment and logical at the next. Although, like the large majority of the Whig party opposed to the declaration of war with Mexico by the President, he never failed to vote for any resolution or bill which had for its object the sending of supplies to our troops who had been ordered to the seat of war. The resolutions read as follows:

"*Whereas*, The President of the United States, in his message of May 11th, 1846, has declared 'that the Mexican Government not only refused to receive him (the envoy of the United States) or listen to his propositions, but, after a long-continued series of menaces, have at last invaded our territory and shed the blood of our fellow-citizens on our own soil.'

"And again, in his message of December 8th, 1846, that 'we

had ample cause of war against Mexico long before the breaking out of hostilities, but even then we forbore to take redress into our own hands until Mexico herself became the aggressor by invading our soil in hostile array, and shedding the blood of our citizens.'

"And yet again, in the message of December 7th, 1847, that 'the Mexican Government refused even to hear the terms of adjustment which he (our minister of peace) was authorized to propose; and, finally, under wholly unjustifiable pretexts, involved the two countries in war by invading the territory of the State of Texas, striking the first blow, and shedding the blood of our citizens on our own soil.'

"*And whereas*, This House is desirous to obtain a full knowledge of all the facts which go to establish whether the particular spot on which the blood of our citizens was so shed, was or was not at that time our own soil. Therefore,

"*Resolved, by the House of Representatives*, That the President of the United States be respectfully requested to inform this House,

"*1st*. Whether the spot on which the blood of our citizens was shed, as in his messages declared, was or was not within the Territory of Spain, at least after the treaty of 1819, until the Mexican revolution.

"*2nd*. Whether that spot is or is not within the territory which was wrested from Spain by the revolutionary Government of Mexico.

"*3rd*. Whether that spot is or is not within a settlement of people, which settlement has existed ever since long before the Texas revolution, and until its inhabitants fled before the approach of the United States Army.

"*4th*. Whether that settlement is or is not isolated from any and all other settlements by the Gulf and the Rio Grande on the south and west, and by wide uninhabited regions on the north and east.

"*5th*. Whether the people of that settlement, or a majority of them, or any of them, have ever submitted themselves to the Government or laws of Texas or of the United States, by consent or by compulsion, either by accepting office, or voting at elections, or paying tax or serving on juries, or having process served upon them, or in any other way.

"*6th*. Whether the people of that settlement did or did not flee from the approach of the United States Army, leaving unprotected their homes and their growing crops, before the blood was shed, as in the message stated; and whether the first blood, so shed, was or was not shed within the enclosure of one of the people who had thus fled from it.

"*7th*. Whether our citizens, whose blood was shed, as in his messages declared, were or were not, at that time, armed officers and soldiers, sent into that settlement by the military order of the President, through the Secretary of War.

"*8th.* Whether the military force of the United States was or was not so sent into that settlement after General Taylor had more than once intimated to the War Department that, in his opinion, no such movement was necessary to the defence or protection of Texas."

On several occasions during the session, he voted for the reception of petitions and memorials in favor of the abolition of slavery in the District of Columbia, against the slave-trade, and advocating the prohibition of slavery in the territory that might be acquired from Mexico.

On the seventeenth of February, 1848, Mr. Lincoln voted for a Loan bill reported by the Committee of Ways and Means, authorizing the raising of sixteen millions of dollars to enable the Government to provide for its debts, principally incurred in Mexico.

On the eleventh of May, in moving to reconsider a vote by which a bill having reference to the public lands had passed, he made the following remarks:

"He stated to the House that he had made this motion for the purpose of obtaining an opportunity to say a few words in relation to a point raised in the course of the debate on this bill, which he would now proceed to make, if in order. The point in the case to which he referred, arose on the amendment that was submitted by the gentleman from Vermont (Mr. Collamer), in Committee of the Whole on the State of the Union, and which was afterwards renewed in the House, in relation to the question whether the reserved sections, which, by some bills heretofore passed, by which an appropriation of land had been made to Wisconsin, had been enhanced in value, should be reduced to the minimum price of the public lands. The question of the reduction in value of those sections was, to him, at this time, a matter very nearly of indifference. He was inclined to desire that Wisconsin should be obliged by having it reduced. But the gentleman from Indiana (Mr. C. B. Smith), the Chairman of the Committee on the Territories, associated that question with the general question, which is now, to some extent, agitated in Congress, of making appropriations of alternate sections of land to aid the States in making internal improvements and enhancing the prices of the section reserved, and the gen tleman from Indiana took ground against that policy. He did not make any special argument in favor of Wisconsin; but he took ground generally against the policy of giving alternate sections of land, and enhancing the price of the reserved sections. Now, he (Mr. L.) did not at this time, take the floor for the purpose of attempting to make an argument on the general subject. He rose simply to protest against the doctrine which the gentleman from Indiana had avowed in the course of what he (Mr. L.) could not but consider an unsound argument.

"It might however be true, for any thing he knew, that the gentleman from Indiana might convince him that his argument was sound; but he (Mr. L.) feared that gentleman would not be able to convince a majority in Congress that it was sound. It was true, the question appeared in a different aspect to persons in consequence of a difference in the point from which they looked at it. It did not look to persons residing east of the mountains as it did to those who lived among the public lands. But, for his part, he would state that if Congress would make a donation of alternate sections of public lands for the purpose of internal improvement in his State, and forbid the reserved sections being sold at $1.25, he should be glad to see the appropriation made, though he should prefer it if the reserved sections were not enhanced in price. He repeated, he should be glad to have such appropriations made, even though the reserved sections should be enhanced in price. He did not wish to be understood as concurring in any intimation that they would refuse to receive such an appropriation of alternate sections of land because a condition enhancing the price of the reserved sections should be attached thereto. He believed his position would now be understood, if not, he feared he should not be able to make himself understood.

"But before he took his seat he would remark that the Senate, during the present session, had passed a bill making appropriations of land on that principle for the benefit of the State in which he resided—the State of Illinois. The alternate sections were to be given for the purpose of constructing roads, and the reserved sections were to be enhanced in value in consequence. When the bill came here for the action of this House, it had been received, and was now before the Committee on Public Lands—he desired much to see it passed as it was, if it could be put in a more favorable form for the State of Illinois. When it should be before this House, if any member from a section of the Union in which these lands did not lie, whose interest might be less than that which he felt, should propose a reduction of the price of the reserved sections to $1.25, he should be much obliged; but he did not think it would be well for those who came from the section of the Union in which the lands lay, to do so. He wished it, then, to be understood, that he did not join in the warfare against the principle which had engaged the minds of some members of Congress who were favorable to improvements in the western country.

"There was a good deal of force, he admitted, in what fell from the Chairman of the Committee on Territories. It might be that there was no precise justice in raising the price of the reserved sections to $2.50 per acre. It might be proper that the price should be enhanced to some extent, though not to double the usual price; but he should be glad to have such an appropriation with the reserved sections at $2.50; he should be better pleased to have the price of those sections at something less; and he should be still better pleased to have them without any enhancement at all.

"There was one portion of the argument of the gentleman from Indiana, the Chairman of the Committee on Territories (Mr. Smith), which he wished to take occasion to say that he did not view as unsound. He alluded to the statement that the General Government was interested in these internal improvements being made, inasmuch as they increased the value of the lands that were unsold, and they enabled the Government to sell lands which could not be sold without them. Thus, then, the Government gained by internal improvements, as well as by the general good which the people derived from them, and it might be, therefore, that the lands should not be sold for more than $1.50, instead of the price being doubled. He, however, merely mentioned this in passing, for he only rose to state, as the principle of giving these lands for the purposes which he had mentioned had been laid hold of and considered favorably, and as there were some gentlemen who had constitutional scruples about giving money for these purposes, who would not hesitate to give land, that he was not willing to have it understood that he was one of those who made war against that principle. This was all he desired to say, and having accomplished the object with which he rose, he withdrew his motion to reconsider."

On the nineteenth of the following month he first had an opportunity to record his views upon the Tariff question, by voting in favor of a resolution instructing the Committee of Ways and Means to inquire into the expediency of reporting a bill increasing the duties on foreign luxuries of all kinds, and on "such foreign manufactures as are now coming into ruinous competition with American labor." He subsequently voted for a resolution instructing the Committee of Ways and Means to inquire into the expediency of reporting a Tariff bill based upon the principles of the Tariff of 1842.

On the 28th of July, 1848, the celebrated bill establishing Territorial governments for Oregon, California and New Mexico, the peculiar feature of which was a provision prohibiting the Legislatures of California and New Mexico from passing laws in favor of or against slavery, and providing that the laws of the Legislatures should be subject to the sanction of Congress, was argued, and after an exciting debate, laid on the table, Mr. Lincoln voting with Mr. Webster, Mr. Corwin, and other illustrious colleagues for this disposition of the bill.

On the sixteenth of January, 1849, Mr. Lincoln offered the following substitute for a resolution which he had voted against, not being satisfied with all its provisions:

"*Resolved*, That the Committee on the District of Columbia be instructed to report a bill in substance, as follows:

"*Sec.* 1. *Be it enacted by the Senate and House of Representatives of the United States in Congress assembled*, That no person not now within the District of Columbia, nor now owned by any person or persons now resident within it, nor hereafter born within it, shall ever be held in slavery within said District.

"*Sec.* 2. That no person now within said District, or now owned by any person or persons now resident within the same, or hereafter born within it, shall ever be held in slavery without the limits of said District: Provided, That officers of the Government of the United States, being citizens of the slaveholding States, coming into said District on public business, and remaining only so long as may be reasonably necessary for that object, may be attended into and out of said District, and while there, by the necessary servants of themselves and their families, without their right to hold such servants in service being impaired.

"*Sec.* 3. That all children born of slave mothers within said District, on or after the 1st day of January, in the year of our Lord 1850, shall be free; but shall be reasonably supported and educated by the respective owners of their mothers, or by their heirs or representatives, and shall serve reasonable service as apprentices to such owners, heirs, or representatives, until they respectively arrive at the age of ——— years, when they shall be entirely free: And the municipal authorities of Washington and Georgetown, within their respective jurisdictional limits, are hereby empowered and required to make all suitable and necessary provision for enforcing obedience to this section, on the part of both masters and apprentices.

"*Sec.* 4. That all persons now within this District, lawfully held as slaves, or now owned by any person or persons now resident within said District, shall remain such at the will of their respective owners, their heirs or legal representatives: Provided that such owner, or his legal representatives, may at any time receive from the Treasury of the United States the full value of his or her slave, of the class in this section mentioned, upon which such slave shall be forthwith and forever free: And provided further, That the President of the United States, the Secretary of State, and the Secretary of the Treasury, shall be a board for determining the value of such slaves as their owners desire to emancipate under this section, and whose duty it shall be to hold a session for the purpose on the first Monday of each calendar month, to receive all applications, and, on satisfactory evidence in each case that the person presented for valuation is a slave, and of the class in the section mentioned, and is owned by the applicant, shall value such slave at his or her full cash value, and give to the applicant an order on the Treasury for the amount, and also to such slave a certificate of freedom.

"*Sec.* 5. That the municipal authorities of Washington and Georgetown, within their respective jurisdictional limits, are hereby empowered and required to provide active and efficient means to arrest and deliver up to their owners all fugitive slaves escaping into said District.

"*Sec.* 6. That the elective officers within said District of Columbia are hereby empowered and required to open polls at all the usual places of holding elections, on the first Monday of April next, and receive the vote of every free white male citizen above the age of twenty-one years, having resided within said District for the period of one year or more next preceding the time of such voting for or against this act, to proceed in taking said votes in all respects not herein specified, as at elections under the municipal laws, and with as little delay as possible to transmit correct statements of the votes so cast to the President of the United States; and it shall be the duty of the President to count such votes immediately, and if a majority of them be found to be for this act, to forthwith issue his proclamation giving notice of the fact; and this act shall only be in full force and effect on and after the day of such proclamation.

"*Sec.* 7. That involuntary servitude for the punishment of crime, whereof the party shall have been duly convicted, shall in nowise be prohibited by this act.

"*Sec.* 8. That for all purposes of this act, the jurisdictional limits of Washington are extended to all parts of the District of Columbia not included within the present limits of Georgetown."

We have given a sufficient record of Mr. Lincoln's services as a Representative in Congress, to show that in his numerous votes and remarks upon the slavery question, he was uniformly consistent, and a determined opponent to that peculiar institution which, Mr. Corwin truly remarked, was an exotic that blights with its shade the soil in which it is planted. He with almost equal determination opposed the annexation of Texas, and voted more than forty different times in favor of the Wilmot Proviso.

BECOMES A DELEGATE TO THE NATIONAL CONVENTION OF 1848.

In the Whig National Convention of 1848, he was an active delegate, and earnestly advocated the selection of General Zachary Taylor as the nominee for the Presidency, and during the canvass which followed, he traversed the States of Indiana and Illinois, speaking in behalf of his favorite candidate and the choice of his party.

HE IS NOMINATED FOR UNITED STATES SENATOR, BUT WITHDRAWS.

In 1849 he was a candidate before the Legislature of Illinois for United States Senator, but his political opponents being in the majority, General Shields was chosen. From that time until 1854, he confined himself almost exclusively to the practice of his profession, but in that year he again entered the political arena, and battled indefatigably in the celebrated campaign which resulted in victory for the first time to the opposition of the Democratic party in Illinois, and gave that State a Republican Legislature, and sent Mr. Trumbull to the United States Senate. During the canvass, Mr. Lincoln was frequently brought into controversy upon the stand with Stephen A. Douglas, one of the discussions, that was held on the fourth of October, 1854, during the progress of the annual State Fair, being particularly remarkable as *the* great discussion of the campaign.

At the election of United States Senator, nine-tenths of the majority were Whigs and in favor of Mr. Lincoln, and the other tenth were Democrats, but not in favor of voting for a Whig, and for the purpose of securing the success of a man whom he knew was opposed to the Nebraska bill, and thus preventing the election of a third person who had little or nothing in common with the Republican party, which was then in its conception, he entreated his friends to vote for Mr. Trumbull. Mr. Lincoln was subsequently offered the nomination for Governor of Illinois, but declined the honor in favor of Mr. Bissell; was also presented, but ineffectually, at the first Republican National Convention for Vice-President; and at the next Presidential election headed the Fremont electoral ticket, and labored industriously in support of that candidate.

AGAIN NOMINATED FOR THE SENATE—HIS SPEECHES IN THE CELEBRATED LINCOLN-DOUGLAS CAMPAIGN.

On the second of June, 1858, the Republican State Convention met at Springfield, and nominated Mr. Lincoln as their candidate for the United States Senate. At the close of their proceedings the honored recipient of their suffrage delivered a speech, which was a forcible exposition of the views and aims of the party of which he was to be the standard-bearer.

The contest which followed was one of the most exciting and remarkable ever witnessed in this country. Mr Stephen A. Douglas, his opponent, had few superiors as a political debater, and while he had made many enemies by his course upon the Nebraska bill, his personal popularity had been greatly increased by his independence, and by the opposition manifested to him by the Administration. His re-election, however, to the Senate would have been equivalent to an indorsement of his acts and views by his Commonwealth, and at the same time would have promoted his prospects for the Presidential nomination. The Republicans, therefore, determined to defeat him if possible, and to increase the probabilities of success in the movement, selected Mr. Lincoln as the man who was most certain of securing the election. Illinois was stumped throughout its length and breadth by both candidates and their respective advocates, and the people of the entire country watched with interest the struggle. From county to county, township to township, and village to village, the two leaders travelled, frequently in the same car or carriage, and in the presence of immense crowds of men, women and children—for the wives and daughters of the hardy yeomanry were naturally interested—face to face, these two opposing champions argued the important points of their political belief, and contended nobly for the mastery.

During the campaign, Mr. Lincoln paid the following tribute to the Declaration of Independence

"These communities, (the thirteen colonies,) by their representatives in old Independence Hall, said to the world of men, 'We hold these truths to be self-evident, that all men are born equal; that they are endowed by their Creator with inalienable rights; that among these are life, liberty, and the pursuit of happiness.' This was their majestic interpretation of the economy of the universe. This was their lofty, and wise, and noble understanding of the justice of the Creator to His creatures. Yes, gentlemen, to all His creatures, to the whole great family of man. In their enlightened belief, nothing stamped with the Divine image and likeness was sent into the world to be trodden on, and degraded, and imbruted by its fellows. They grasped not only the race of men then living, but they reached forward and seized upon the furthest posterity. They created a beacon to guide their children and their children's children, and the countless myriads who should inhabit the earth in other ages. Wise statesmen as they were, they knew the tendency of prosperity to breed tyrants, and so they established these great self-evident truths that when, in the distant future, some man, some faction, some interest, should set up the doctrine that none but rich men, or none but white men, or none but Anglo-Saxon white men, were entitled to life, liberty, and the pursuit of happiness, their posterity might look up again to the Declaration of Independence, and take courage to renew the battle which their fathers began, so that truth, and justice and mercy, and all the humane and Christian virtues might not be extinguished from the land; so that no man would hereafter dare to limit and circumscribe the great principles on which the temple of liberty was being built.

"Now, my countrymen, if you have been taught doctrines conflicting with the great landmarks of the Declaration of Independence; if you have listened to suggestions which would take away from its grandeur, and mutilate the fair symmetry of its proportions; if you have been inclined to believe that all men are not created equal in those inalienable rights enumerated by our chart of liberty, let me entreat you to come back—return to the fountain whose waters spring close by the blood of the Revolution. Think nothing of me, take no thought for the political fate of any man whomsoever, but come back to the truths that are in the Declaration of Independence.

"You may do any thing with me you choose, if you will but heed these sacred principles. You may not only defeat me for the Senate, but you may take me and put me to death. While pretending no indifference to earthly honors, I *do claim* to be actuated in this contest by something higher than an anxiety for office. I charge you to drop every paltry and insignificant thought for any man's success. It is nothing; I am nothing; Judge Douglas is nothing. *But do not destroy that immortal emblem of humanity—the Declaration of American Independence.*"

PEN-PORTRAITS OF ABRAHAM LINCOLN.

As we have stated, the exciting struggle was watched with intense interest, not only by the members of the respective political parties of which the two orators were recognized leaders and champions, but by that portion of the different communities of the Union who do not generally trouble their minds with political contests. Copious extracts from the speeches of both Mr. Lincoln and Mr. Douglas were published in the journals of the day, and criticisms of the orators and their discussions appeared in the leading magazines and newspapers.

From some of the latter we select the following, for the purpose of showing in what estimation the talents and ability of the honorable subject of our sketch were held at the time of which we now more particularly speak, and to give those readers of this work who have not had the opportunity to see Mr. Lincoln, an idea of his personal appearance :

One writer gives the following pen-portrait:

"Mr. Lincoln stands six feet and four inches high in his stockings. His frame is not muscular, but gaunt and wiry; his arms are long, but not unreasonably so for a person of his height; his lower limbs are not disproportioned to his body. In walking, his gait, though firm, is never brisk. He steps slowly and deliberately, almost always with his head inclined forward, and his hands clasped behind his back. In matters of dress he is by no means precise. Always clean, he is never fashionable; he is careless, but not slovenly. In manner he is remarkably cordial, and, at the same time, simple. His politeness is always sincere, but never elaborate and oppressive. A warm shake of the hand, and a warmer smile of recognition, are his methods of greeting his friends. At rest, his features, though those of a man of mark, are not such as belong to a handsome man; but when his fine dark gray eyes are lighted up by any emotion, and his features begin their play, he would be chosen from among a crowd as one who had in him not only the kindly sentiments which women love, but the heavier metal of which full-grown men and Presidents are made. His hair is black, and though thin is wiry. His head sits well on his shoulders, but beyond that it defies description. It nearer resembles that of Clay than that of Webster; but it is unlike either. It is very large, and, phrenologically, well proportioned, betokening power in all its developments. A slightly Roman nose, a wide-cut mouth, and a dark complexion, with the appearance of having been weather-beaten, complete the description.

"In his personal habits, Mr. Lincoln is as simple as a child. He loves a good dinner, and eats with the appetite which goes with a great brain; but his food is plain and nutritious. He never drinks intoxicating liquors of any sort, not even a glass of wine. He is not addicted to tobacco in any of its shapes. He never was accused of a licentious act in all his life. He never uses profane language.

"A friend says that once, when in a towering rage, in consequence of the efforts of certain parties to perpetrate a fraud on the State, he was heard to say: 'They sha'n't do it, d—n 'em!' but beyond an expression of that kind, his bitterest feelings never carry him. He never gambles; we doubt if he ever indulges in any games of chance. He is particularly cautious about incurring pecuniary obligations for any purpose whatever, and in debt, he is never content until the score is discharged. We presume he owes no man a dollar. He never speculates. The rage for the sudden acquisition of wealth never took hold of him. His gains from his profession have been moderate, but sufficient for his purposes. While others have dreamed of gold, he has been in pursuit of knowledge. In all his dealings he has the reputation of being generous but exact, and, above all, religiously honest. He would be a bold man who would say that Abraham Lincoln ever wronged any one out of a cent, or ever spent a dollar that he had not honestly earned. His struggles in early life have made him careful of money; but his generosity with his own is proverbial. He is a regular attendant upon religious worship, and though not a communicant, is a pew-holder and liberal supporter of the Presbyterian Church, in Springfield, to which Mrs. Lincoln belongs. He is a scrupulous teller of the truth—too exact in his notions to suit the atmosphere of Washington, as it now is. His enemies may say that he tells Black Republican lies; but no man ever charged that, in a professional capacity, or as a citizen dealing with his neighbors, he would depart from the Scriptural command. At home, he lives like a gentleman of modest means and simple tastes. A good-sized house of wood, simply but tastefully furnished, surrounded by trees and flowers, is his own, and there he lives, at peace with himself, the idol of his family, and for his honesty, ability, and patriotism, the admiration of his countrymen."

Another person gives the subjoined sketch of him:

"In personal appearance, Mr. Lincoln, or, as he is more familiarly termed among those who know him best, 'Old Uncle Abe,' is long, lean, and wiry. In motion he has a great deal of the elasticity and awkwardness which indicates the rough training of his early life, and his conversation savors strongly of Western idioms and pronunciation. His height is six feet four inches. His complexion is about that of an octoroon; his face, without being by any means beautiful, is genial-looking, and good humor seems to lurk in every corner of its innumerable angles. He has dark hair tinged with gray, a good forehead, small eyes, a long penetrating nose, with nostrils such as Napoleon always liked to find in his best generals, because they indicated a long head and clear thoughts; and a mouth, which, aside from being of magnificent proportions, is probably the most expressive feature of his face.

"As a speaker he is ready, precise, and fluent. His manner before a popular assembly is as he pleases to make it, being either superlatively ludicrous, or very impressive. He employs but little gesticulation, but when he desires to make a point, produces a shrug of his shoulders, an elevation of his eyebrows, a depression of his mouth, and a general malformation of countenance so comically awkward that it never fails to 'bring down the house.' His enunciation is slow and emphatic, and his voice, though sharp and powerful, at times has a frequent tendency to dwindle into a shrill and unpleasant sound ; but as before stated, the peculiar characteristic of his delivery is the remarkable mobility of his features, the frequent contortions of which excite a merriment his words could not produce."

A third says :

"In perhaps the severest test that could have been applied to any man's temper—his political contest with Senator Douglas in 1858—Mr. Lincoln not only proved himself an able speaker and a good tactician, but demonstrated that it is possible to carry on the fiercest political warfare without once descending to rude personality and course denunciation. We have it on the authority of a gentleman who followed Abraham Lincoln throughout the whole of that campaign, that, in spite of all the temptations to an opposite course to which he was continuously exposed, no personalities against his opponent, no vituperation or coarseness, ever defiled his lips. His kind and genial nature lifted him above a resort to any such weapons of political warfare, and it was the commonly-expressed regret of fiercer natures that he treated his opponent too courteously and urbanely. Vulgar personalities and vituperation are the last thing that can be truthfully charged against Abraham Lincoln. His heart is too genial, his good sense too strong, and his innate self-respect too predominant to permit him to indulge in them. His nobility of nature—and we may use the term advisedly—has been as manifest throughout his whole career as his temperate habits, his self-reliance, and his mental and intellectual power."

And a fourth, a distinguished scholar, after listening to a speech delivered at Galesburgh, thus wrote :

"The men are entirely dissimilar. Mr. Douglas is a thick-set, finely-built, courageous man, and has an air of self-confidence that does not a little to inspire his supporters with hope. Mr. Lincoln is a tall, lank man, awkward, apparently diffident, and when not speaking has neither firmness in his countenance nor fire in his eye.

"Mr. Lincoln has a rich, silvery voice, enunciates with great distinctness, and has a fine command of language. He commenced by a review of the points Mr. Douglas had made. In this he showed great tact, and his retorts, though gentlemanly, were sharp, and reached to the core the subject in dispute. While he gave but little time to the work of review, we did not feel that any thing was omitted which deserved attention.

"He then proceeded to defend the Republican party. Here he charged Mr. Douglas with doing nothing for freedom; with disregarding the rights and interests of the colored man: and for about forty minutes he spoke with a power that we have seldom heard equalled. There was a grandeur in his thoughts, a comprehensiveness in his arguments, and a binding force in his conclusions, which were perfectly irresistible. The vast throng were silent as death; every eye was fixed upon the speaker, and all gave him serious attention. He was the tall man eloquent; his countenance glowed with animation, and his eye glistened with an intelligence that made it lustrous. He was no longer awkward and ungainly; but graceful, bold, commanding

"Mr. Douglas had been quietly smoking up to this time; but here he forgot his cigar and listened with anxious attention. When he rose to reply he appeared excited, disturbed, and his second effort seemed to us vastly inferior to his first. Mr. Lincoln had given him a great task, and Mr. Douglas had not time to answer him, even if he had the ability."

MR. LINCOLN DEFEATED BY MR. DOUGLAS.

The election-day at length arrived, and although the efforts of Mr. Lincoln resulted in an immense increase of the Republican vote, whatever aspirations he had for personal success were frustrated. A vote of 126,084 was cast for the Republican candidates, 121,940 for the Douglas Democrats, and 5,091 for the Lecompton candidates, but Mr. Douglas was elected United States Senator by the Legislature, in which his supporters had a majority of eight on joint ballot.

Although defeated in the hope of securing Mr. Lincoln as their representative in the United States Senate, the Republicans were not discouraged, and from that time determined that their favorite leader should be rewarded with even more exalted honors.

IS NAMED FOR THE PRESIDENCY—EVIDENCE OF HIS SKILL AS A RAIL-SPLITTER.

He was immediately mentioned prominently for the Presidency, and at a meeting of the Illinois State Republican Convention, where he was present as a spectator, a veteran Democrat of Macon county brought in and presented to the Convention two old fence-rails, gayly decorated with flags and ribbons, and upon which the following words were inscribed:

> ABRAHAM LINCOLN,
>
> THE RAIL CANDIDATE
>
> FOR PRESIDENT IN 1860
>
> Two rails from a lot of 3,000 made in 1830, by Thos. Hanks and Abe Lincoln—whose father was the first pioneer of Macon county.

The event occasioned the most unbounded enthusiasm, and for several minutes the most deafening applause resounded through the building. Mr. Lincoln was vociferously called for, and arising from his seat, modestly acknowledged that he had split rails some thirty years previous in Macon county, and he was informed that those before him were a small portion of the product of his labor with the axe.

The fame of the able advocate of Republican principles induced the members of that party in other States to secure his voice and influence in their behalf, and in the fall of 1859 he made several effective speeches in favor of the cause.

HIS GREAT SPEECH AT THE COOPER INSTITUTE, NEW YORK.

On the twenty-seventh of February, 1860, he made the following forcible speech at the Cooper Institute, New York, before an immense audience:

"MR. PRESIDENT AND FELLOW-CITIZENS OF NEW YORK: The facts with which I shall deal this evening are mainly old and familiar; nor is there any thing new in the general use I shall make of them. If there shall be any novelty, it will be in the mode of presenting the facts, and the inferences and observations following that presentation.

"In his speech last autumn, at Columbus, Ohio, as reported in *The New York Times*, Senator Douglas said:

"'Our fathers, when they framed the Government under which we live, understood this question just as well, and even better than we do now.'

"I fully indorse this and I adopt it as a text for this discourse I so adopt it because it furnishes a precise and agreed starting point for the discussion between Republicans and that wing of Democracy headed by Senator Douglas. It simply leaves the inquiry: 'What was the understanding those fathers had of the questions mentioned?'

"What is the frame of Government under which we live?

"The answer must be: 'The Constitution of the United States.' That Constitution consists of the original, framed in 1787 (and under which the present Government first went into operation), and twelve subsequently framed amendments, the first ten of which were framed in 1789.

"Who were our fathers that framed the Constitution? I suppose the 'thirty-nine' who signed the original instrument may be fairly called our fathers who framed that part of the present Government. It is almost exactly true to say they framed it, and it is altogether true to say they fairly represented the opinion and sentiment of the whole nation at that time. Their names being familiar to nearly all, and accessible to quite all, need not now be repeated.

"I take these 'thirty-nine,' for the present, as being 'our fathers who framed the Government under which we live.'

"What is the question which according to the text, those fathers understood just as well, and even better than we do now?

"It is this: Does the proper division of local from federal authority, or any thing in the Constitution, forbid our Federal Government control as to slavery in our Federal Territories?

"Upon this, Douglas holds the affirmative, and Republicans the negative. This affirmative and denial form an issue; and this issue—this question—is precisely what the text declares our fathers understood better than we.

"Let us now inquire whether the 'thirty-nine,' or any of them, ever acted upon this question; and if they did, how they acted upon it—how they expressed that better understanding.

"In 1784—three years before the Constitution—the United States then owning the Northwestern Territory, and no other—the Congress of the Confederation had before them the question of prohibiting slavery in that Territory; and four of the 'thirty-nine' who afterward framed the Constitution were in that

Congress, and voted on that question. Of these, Roger Sherman, Thomas Mifflin, and Hugh Williamson voted for the prohibition—thus showing that, in their understanding, no line dividing local from federal authority, nor any thing else, properly forbade the Federal Government to control as to slavery in federal territory. The other of the four—James McHenry—voted against the prohibition, showing that, for some cause, he thought it improper to vote for it.

"In 1787, still before the Constitution, but while the Convention was in session framing it, and while the Northwestern Territory still was the only territory owned by the United States—the same question of prohibiting slavery in the territory again came before the Congress of the Confederation; and three more of the 'thirty-nine' who afterward signed the Constitution, were in that Congress, and voted on the question. They were William Blount, William Few and Abraham Baldwin; and they all voted for the prohibition—thus showing that, in their understanding, no line dividing local from federal authority, nor any thing else, properly forbids the Federal Government to control as to slavery in federal territory. This time the prohibition became a law, being part of what is now well known as the Ordinance of '87.

"The question of federal control of slavery in the territories, seems not to have been directly before the Convention which framed the original Constitution; and hence it is not recorded that the 'thirty-nine' or any of them, while engaged on that instrument, expressed any opinion on that precise question.

"In 1789, by the first Congress which sat under the Constitution, an act was passed to enforce the Ordinance of '87 including the prohibition of slavery in the Northwestern Territory. The bill for this act was reported by one of the 'thirty-nine,' Thomas Fitzsimmons, then a member of the House of Representatives from Pennsylvania. It went through all its stages without a word of opposition, and finally passed both branches without yeas and nays, which is equivalent to an unanimous passage. In this Congress there were sixteen of the 'thirty-nine' fathers who framed the original Constitution. They were John Langdon, Nicholas Gilman, Wm. S. Johnson, Roger Sherman, Robert Morris, Thos. Fitzsimmons, William Few, Abraham Baldwin, Rufus King, William Patterson, George Clymer, Richard Bassett, George Read, Pierce Butler, Daniel Carrol, James Madison.

"This shows that, in their understanding, no line dividing local from federal authority, nor any thing in the Constitution, properly forbade Congress to prohibit slavery in the federal territory; else both their fidelity to correct principle, and their oath to support the Constitution, would have constrained them to oppose the prohibition.

"Again, George Washington, another of the 'thirty-nine,

was then President of the United States, and, as such, approved and signed the bill, thus completing its validity as a law, and thus showing that, in his understanding, no line dividing local from federal authority, nor any thing in the Constitution, forbade the Federal Government to control as to slavery in federal territory.

"No great while after the adoption of the original Constitution, North Carolina ceded to the Federal Government the country now constituting the State of Tennessee; and a few years later Georgia ceded that which now constitutes the States of Mississippi and Alabama. In both deeds of cession it was made a condition by the ceding States that the Federal Government should not prohibit slavery in the ceded country. Besides this, slavery was then actually in the ceded country. Under these circumstances, Congress, on taking charge of these countries did not absolutely prohibit slavery within them. But they did interfere with it—take control of it—even there, to a certain extent. In 1798, Congress organized the Territory of Mississippi. In the act of organization they prohibited the bringing of slaves into the Territory, from any place without the United States, by fine and giving freedom to slaves so brought. This act passed both branches of Congress without yeas and nays. In that Congress were three of the 'thirty-nine' who framed the original Constitution. They were John Langdon, George Read, and Abraham Baldwin. They all, probably, voted for it. Certainly they would have placed their opposition to it upon record, if, in their understanding, any line dividing local from federal authority, or any thing in the Constitution, properly forbade the Federal Government to control as to slavery in federal territory.

"In 1803, the Federal Government purchased the Louisiana country. Our former territorial acquisitions came from certain of our own States; but this Louisiana country was acquired from a foreign nation. In 1804, Congress gave a territorial organization to that part of it which now constitutes the State of Louisiana. New Orleans, lying within that part, was an old and comparatively large city. There were other considerable towns and settlements, and slavery was extensively and thoroughly intermingled with the people. Congress did not, in the Territorial Act, prohibit Slavery; but they did interfere with it—take control of it—in a more marked and extensive way than they did in the case of Mississippi. The substance of the provision therein made, in relation to slaves, was:

"*First.* That no slave should be imported into the territory from foreign parts.

"*Second.* That no slave should be carried into it who had been imported into the United States since the first day of May, 1798.

"*Third.* That no slave should be carried into it, except by the owner, and for his own use as a settler; the penalty in all the cases being a fine upon the violator of the law, and freedom to the slave.

"This act also was passed without yeas and nays. In the Congress which passed it, there were two of the 'thirty-nine.' They were Abraham Baldwin and Jonathan Dayton. As stated in the case of Mississippi, it is probable they both voted for it. They would not have allowed it to pass without recording their opposition to it, if, in their understanding, it violated either the line proper dividing local from Federal authority or any provision of the Constitution.

"In 1819-20, came and passed the Missouri question. Many votes were taken, by yeas and nays, in both branches of Congress, upon the various phases of the general question. Two of the 'thirty-nine'—Rufus King and Charles Pinckney—were members of that Congress. Mr. King steadily voted for slavery prohibition and against all compromises, while Mr. Pinckney as steadily voted against slavery prohibition and against all compromises. By this Mr. King showed that, in his understanding, no line dividing local from Federal authority, nor any thing in the Constitution, was violated by Congress prohibiting slavery in federal territory; while Mr. Pinckney, by his votes, showed that in his understanding there was some sufficient reason for opposing such prohibition in that case.

"The cases I have mentioned are the only acts of the 'thirty-nine,' or of any of them, upon the direct issue, which I have been able to discover.

"To enumerate the persons who thus acted, as being four in 1784, three in 1787, seventeen in 1789, three in 1798, two in 1804, and two in 1819-20—there would be thirty-one of them. But this would be counting John Langdon, Roger Sherman, William Few, Rufus King, and George Read, each twice, and Abraham Baldwin four times. The true number of those of the 'thirty-nine' whom I have shown to have acted upon the question, which, by the text they understood better than we, is twenty-three, leaving sixteen not shown to have acted upon it in any way.

"Here, then, we have twenty-three out of our 'thirty-nine' fathers who framed the government under which we live, who have, upon their official responsibility and their corporal oaths, acted upon the very question which the text affirms they 'understood just as well, and even better than we do now;' and twenty-one of them—a clear majority of the 'thirty-nine'—so acting upon it as to make them guilty of gross political impropriety, and wilful perjury, if, in their understanding, any proper division between local and Federal authority, or any thing in the Constitution they had made themselves, and sworn to support, forbade the Federal government to control as to slavery in the Federal territories Thus the twenty-one acted; and, as actions speak louder than words, so actions under such responsibility speak still louder.

"Two of the twenty-three voted against Congressional prohibition of slavery in the Federal territories, in the instances in which they acted upon the question. But for what reasons they so voted is not known. They may have done so because they thought a proper division of local from Federal authority, or some provision or principle of the Constitution, stood in the way; or they may, without any such question, have voted against the prohibition, on what appeared to them to be sufficient grounds of expediency. No one who has sworn to support the Constitution, can conscientiously vote for what he understands to be an unconstitutional measure, however expedient he may think it; but one may and ought to vote against a measure which he deems constitutional, if, at the same time, he deems it inexpedient. It, therefore, would be unsafe to set down even the two who voted against the prohibition, as having done so because, in their understanding, any proper division of local from Federal authority, or any thing in the Constitution, forbade the Federal government to control as to slavery in Federal territory.

"The remaining sixteen of the 'thirty-nine,' so far as I have discovered, have left no record of their understanding upon the direct question of Federal control of slavery in the Federal territories. But there is much reason to believe that their understanding upon that question would not have appeared different from that of their twenty-three compeers, had it been manifested at all.

"For the purpose of adhering rigidly to the text, I have purposely omitted whatever understanding may have been manifested, by any person, however distinguished, other than the 'thirty-nine' fathers who framed the original Constitution; and, for the same reason, I have also omitted whatever understanding may have been manifested by any of the 'thirty-nine' even, on any other phase of the general question of slavery. If we should look into their acts and declarations on those other phases, as the foreign slave-trade, and the morality and policy of slavery generally, it would appear to us that on the direct question of Federal control of slavery in Federal territories, the sixteen, if they had acted at all, would probably have acted just as the twenty-three did. Among that sixteen were several of the most noted anti-slavery men of those times—as Dr. Franklin, Alexander Hamilton, and Governeur Morris—while there was not one now known to have been otherwise, unless it may be John Rutledge, of South Carolina.

"The sum of the whole is, that of our 'thirty-nine' fathers who framed the original Constitution, twenty-one—a clear majority of the whole—certainly understood that no proper division of local from Federal authority nor any part of the Constitution, forbade the Federal government to control slavery in the Federal territories, while all the rest probably had the same understanding. Such, unquestionably, was the understanding of our fathers who framed the original Constitution; and the text affirms that they understood the question better than we.

"But, so far, I have been considering the understanding of the question manifested by the framers of the original Constitution. In and by the original instrument, a mode was provided for amending it; and, as I have already stated, the present frame of government under which we live consists of that original, and twelve amendatory articles framed and adopted since. Those who now insist that Federal control of slavery in Federal territories violates the Constitution, point us to the provisions which they suppose it thus violates; and, as I understand, they all fix upon provisions in these amendatory articles, and not in the original instrument. The Supreme Court, in the Dred Scott case, plant themselves upon the fifth amendment, which provides that 'no person shall be deprived of property without due process of law;' while Senator Douglas and his peculiar adherents plant themselves upon the tenth amendment, providing that 'the powers not granted by the Constitution are reserved to the States respectively, and to the people.'

"Now, it so happens that these amendments were framed by the first Congress which sat under the Constitution—the identical Congress which passed the act already mentioned, enforcing the prohibition of slavery in the northwestern territory. Not only was it the same Congress, but they were the identical, same individual men who, at the same session, and at the same time within the session, had under consideration, and in progress toward maturity, these Constitutional amendments, and this act prohibiting slavery in all the territory the nation then owned. The Constitutional amendments were introduced before, and passed after the act enforcing the Ordinance of '87; so that during the whole pendency of the act to enforce the Ordinance, the Constitutional amendments were also pending.

"That Congress, consisting in all of seventy-six members, including sixteen of the framers of the original Constitution, as before stated, were pre-eminently our fathers who framed that part of the government under which we live, which is now claimed as forbidding the Federal government to control slavery in the Federal territories.

"Is it not a little presumptuous in any one at this day to affirm that the two things which that Congress deliberately framed, and carried to maturity at the same time, are absolutely inconsistent with each other? And does not such affirmation become impudently absurd when coupled with the other affirmation, from the same mouth, that those who did the two things alleged to be inconsistent understood whether they really were inconsistent better than we—better than he who affirms that they are inconsistent?

"It is surely safe to assume that the 'thirty-nine' framers of the original Constitution, and the seventy-six members of the Congress which framed the amendments thereto, taken together, do certainly include those who may be fairly called 'our fathers who framed the government under which we live.' And so assuming, I defy any man to show that any one of them ever, in his whole life, declared that, in his understanding, any proper division of local from Federal authority, or any part of the Constitution, forbade the Federal government to control as to slavery in the Federal territories. I go a step further. I defy any one to show that any living man in the whole world ever did, prior to the beginning of the present century (and I might almost say prior to the beginning of the last half of the present century), declare that, in his understanding, any proper division of local from Federal authority, or any part of the Constitution, forbade the Federal government to control as to slavery in the Federal territories. To those who now so declare, I give, not only 'our fathers who framed the government under which we live,' but with them all other living men within the century in which it was framed, among whom to search, and they shall not be able to find the evidence of a single man agreeing with them.

"Now, and here, let me guard a little against being misunderstood. I do not mean to say we are bound to follow implicitly in whatever our fathers did. To do so, would be to discard all the lights of current experience—we reject all progress—all improvement. What I do say is, that if we would supplant the opinions and policy of our fathers in any case, we should do so upon evidence so conclusive, and argument so clear, that even their great authority, fairly considered and weighed, cannot stand; and most surely not in a case whereof we ourselves declare they understood the question better than we.

"If any man, at this day, sincerely believes that a proper division of local from Federal authority, or any part of the Constitution, forbids the Federal government to control as to slavery in the Federal territories, he is right to say so, and to enforce his position by all truthful evidence and fair argument which he can. But he has no right to mislead others, who have less access to history and less leisure to study it, into the false belief that 'our fathers, who framed the government under which we live,' were of the same opinion—thus substituting falsehood and deception for truthful evidence and fair argument. If any man, at this day, sincerely believes 'our fathers, who framed the government under which we live,' used and applied principles, in other cases, which ought to have led them to understand that a proper division of local from Federal authority, or some part of the Constitution, forbids the Federal government to control as to slavery in the Federal territories, he is right to say so. But he should, at the same time, brave the responsibility of declaring that, in his opinion, he understands their principles better than they did themselves; and especially should he not shirk that responsibility by asserting that they 'understood the question just as well, and even better than we do now.'

"But enough. Let all who believe that 'our fathers, who framed the government under which we live, understood this question just as well, and even better than we do now,' speak as they spoke, and act as they acted upon it. This is all Republicans ask, all Republicans desire, in relation to slavery. As those fathers marked it, so let it be again marked, as an evil not to be extended, but to be tolerated and protected only because of and so far as its actual presence among us makes that toleration and protection a necessity. Let all the guaranties those fathers gave it, be, not grudgingly, but fully and fairly maintained. For this Republicans contend, and with this, so far as I know or believe, they will be content.

"And now, if they would listen—as I suppose they will not—I would address a few words to the Southern people.

"I would say to them: You consider yourselves a reasonable and a just people; and I consider that, in the general qualities of reason and justice, you are not inferior to any other people. Still, when you speak of us Republicans, you do so only to denounce us as reptiles, or, at the best, as no better than outlaws. You will grant a hearing to pirates or murderers, but nothing like it to 'Black Republicans.' In all your contentions with one another, each of you deems an unconditional condemnation of 'Black Republicanism' as the first thing to be attended to. Indeed, such condemnation of us seems to be an indispensable prerequisite—license, so to speak—among you to be admitted or permitted to speak at all.

"Now can you, or not, be prevailed upon to pause and to consider whether this is quite just to us, or even to yourselves?

"Bring forward your charges and specifications, and then be patient long enough to hear us deny or justify.

"You say we are sectional. We deny it. That makes an issue; and the burden of proof is upon you. You produce your proof; and what is it? Why, that our party has no existence in your section—gets no votes in your section. The fact is substantially true; but does it prove the issue? If it does, then, in case we should, without change of principle, begin to get votes in your section, we should thereby cease to be sectional You cannot escape this conclusion; and yet, are you willing to abide by it? If you are, you will probably soon find that we have ceased to be sectional, for we shall get votes in your section this very year. You will then begin to discover, as the truth plainly is, that your proof does not touch the issue. The fact that we get no votes in your section is a fact of your making, and not of ours. And if there be fault in that fact, that fault is primarily yours, and remains so until you show that we repel you by some wrong principle or practice. If we do repel you by any wrong principle or practice, the fault is ours; but this brings us to where you ought to have started—to a discussion of the right or wrong of our principle. If our principle, put in practice, would wrong your section for the benefit of ours, or for any other object, then our principle, and we with it, are sectional, and are justly opposed and denounced as such. Meet us, then, on the question of whether our principle, put in practice, would wrong your section; and so meet it as if it were possible that something may be said on our side. Do you accept the challenge? No? Then you really believe that the principle which our fathers, who framed the government under which we live, thought so clearly right as to adopt it, and indorse it again and again upon their official oaths, is, in fact, so clearly wrong as to demand your condemnation without a moment's consideration.

"Some of you delight to flaunt in our faces the warning against sectional parties given by Washington in his Farewell Address. Less than eight years before Washington gave that warning, he had, as President of the United States, approved and signed an act of Congress enforcing the prohibition of slavery in the Northwestern Territory, which act embodied the policy of the government upon that subject, up to and at the very moment he penned that warning; and about one year after he penned it he wrote Lafayette that he considered that prohibition a wise measure, expressing, in the same connection, his hope that we should some time have a confederacy of free States.

"Bearing this in mind, and seeing that sectionalism has since arisen upon this same subject, is that warning a weapon in your hands against us, or in our hands against you? Could Washington himself speak, would he cast the blame of that sectionalism upon us, who sustain his policy, or upon you, who repudiate it? We respect that warning of Washington, and we commend it to you, together with his example pointing to the right application of it.

"But you say you are conservative—eminently conservative—while we are revolutionary, destructive, or something of the sort. What is conservatism? Is it not adherence to the old and tried against the new and untried? We stick to, contend for, the identical old policy on the point in controversy which was adopted by our fathers who framed the government under which we live; while you, with one accord, reject, and scout, and spit upon that old policy, and insist upon substituting something new. True, you disagree among yourselves as to what that substitute shall be. You have considerable variety of new propositions and plans, but you are unanimous in rejecting and denouncing the old policy of the fathers. Some of you are for reviving the foreign slave-trade; some for a Congressional Slave-Code for the Territories; some for Congress forbidding the Territories to prohibit slavery within their limits; some for maintaining slavery in the Territories through the Judiciary; some for the 'gur-reat pur-rinciple' that, 'if one man would enslave another, no third man should object,' fantastically called 'Popular Sovereignty;' but never a man among you in favor of Federal prohibition of slavery in Federal Territories, according to the practice of our fathers who framed the government under which we live. Not one of all your various plans can show a precedent or an advocate in the century within which our government originated. Consider, then, whether your claim of conservatism for yourselves, and your charge of destructiveness against us, are based on the most clear and stable foundations.

"Again, you say we have made the slavery question more prominent than it formerly was. We deny it. We admit that it is more prominent, but we deny that we made it so. It was not we, but you, who discarded the old policy of the fathers. We resisted, and still resist, your innovation; and thence comes the greater prominence of the question. Would you have that question reduced to its former proportions? Go back to that old policy. What has been will be again, under the same conditions. If you would have the peace of the old times, re-adopt the precepts and policy of the old times.

"You charge that we stir up insurrections among your slaves. We deny it. And what is your proof? Harper's Ferry! John Brown! John Brown was no Republican; and you have failed to implicate a single Republican in his Harper's Ferry enterprise. If any member of our party is guilty in that matter, you know it, or you do not know it. If you do know it, you are inexcusable to not designate the man, and prove the fact. If you do not know it, you are inexcusable to assert it, and especially to persist in the assertion after you have tried and failed to make the proof. You need not be told that persisting in a charge which one does not know to be true is simply malicious slander.

"Some of you admit that no Republican designedly aided or encouraged the Harper's Ferry affair; but still insist that our doctrines and declarations necessarily lead to such results. We do not believe it. We know we hold to no doctrine, and make no declarations which were not held to and made by our fathers who framed the government under which we live. You never deal fairly by us in relation to this affair. When it occurred, some important State elections were near at hand, and you were in evident glee with the belief that, by charging the blame upon us, you could get an advantage of us in those elections. The elections came, and your expectations were not quite fulfilled. Every Republican man knew that, as to himself, at least, your charge was a slander, and he was not much inclined by it to cast his vote in your favor. Republican doctrines and declarations are accompanied with a continual protest against any interference whatever with your slaves, or with you about your slaves. Surely, this does not encourage them to revolt. True, we do, in common with our fathers, who framed the government under which we live, declare our belief that slavery is wrong; but the slaves do not hear us declare even this. For any thing we say or do, the slaves would scarcely know there is a Republican party. I believe they would not, in fact, generally know it but for your misrepresentations of us in their hearing. In your political contests among yourselves, each faction charges the other with sympathy with Black Republicanism; and then, to give point to the charge, defines Black Republicanism to simply be insurrection, blood and thunder among the slaves.

"Slave insurrections are no more common now than they were before the Republican party was organized. What induced the Southampton insurrection, twenty-eight years ago, in which, at least, three times as many lives were lost as at Harper's Ferry? You can scarcely stretch your very elastic fancy to the conclusion that Southampton was got up by Black Republicanism. In the present state of things in the United States, I do not think a general, or even a very extensive slave insurrection, is possible. The indispensable concert of action cannot be attained. The slaves have no means of rapid communication; nor can incendiary free men, black or white, supply it. The explosive materials are everywhere in parcels; but there neither are, nor can be supplied, the indispensable connecting trains.

"Much is said by southern people about the affection of slaves for their masters and mistresses; and a part of it, at least, is true. A plot for an uprising could scarcely be devised and communicated to twenty individuals before some one of them, to save the life of a favorite master or mistress, would divulge it. This is the rule; and the slave revolution in Hayti was not an exception to it, but a case occurring under peculiar circumstances. The gunpowder-plot of British history, though not connected with the slaves, was more in point. In that case, only about twenty were admitted to the secret; and yet one of them, in his anxiety to save a friend, betrayed the plot to that friend, and, by consequence, averted the calamity. Occasional poisonings from the kitchen, and open or stealthy assassinations in the field, and local revolts extending to a score or so, will continue to occur as the natural results of slavery; but no general insurrection of slaves, as I think, can happen in this country for a long time. Whoever much fears, or much hopes, for such an event, will be alike disappointed.

"In the language of Mr. Jefferson, uttered many years ago, 'It is still in our power to direct the process of emancipation, and deportation, peaceably and in such slow degrees, as that the evil will wear off insensibly; and their place be, *pari passu*, filled up by free white laborers. If, on the contrary, it is left to force itself on, human nature must shudder at the prospect held up.'

"Mr. Jefferson did not mean to say, nor do I, that the power of emancipation is in the Federal Government. He spoke of Virginia; and, as to the power of emancipation, I speak of the slaveholding States only.

"The Federal Government, however, as we insist, has the power of restraining the extension of the institution—the power to insure that a slave insurrection shall never occur on any American soil which is now free from slavery.

"John Brown's effort was peculiar. It was not a slave insurrection. It was an attempt by white men to get up a revolt among slaves, in which the slaves refused to participate. In fact, it was so absurd that the slaves, with all their ignorance, saw plainly enough it could not succeed. That affair, in its philosophy, corresponds with the many attempts, related in history, at the assassination of kings and emperors. An enthusiast broods over the oppression of a people till he fancies himself commissioned by Heaven to liberate them. He ventures the attempt, which ends in little else than in his own execution. Orsini's attempt on Louis Napoleon, and John Brown's attempt at Harper's Ferry were, in their philosophy, precisely the same. The eagerness to cast blame on old England in the one case, and on New England in the other, does not disprove the sameness of the two things.

"And how much would it avail you, if you could, by the use of John Brown, Helper's book, and the like, break up the Republican organization? Human action can be modified to some extent, but human nature cannot be changed. There is a judgment and a feeling against slavery in this nation, which cast at least a million and a-half of votes. You cannot destroy that judgment and feeling—that sentiment—by breaking up the political organization which rallies around it. You can scarcely scatter and disperse an army which has been formed into order in the face of your heaviest fire; but if you could, how much would you gain by forcing the sentiment which created it out of the peaceful channel of the ballot-box, into some other channel? What would that other channel probably be? Would the number of John Browns be lessened or enlarged by the operation.

"But you will break up the Union rather than submit to a denial of your Constitutional rights.

"That has a somewhat reckless sound; but it would be palliated, if not fully justified, were we proposing, by the mere force of numbers, to deprive you of some right plainly written down in the Constitution. But we are proposing no such thing.

"When you make these declarations, you have a specific and well-understood allusion to an assumed Constitutional right of yours, to take slaves into the federal territories, and hold them there as property. But no such right is specifically written in the Constitution. That instrument is literally silent about any such right. We, on the contrary, deny that such a right has any existence in the Constitution, even by implication.

"Your purpose, then, plainly stated, is, that you will destroy the Government, unless you be allowed to construe and enforce the Constitution as you please, on all points in dispute between you and us. You will rule or ruin in all events.

"This, plainly stated, is your language to us. Perhaps you will say the Supreme Court has decided the disputed Constitutional question in your favor. Not quite so. But waiving the lawyer's distinction between dictum and decision, the Courts have decided the question for you in a sort of way. The Courts have substantially said, it is your Constitutional right to take slaves into the Federal Territories, and to hold them there as property.

"When I say the decision was made in a sort of way, I mean it was made in a divided Court by a bare majority of the Judges, and they not quite agreeing with one another in the reasons for making it; that it is so made as that its avowed supporters disagree with one another about its meaning, and that it was mainly based upon a mistaken statement of fact—the statement in the opinion that 'the right of property in a slave is distinctly and expressly affirmed in the Constitution.'

"An inspection of the Constitution will show that the right of property in a slave is not distinctly and expressly affirmed in it. Bear in mind the Judges do not pledge their judicial opinion that such right is impliedly affirmed in the Constitution; but they pledge their veracity that it is distinctly and expressly affirmed there—'distinctly' that is, not mingled with any thing else—'expressly' that is, in words meaning just that, without the aid of any inference, and susceptible of no other meaning.

"If they had only pledged their judicial opinion that such right is affirmed in the instrument by implication, it would be open to others to show that neither the word 'slave' nor 'slavery' is to be found in the Constitution, nor the word 'property' even, in any connection with language alluding to the things slave, or slavery, and that wherever in that instrument the slave is alluded to, he is called a 'person;' and wherever his master's legal right in relation to him is alluded to, it is spoken of as 'service or labor due,' as a 'debt' payable in service or labor. Also, it would be open to show, by contemporaneous history, that this mode of alluding to slaves and slavery, instead of speaking of them, was employed on purpose to exclude from the Constitution the idea that there could be property in man.

"To show all this is easy and certain.

"When this obvious mistake of the Judges shall be brought to their notice, is it not reasonable to expect that they will withdraw the mistaken statement, and reconsider the conclusion based upon it?

"And then it is to be remembered that 'our fathers, who framed the Government under which we live'—the men who made the Constitution—decided this same Constitutional question in our favor, long ago—decided it without a division among themselves, when making the decision; without division among themselves about the meaning of it after it was made, and so far as any evidence is left, without basing it upon any mistaken statement of facts.

"Under all these circumstances, do you really feel yourselves justified to break up this Government, unless such a court decision as yours is, shall be at once submitted to, as a conclusive and final rule of political action.

"But you will not abide the election of a Republican President. In that supposed event, you say, you will destroy the Union; and then, you say, the great crime of having destroyed it will be upon us!

"That is cool. A highwayman holds a pistol to my ear, and mutters through his teeth, 'stand and deliver, or I shall kill you, and then you will be a murderer!'

"To be sure, what the robber demanded of me—my money—was my own; and I had a clear right to keep it; but it was no more my own than my vote is my own; and threat of death to me, to extort my money, and threat of destruction to the Union, to extort my vote, can scarcely be distinguished in principle.

"A few words now to Republicans. It is exceedingly desirable that all parts of this great Confederacy shall be at peace, and in harmony, one with another. Let us Republicans do our part to have it so. Even though much provoked, let us do nothing through passion and ill temper. Even though the southern people will not so much as listen to us, let us calmly consider their demands, and yield to them if, in our deliberate view of our duty, we possibly can. Judging by all they say and do, and by the subject and nature of their controversy with us, let us determine, if we can, what will satisfy them?

"Will they be satisfied if the Territories be unconditionally surrendered to them? We know they will not. In all their present complaints against us, the Territories are scarcely mentioned. Invasions and insurrections are the rage now. Will it satisfy them if, in the future, we have nothing to do with invasions and insurrections? We know it will not. We so know because we know we never had any thing to do with invasions and insurrections; and yet this total abstaining does not exempt us from the charge and the denunciation.

"The question recurs, what will satisfy them? Simply this: We must not only let them alone, but we must, somehow, convince them that we do let them alone. This, we know by experience, is no easy task. We have been so trying to convince them from the very beginning of our organization, but with no success. In all our platforms and speeches we have constantly protested our purpose to let them alone; but this has had no tendency to convince them. Alike unavailing to convince them is the fact that they have never detected a man of us in any attempt to disturb them.

"These natural, and apparently adequate means all failing, what will convince them? This, and this only: cease to call slavery *wrong*, and join them in calling it *right*. And this must be done thoroughly—done in *acts* as well as in *words*. Silence will not be tolerated—we must place ourselves avowedly with them. Douglas's new sedition law must be enacted and enforced, suppressing all declarations that slavery is wrong, whether made in politics, in presses, in pulpits, or in private. We must arrest and return their fugitive slaves with greedy pleasure. We must pull down our Free-State Constitutions. The whole atmosphere must be disinfected from all taint of opposition to slavery, before they will cease to believe that all their troubles proceed from us.

"I am quite aware they do not state their case precisely in this way. Most of them would probably say to us, 'Let us alone, do nothing to us, and say what you please about slavery.' But we do let them alone—have never disturbed them—so that, after all, it is what we say, which dissatisfies them. They will continue to accuse us of doing, until we cease saying.

"I am also aware they have not, as yet, in terms demanded the overthrow of our Free-State Constitutions. Yet those Constitutions declare the wrong of slavery, with more solemn emphasis, than do all other sayings against it; and when all these other sayings shall have been silenced, the overthrow of these Constitutions will be demanded, and nothing be left to resist the demand. It is nothing to the contrary, that they do not demand the whole of this just now. Demanding what they do, and for the reason they do, they can voluntarily stop nowhere short of this consummation. Holding, as they do, that slavery is morally right, and socially elevating, they cannot cease to demand a full national recognition of it, as a legal right, and a social blessing.

"Nor can we justifiably withhold this, on any ground save our conviction that slavery is wrong. If slavery is right, all words, acts, laws, and constitutions against it, are themselves wrong, and should be silenced, and swept away. If it is right, we cannot justly object to its nationality—its universality; if it is wrong, they cannot justly insist upon its extension—its enlargement. All they ask, we could readily grant, if we thought slavery right; all we ask, they could as readily grant, if they thought it wrong. Their thinking it right, and our thinking it wrong, is the precise fact upon which depends the whole controversy. Thinking it right, as they do, they are not to blame for desiring its full recognition, as being right; but, thinking it wrong, as we do, can we yield to them? Can we cast our votes with their view, and against our own? In view of our moral, social, and political responsibilities, can we do this?

"Wrong as we think slavery is, we can yet afford to let it alone where it is, because that much is due to the necessity arising from its actual presence in the nation; but can we, while our votes will prevent it, allow it to spread into the National Territories, and to overrun us here in these Free States?

"If our sense of duty forbids this, then let us stand by our duty, fearlessly and effectively. Let us be diverted by none of those sophistical contrivances wherewith we are so industriously plied and belabored—contrivances such as groping for some middle ground between the right and the wrong, vain as the search for a man who should be neither a living man nor a dead man—such as a policy of 'don't care' on a question about which all true men do care—such as Union appeals beseeching true Union men to yield to Disunionists, reversing the divine rule, and calling, not the sinners, but the righteous to repentance—such as invocations to Washington, imploring men to unsay what Washington said, and undo what Washington did.

"Neither let us be slandered from our duty by false accusations against us, not frightened from it by menaces of destruction to the Government, nor of dungeons to ourselves. Let us have faith that right makes might, and in that faith, let us, to the end, dare to do our duty, as we understand it."

IS NOMINATED FOR PRESIDENT OF THE UNITED STATES BY THE REPUBLICAN CONVENTION.

On the sixteenth of May, 1860, the Republican National Convention assembled in Chicago, for the purpose of nominating candidates for the Presidency and Vice-Presidency. The first day was spent in organizing, and the second, in adopting rules for the government of the Convention and the platform of the party, and on the third, the body proceeded to ballot for the two candidates. Mr. Lincoln was nominated for President by Mr. Judd, of Illinois, and on the first ballot, received 102 votes, Mr. Seward receiving, on the same ballot, 173½ votes, and the balance being divided between the other candidates. On the second ballot, the vote stood: Lincoln, 181; Seward, 184½; and on the third, Mr. Lincoln received 230½ votes, or within one and one-half of a nomination. One of the delegates then changed four votes of his State, giving them to Mr. Lincoln, thus nominating him, and then, amid a scene of the most intense excitement, vote after vote was changed to the successful candidate, until at length the nomination was made unanimous. The selection was received by the Republican voters of the country with the most unbounded enthusiasm, and immediate preparations were made for an arduous campaign. The antecedents of their standard-bearer were of such an honorable and noble character, that they felt convinced the different factions among the opposition—indeed, all who were inspired more by patriotism than party predilections—would support him in the canvass and at the ballot-box. The architect of his own fortunes, he had raised himself from obscurity to eminence and distinction. Born in a floorless log-cabin, in a Kentucky wilderness; the child of humble and uneducated, but Christian parents; and with no education save that received during six months tuition in an unpretending school-house, and from attentive study at home by the light of a log fire, Abraham Lincoln, by his indefatigable perseverance and energy, rapidly rose from one position of trust and responsibility to another, until he attained the nomination of a great political party for the highest office in the gift of the American people.

IS NOTIFIED OF HIS NOMINATION—THE ADDRESSES ON THE OCCASION.

The committee appointed by the Convention to notify Mr. Lincoln of his nomination, performed their duty without delay, and upon arriving at his residence in Springfield, whither they were escorted by an immense concourse of citizens, the President of the Convention addressed the nominee as follows:

SPEECH OF THE PRESIDENT OF THE CONVENTION.

"I have, sir, the honor, in behalf of the gentlemen who are present, a Committee appointed by the Republican Convention, recently assembled at Chicago, to discharge a most pleasant duty. We have come, sir, under a vote of instructions to that Committee, to notify you that you have been selected by the Convention of the Republicans at Chicago, for President of the United States. They instruct us, sir, to notify you of that selection, and that Committee deem it not only respectful to yourself, but appropriate to the important matter which they have in hand, that they should come in person, and present to you the authentic evidence of the action of that Convention; and, sir, without any phrase which shall either be considered personally plauditory to yourself, or which shall have any reference to the principles involved in the questions which are connected with your nomination, I desire to present to you the letter which has been prepared, and which informs you of the nomination, and with it the platform, resolutions and sentiments, which the Convention adopted. Sir, at your convenience, we shall be glad to receive from you such a response as it may be your pleasure to give us."

REPLY OF MR. LINCOLN.

In response, Mr. Lincoln said:

"*Mr. Chairman and Gentlemen of the Committee:* I tender to you, and through you to the Republican National Convention, and all the people represented in it, my profoundest thanks for the high honor done me, which you now formally announce. Deeply, and even painfully sensible of the great responsibility which is inseparable from this high honor—a responsibility which I could almost wish had fallen upon some one of the far more eminent men and experienced statesmen whose distinguished names were before the Convention, I shall, by your leave, consider more fully the resolutions of the Convention, denominated the platform, and without unnecessary or unreasonable delay, respond to you, Mr. Chairman, in writing, not doubting that the platform will be found satisfactory, and the nomination gratefully accepted. And now I will not longer defer the pleasure of taking you, and each of you, by the hand."

CORRESPONDENCE BETWEEN THE CONVENTION AND MR. LINCOLN.

The following letter was addressed to Mr. Lincoln by

the President of the Convention, and a committee appointed for that purpose:

"CHICAGO, *May 18th*, 1860.

"TO THE HON. ABRAHAM LINCOLN, OF ILLINOIS.

"SIR: The representatives of the Republican party of the United States, assembled in Convention at Chicago, have this day by a unanimous vote, selected you as the Republican candidate for the office of President of the United States to be supported at the next election; and the undersigned were appointed a Committee of the Convention to apprise you of this nomination, and respectfully to request that you will accept it. A declaration of the principles and sentiments adopted by the Convention accompanies this communication.

"In the performance of this agreeable duty we take leave to add our confident assurance that the nomination of the Chicago Convention will be ratified by the suffrages of the people.

"We have the honor to be, with great respect and regard, your friends and fellow-citizens."

On the 23d, Mr. Lincoln addressed the following letter to the President of the Convention:

"SPRINGFIELD, ILLINOIS, *May 23rd*, 1860.

"HON. GEORGE ASHMAN, *President of the Republican National* "*Convention.*

"SIR: I accept the nomination tendered me by the Convention over which you presided, and of which I am formally apprised in the letter of yourself and others, acting as a Committee of the Convention for that purpose.

"The declaration of principles and sentiments, which accompanies your letter, meets my approval; and it shall be my care not to violate, or disregard it, in any part.

"Imploring the assistance of Divine Providence, and with due regard to the views and feelings of all who were represented in the Convention; to the rights of all the States and Territories, and people of the nation; to the inviolability of the Constitution, and the perpetual union, harmony and prosperity of all, I am most happy to co-operate for the practical success of the principles declared by the Convention,

"Your obliged friend and fellow-citizen,

"ABRAHAM LINCOLN."

On the sixth of November, 1860, the election for President took place, with the following result: Mr. Lincoln received 491,275 over Mr. Douglas; 1,018,499 over Mr. Breckenridge, and 1,275,821 over Mr. Bell; and the vote was subsequently proclaimed by Congress to be as follows:

For Abraham Lincoln, of Illinois..................	180
For John C. Breckenridge, of Kentucky............	72
For John Bell, of Tennessee.......................	39
For Stephen A. Douglas, of Illinois................	12

To describe the various movements and projects which were devised and consummated in the South between the time that Mr. Lincoln was elected and the date of his inauguration, would require a much larger work than that which we now offer to the public, and we will therefore confine our account merely to those which it is unavoidably necessary to mention. The principal and most diabolical plot conceived and recommended by the traitors, was to prevent the inauguration by obtaining possession of the Federal Capital, or by assassinating Mr. Lincoln while on his way thither, or upon the day that the ceremonies were to take place. Whatever may have been the plan, or however large the reward offered to the villain who would accomplish the murderous deed, the object of their vindictiveness escaped their machinations, and still continues to administer the government wisely and faithfully.

LEAVES SPRINGFIELD FOR WASHINGTON—OVATIONS ON THE ROUTE.

The President Elect left his home in Springfield, Illinois, on the eleventh of February, 1861, for Washington, having before leaving the depot addressed the following words of farewell to the thousands of his fellow-citizens who had assembled at the place of departure:

"*My friends:* No one not in my position can appreciate the sadness I feel at this parting. To this people I owe all that I am. Here I have lived more than a quarter of a century. Here my children were born, and here one of them lies buried. I know not how soon I shall see you again. A duty devolves upon me which is perhaps greater than that which has devolved upon any other man since the days of Washington. He never would have succeeded except for the aid of Divine Providence, upon which he at all times relied. I feel that I cannot succeed without the same Divine aid which sustained him, and in the same Almighty Being I place my reliance for support; and I hope you, my friends, will all pray that I may receive that Divine assistance, without which I cannot succeed, but with which success is certain. Again, I bid you all an affectionate farewell."

Along the route, multitudes assembled at the railway stations to greet him. At Toledo, in response to repeated calls, Mr. Lincoln appeared on the platform and said:

"I am leaving you on an errand of national importance, attended, as you are aware, with considerable difficulties. Let us believe, as some poet has expressed it, 'Behind the cloud the sun is shining still.' I bid you an affectionate farewell."

He next proceeded to Indianapolis, where Mr. Lincoln was welcomed by the Governor of the State, and escorted by a procession composed of both Houses of the Legislature, the public officers, municipal authorities, military, and firemen. On reaching the Hotel he addressed the people as follows:

"*Fellow-citizens of the State of Indiana:* I am here to thank you much for this magnificent welcome, and still more for the very generous support given by your State to that political cause, which I think is the true and just cause of the whole country and the whole world. Solomon says 'there is a time to keep silence;' and when men wrangle by the mouth, with no certainty that they mean the same thing while using the same words, it perhaps were as well if they would keep silence. The words 'coercion' and 'invasion' are much used in these days, and often with some temper and hot blood. Let us make sure, if we can, that we do not misunderstand the meaning of those who use them. Let us get the exact definitions of these words, not from dictionaries, but from the men themselves, who certainly deprecate the things they would represent by the use of the words. What, then, is 'coercion?' What is 'invasion?' Would the marching of an army into South Carolina, without the consent of her people, and with hostile intent towards them, be invasion? I certainly think it would, and it would be 'coercion' also if the South Carolinians were forced to submit. But if the United States should merely hold and retake its own forts and other property, and collect the duties on foreign importations, or even withhold the mails from places where they were habitually violated, would any or all of these things be 'invasion' or 'coercion?' Do our professed lovers of the Union, but who spitefully resolve that they will resist coercion and invasion, understand that such things as these, on the part of the United States, would be coercion or invasion of a State? If so, their idea of means to preserve the object of their great affection would seem to be exceedingly thin and airy. If sick, the little pills of the homœopathist would be much too large for it to swallow. In their view, the Union, as a family relation, would seem to be no regular marriage, but rather a sort of 'free-love' arrangement, to be maintained on passional attraction. By the way, in what consists the special sacredness of a State? I speak not of the position assigned to a State in the Union by the Constitution, for that is the bond we all recognize. That position, however, a State cannot carry out of the Union with it. I speak of that assumed primary right of a State to rule all which is less than itself, and to ruin all which is larger than itself. If a State and a County, in a given case, should be equal in extent of territory and equal in number of inhabitants, in what, as a matter of principle, is the State better than the County? Would an exchange of name be an exchange of rights? Upon what principle, upon what rightful principle, may a State, being no more than one-fiftieth part of the nation in soil and population, break up the nation, and then coerce a proportionably larger subdivision of itself in the most arbitrary way? What mysterious right to play tyrant is conferred on a district of country with its people, by merely calling it a State? Fellow-citizens, I am not asserting any thing. I am merely asking questions for you to consider. And now allow me to bid you farewell."

Proceeding to Cincinnati, he received a most enthusiastic welcome. Having been addressed by the mayor of the city, and escorted by a civic and military procession to the Burnet House, he addressed the assemblage in these words:

"*Fellow-citizens:* I have spoken but once before this in Cincinnati. That was a year previous to the late Presidential election. On that occasion, in a playful manner, but with sincere words, I addressed much of what I said to the Kentuckians. I gave my opinion that we, as Republicans, would ultimately beat them as Democrats, but that they could postpone the result longer by nominating Senator Douglas for the Presidency than they could in any other way. They did not, in any true sense of the word, nominate Mr. Douglas, and the result has come certainly as soon as ever I expected.

"I also told them how I expected they would be treated after they should have been beaten, and now wish to call their attention to what I then said:

"'When we do, as we say we will, beat you, you perhaps want to know what we will do with you. I will tell you—as far as I am authorized to speak for the opposition—what we mean to do with you. We mean to treat you as near as we possibly can, as Washington, Jefferson, and Madison treated you. We mean to leave you alone, and in no way to interfere with your institutions; to abide by all and every compromise of the Constitution. In a word, coming back to the original proposition, to treat you, as far as degenerate men—if we have degenerated—may, according to the example of those noble fathers, Washington, Jefferson, and Madison. We mean to remember that you are as good as we; that there is no difference between us other than the difference of circumstances. We mean to recognize and bear in mind always that you have as good hearts in your bosoms as other people, or as we claim to have, and to treat you accordingly.'

"Fellow-citizens of Kentucky, friends, brethren: May I call you such? In my new position I see no occasion and feel no inclination to retract a word of this. If it shall not be made good be assured that the fault shall not be mine.'

In the evening he had a reception, when large crowds called upon him.

On the next morning he left Cincinnati, and arrived at Columbus, where he was received with every demonstration of enthusiasm. He visited the Governor in the Executive Chamber, and was subsequently introduced to the members of the Legislature in joint session, when he was formally welcomed by the Lieutenant-Governor, to whom Mr. Lincoln responded in these words:

"It is true, as has been said by the President of the Senate, that very great responsibility rests upon me in the position to which the votes of the American people have called me. I am deeply sensible of that weighty responsibility. I cannot but know, what you all know, that without a name—perhaps without a reason why I should have a name—there has fallen upon me a task such as did not rest upon the Father of his Country. And so feeling, I cannot but turn and look for the support without which it will be impossible for me to perform that great task I turn, then, and look to the American people, and to that God who has never forsaken them.

"Allusion has been made to the interest felt in relation to the policy of the new Administration. In this, I have received from some a degree of credit for having kept silence, from others some depreciation. I still think I was right. In the varying and repeatedly shifting scenes of the present, without a precedent which could enable me to judge for the past, it has seemed fitting, that before speaking upon the difficulties of the country I should have gained a view of the whole field. To be sure, after all, I would be at liberty to modify and change the course of policy as future events might make a change necessary.

"I have not maintained silence from any want of real anxiety. It is a good thing that there is no more than anxiety, for there is nothing going wrong. It is a consoling circumstance that when we look out there is nothing that really hurts anybody. We entertain different views upon political questions, but nobody is suffering any thing. This is a most consoling circumstance, and from it I judge that all we want is time and patience, and a reliance on that God who has never forsaken this people."

On the 14th of February, Mr. Lincoln proceeded to Pittsburgh. At Steubenville, on the route, in reply to an address, he said:

"I fear the great confidence placed in my ability is unfounded. Indeed, I am sure it is. Encompassed by vast difficulties, as I am, nothing shall be wanted on my part, if sustained by the American people and God. I believe the devotion to the Constitution is equally great on both sides of the river. It is only the different understanding of that instrument that causes difficulties. The only dispute is 'What are their rights?' If the majority should not rule who should be the judge? Where is such a judge to be found? We should all be bound by the majority of the American people—if not, then the minority must control. Would that be right? Would it be just or generous? Assuredly not." He reiterated, the majority should rule. If he adopted a wrong policy, then the opportunity to condemn him would occur in four years' time. "Then I can be turned out and a better man with better views put in my place."

The next morning he left for Cleveland, but before his departure he made an address to the people of Pittsburgh, in which he said:

"In every short address I have made to the people, and in every crowd through which I have passed of late, some allusion has been made to the present distracted condition of the country. It is naturally expected that I should say something upon this subject, but to touch upon it at all would involve an elaborate discussion of a great many questions and circumstances, would require more time than I can at present command, and would perhaps unnecessarily commit me upon matters which have not yet fully developed themselves.

"The condition of the country, fellow-citizens, is an extraordinary one, and fills the mind of every patriot with anxiety and solicitude. My intention is to give this subject all the consideration which I possibly can before I speak fully and definitely in regard to it, so that, when I do speak, I may be as nearly right as possible. And when I do speak, fellow-citizens, I hope to say nothing in opposition to the spirit of the Constitution, contrary to the integrity of the Union, or which will in any way prove inimical to the liberties of the people or to the peace of the whole country. And, furthermore, when the time arrives for me to speak on this great subject, I hope to say nothing which will disappoint the reasonable expectations of any man, or disappoint the people generally throughout the country, especially if their expectations have been based upon any thing which I may have heretofore said.

"Notwithstanding the troubles across the river, [the speaker, smiling, pointed southwardly to the Monongahela River,] there is really no crisis springing from any thing in the Government itself. In plain words, there is really no crisis except an artificial one. What is there now to warrant the condition of affairs presented by our friends 'over the river'? Take even their own view of the questions involved, and there is nothing to justify the course which they are pursuing. I repeat it, then, there is no crisis, except such a one as may be gotten up at any time by turbulent men, aided by designing politicians. My advice, then, under such circumstances, is to keep cool. If the great American people will only keep their temper on both sides of the line, the trouble will come to an end, and the question which now distracts the country will be settled just as surely as all other difficulties of like character which have originated in this Government have been adjusted. Let the people on both sides keep their self-possession, and just as other clouds have cleared away in due time, so will this, and this great nation shall continue to prosper as heretofore."

He then referred to the subject of the tariff, and said:

"According to my political education, I am inclined to believe that the people in the various portions of the country should have their own views carried out through their representatives in Congress. That consideration of the Tariff bill should not be postponed until the next session of the National Legislature. No subject should engage your representatives more closely than that of the tariff. If I have any recommendation to make, it will be that every man who is called upon to serve the people, in a representative capacity, should study the whole subject thoroughly, as I intend to do myself, looking to all the varied interests of the common country, so that, when the time for action arrives, adequate protection shall be extended to the coal and iron of Pennsylvania and the corn of Illinois. Permit me to express the hope that this important subject may receive such consideration at the hands of your representatives that the interests of no part of the country may be overlooked, but that all sections may share in the common benefits of a just and equitable tariff."

Mr. Lincoln, upon his arrival in Cleveland, adverted to the same subject in the following terms:

"It is with you, the people, to advance the great cause of the Union and the Constitution, and not with any one man. It rests with you alone. This fact is strongly impressed on my mind at present. In a community like this, whose appearance testifies to their intelligence, I am convinced that the cause of liberty and the Union can never be in danger. Frequent allusion is made to the excitement at present existing in national politics. I think there is no occasion for any excitement. The crisis, as it is called, is altogether an artificial crisis. In all parts of the nation, there are differences of opinion in politics. There are differences of opinion even here. You did not all vote for the person who now addresses you. And how is it with those who are not here? Have they not all their rights as they ever had? Do they not have their fugitive slaves returned now as ever? Have they not the same Constitution that they have lived under for seventy odd years? Have they not a position as citizens of this common country, and have we any power to change that position? What, then, is the matter with them? Why all this excitement? Why all these complaints? As I said before, this crisis is all artificial. It has no foundation in fact. It was 'argued up,' as the saying is, and cannot be argued down. Let it alone, and it will go down itself."

On Saturday he proceeded to Buffalo, where he arrived at evening, and was met by an immense concourse of citizens, headed by Ex-President Fillmore.

Arriving at the hotel, Mr. Lincoln was welcomed in a brief speech by the acting chief magistrate, to which he made a brief reply, as follows:

"*Mr. Mayor and Fellow-Citizens*:—I am here to thank you briefly for this grand reception given to me, not personally, but as the representative of our great and beloved country. Your worthy mayor has been pleased to mention in his address to me, the fortunate and agreeable journey which I have had from home—only it is rather a circuitous route to the Federal Capital. I am very happy that he was enabled, in truth, to congratulate myself and company on that fact. It is true, we have had nothing thus far to mar the pleasure of the trip. We have not been met alone by those who assisted in giving the election to me; I say not alone, but by the whole population of the country through which we have passed. This is as it should be. Had the election fallen to any other of the distinguished candidates instead of myself, under the peculiar circumstances, to say the least, it would have been proper for all citizens to have greeted him as you now greet me. It is an evidence of the devotion of the whole people to the Constitution, the Union, and the perpetuity of the liberties of this country. I am unwilling, on any occasion, that I should be so meanly thought of as to have it supposed for a moment that these demonstrations are tendered to me personally. They are tendered to the country, to the institutions of the country, and to the perpetuity of the liberties of the country for which these institutions were made and created. Your worthy mayor has thought fit to express the hope that I may be able to relieve the country from the present, or, I should say, the threatened difficulties. I am sure I bring a heart true to the work. For the ability to perform it, I trust in that Supreme Being who has never forsaken this favored land, through the instrumentality of this great and intelligent people. Without that assistance I should surely fail; with it I cannot fail. When we speak of the threatened difficulties to the country, it is natural that it should be expected that something should be said by myself with regard to particular measures. Upon more mature reflection, however—and others will agree with me—that, when it is considered that these difficulties are without precedent, and never have been acted upon by any individual situated as I am, it is most proper I should wait and see the developments, and get all the light possible, so that, when I do speak authoritatively, I may be as near right as possible. When I shall speak authoritatively, I hope to say nothing inconsistent with the Constitution, the Union, the rights of all the States, of each State, and of each section of the country, and not to disappoint the reasonable expectations of those who have confided to me their votes. In this connection, allow me to say that you, as a portion of the great American people, need only to maintain your composure, stand up to your sober convictions of right, to your obligations to the Constitution, and act in accordance with those sober convictions, and the clouds which now arise in the horizon will be dispelled, and we shall have a bright and glorious future; and, when this generation shall have passed away, tens of thousands shall inhabit this country where only thousands inhabit it now. I do not propose to address you at length. I have no voice for it. Allow me again to thank you for this magnificent reception, and bid you farewell."

Mr. Lincoln then proceeded from Buffalo to Albany. Here he was met by the Mayor, the City Councils, and the Legislative Committees, and was conducted to the Capitol, where he was welcomed by Governor Morgan, and responded briefly, as follows:

"*Governor Morgan:*—I was pleased to receive an invitation to visit the capital of the great Empire State of this nation, while on my way to the Federal capital. I now thank you, and you, the people of the capital of the State of New York, for this most hearty and magnificent welcome. If I am not at fault, the great Empire State at this time contains a larger population than did the whole of the United States of America at the time they achieved their national independence; and I was proud to be invited to visit its capital, to meet its citizens as I now have the honor to do. I am notified by your governor that this reception is tendered by citizens without distinction of party. Because of this, I accept it the more gladly. In this country, and in any country where freedom of thought is tolerated, citizens attach themselves to political parties. It is but an ordinary degree of charity to attribute this act to the supposition that, in thus attaching themselves to the various parties, each man, in his own judgment, supposes he thereby best advances the interests of the whole country. And when an election is passed, it is altogether befitting a free people that, until the next election, they should be one people. The reception you have extended me to-day is not given to me personally. It should not be so, but as the representative, for the time being, of the majority of the nation. If the election had fallen to any of the more distinguished citizens, who received the support of the people, this same honor should have greeted him that greets me this day, in testimony of the unanimous devotion of the whole people to the Constitution, the Union, and to the perpetual liberties of succeeding generations in this country. I have neither the voice nor the strength to address you at any greater length. I beg you will, therefore, accept my most grateful thanks for this manifest devotion—not to me but to the institutions of this great and glorious country."

He was then conducted to the Legislative halls, where, in reply to an address of welcome, he again adverted to the troubles of the country in the following terms:

"*Mr. President and Gentlemen of the Legislature of the*

State of New York :—It is with feelings of great diffidence, and, I may say, feelings even of awe, perhaps greater than I have recently experienced, that I meet you here in this place. The history of this great State, the renown of its great men, who have stood in this chamber, and have spoken their thoughts, all crowd around my fancy, and incline me to shrink from an attempt to address you. Yet I have some confidence given me by the generous manner in which you have invited me, and the still more generous manner in which you have received me. You have invited me and received me without distinction of party. I could not for a moment suppose that this has been done in any considerable degree with any reference to my personal self. It is very much more grateful to me that this reception and the invitation preceding it were given to me as the representative of a free people than it could possibly have been were they but the evidence of devotion to me or to any one man. It is true that, while I hold myself, without mock-modesty, the humblest of all the individuals who have ever been elected President of the United States, I yet have a more difficult task to perform than any one of them has ever encountered. You have here generously tendered me the support, the united support, of the great Empire State. For this, in behalf of the nation—in behalf of the President and of the future of the nation—in behalf of the cause of civil liberty in all time to come—I most gratefully thank you. I do not propose now to enter upon any expressions as to the particular line of policy to be adopted with reference to the difficulties that stand before us in the opening of the incoming Administration. I deem that it is just to the country, to myself, to you, that I should see every thing, hear every thing, and have every light that can possibly be brought within my reach to aid me before I shall speak officially, in order that, when I do speak, I may have the best possible means of taking correct and true grounds. For this reason, I do not now announce any thing in the way of policy for the new Administration. When the time comes, according to the custom of the government, I shall speak, and speak as well as I am able for the good of the present and of the future of this country—for the good of the North and of the South—for the good of one and of the other, and of all sections of it. In the meantime, if we have patience, if we maintain our equanimity, though some may allow themselves to run off in a burst of passion, I still have confidence that the Almighty Ruler of the Universe, through the instrumentality of this great and intelligent people, can and will bring us through this difficulty, as he has heretofore brought us through all preceding difficulties of the country. Relying upon this, and again thanking you, as I forever shall, in my heart, for this generous reception you have given me, I bid you farewell."

At Albany, he was met by a delegation from the city authorities of New York, and on the 19th started for that city. At Poughkeepsie, he was welcomed by the Mayor of the city. Mr. Lincoln, in reply, said:

"I am grateful for this cordial welcome, and I am gratified that this immense multitude has come together, not to meet the individual man, but the man who, for the time being, will humbly but earnestly represent the majesty of the nation. These receptions have been given me at other places, and, as here, by men of different parties, and not by one party alone. It shows an earnest effort on the part of all to save, not the country, for the country can save itself, but to save the institutions of the country—those institutions under which, for at least three-quarters of a century, we have become the greatest, the most intelligent, and the happiest people in the world. These manifestations show that we all make common cause for these objects; that if some of us are successful in an election, and others are beaten, those who are beaten are not in favor of sinking the ship in consequence of defeat, but are earnest in their purpose to sail it safely through the voyage in hand, and, in so far as they may think there has been any mistake in the election, satisfying themselves to take their chance at setting the matter right the next time. That course is entirely right. I am not sure—I do not pretend to be sure—that in the selection of the individual who has been elected this term, the wisest choice has been made. I fear it has not. In the purposes and in the principles that have been sustained, I have been the instrument selected to carry forward the affairs of this Government. I can rely upon you, and upon the people of the country; and with their sustaining hand, I think that even I shall not fail in carrying the Ship of State through the storm."

The reception of President Lincoln in New York City was a most imposing demonstration. Places of business were generally closed, and hundreds of thousands were in the streets. On the next day, he was welcomed to the city by Mayor Wood, and replied as follows:

"*Mr. Mayor:* It is with feelings of deep gratitude that I make my acknowledgments for the reception given me in the great commercial city of New York. I cannot but remember that this is done by a people who do not, by a majority, agree with me in political sentiment. It is the more grateful, because in this I see that, for the great principles of our Government, the people are almost unanimous. In regard to the difficulties that confront us at this time, and of which your Honor has thought fit to speak so becomingly and so justly, as I suppose, I can only say that I agree in the sentiments expressed. In my devotion to the Union, I hope I am behind no man in the nation. In the wisdom with which to conduct the affairs tending to the preservation of the Union, I fear that too great confidence may have been reposed in me; but I am sure I bring a heart devoted to the work. There is nothing that could ever bring me to willingly consent to the destruction of this Union, under which not only the great commercial city of New York, but the whole country, acquired its greatness, except it be the purpose for which the Union itself was formed. I understand the ship to be made for the carrying and the preservation of the cargo, and so long as the ship can be saved with the cargo, it should never be abandoned, unless it fails the possibility of its preservation, and shall cease to exist, except at the risk of throwing overboard both freight and passengers. So long, then, as it is possible that the prosperity and the liberties of the people be preserved in this Union, it shall be my purpose at all times to use all my powers to aid in its perpetuation. Again thanking you for the reception given me, allow me to come to a close."

On the next day, he left for Philadelphia. At Trenton, he remained a few hours, and visited both Houses of the Legislature. On being received in the Senate, he thus addressed that body:

"*Mr. President and Gentlemen of the Senate of the State of New Jersey:* I am very grateful to you for the honorable reception of which I have been the object. I cannot but remember the place that New Jersey holds in our early history. In the early Revolutionary struggle, few of the States among the old Thirteen had more of the battle-fields of the country within its limits than old New Jersey. May I be pardoned, if, upon this occasion, I mention, that away back in my childhood, the earliest days of my being able to read, I got hold of a small book, such a one as few of the younger members have ever seen, 'Weems' Life of Washington.' I remember all the accounts there given of the battle-fields and struggles for the liberties of the country, and none fixed themselves upon my imagination so deeply as the struggle here at Trenton, New Jersey. The crossing of the river—the contest with the Hessians—the great hardships endured at that time—all fixed themselves on my memory more than any single revolutionary event; and you all know, for you have all been boys, how these early impressions last longer than any others. I recollect thinking then, boy even though I was, that there must have been something more than common that those men struggled for. I am exceedingly anxious that that thing which they struggled for—that something even more than National Independence—that something that held out a great promise to all the people of the world to all time to come—I am exceedingly anxious that this Union, the Constitution, and the liberties of the people, shall be perpetuated in accordance with the original idea for which that struggle was made, and I shall be most happy indeed if I shall be an humble instrument in the hands of the Almighty, and of this, His almost chosen people, for perpetuating the object of that great struggle. You give me this reception, as I understand, without distinction of party. I learn that this body is composed of a majority of gentlemen who, in the exercise of their best judgment in the choice of a Chief Magistrate, did not think I was the man. I understand, nevertheless, that they came forward here to greet me as the constitutional President of the United States—as citizens of the United States, to meet the man who, for the time being, is the representative man of the nation, united by a purpose to perpetuate the Union and liberties of the people. As such, I accept this reception more gratefully than I could do did I believe it was tendered to me as an individual."

He then passed into the Chamber of the Assembly, and upon being introduced by the Speaker, addressed that body as follows:

"*Mr. Speaker and Gentlemen:* I have just enjoyed the honor of a reception by the other branch of this Legislature, and I return to you and them my thanks for the reception which the people of New Jersey have given, through their chosen representatives, to me, as the representative, for the time being, of the majesty of the people of the United States. I appropriate to myself very little of the demonstrations of respect with which I have been greeted. I think little should be given to any man, but that it should be a manifestation of adherence to the Union and the Constitution. I understand myself to be received here by the representatives of the people of New Jersey, a majority of whom differ in opinion from those with whom I have acted. This manifestation is therefore to be regarded by me as expressing their devotion to the Union, the Constitution, and the liberties of the people. You, Mr. Speaker, have well said, that this is the time when the bravest and wisest look with doubt and awe upon the aspect presented by our national affairs. Under these circumstances, you will readily see why I should not speak in detail of the course I shall deem it best to pursue. It is proper that I should avail myself of all the information and all the time at my command, in order that when the time arrives in which I must speak officially, I shall be able to take the ground which I deem the best and safest, and from which I may have no occasion to swerve. I shall endeavor to take the ground I deem most just to the North, the East, the West, the South, and the whole country. I take it, I hope, in good temper—certainly with no malice towards any section. I shall do all that may be in my power to promote a peaceful settlement of all our difficulties. The man does not live who is more devoted to peace than I am—none who would do more to preserve it. But it may be necessary to put the foot down firmly. And if I do my duty, and do right, you will sustain me, will you not? Received, as I am, by the members of a Legislature, the majority of whom do not agree with me in political sentiments, I trust that I may have their assistance in piloting the Ship of State through this voyage, surrounded by perils as it is; for if it should suffer shipwreck now, there will be no pilot ever needed for another voyage."

On his arrival in Philadelphia, he was received with great enthusiasm, and the Mayor greeted him with the following address:

"*Sir:* In behalf of the Councils of Philadelphia and of its citizens, who, with common respect for their chief Magistrate-elect, have greeted your arrival, I tender you the hospitality of this city. I do this as the official representative of ninety thousand hearths, around which dwell six hundred thousand people, firm and ardent in their devotion to the Union; and yet it may not be withheld, that there are but few of these firesides whose cheer is not straitened and darkened by the calamitous condition of our country. The great mass of this people are heartily weary and sick of the selfish schemes and wily plots of mere politicians, who bear no more relation to true statesmanship than do the barnacles which incrust the ship to the master who stands by the helm. Your fellow-countrymen look to you in the earnest hope that true statesmanship and unalloyed patriotism may, with God's blessing, restore peace and prosperity to this distracted land. It is to be regretted that your short stay precludes that intercourse with the merchants, manufacturers, mechanics, and other citizens of Philadelphia, which might afford you a clear discernment of their great interests. And, sir, it could not be other than grateful to yourself to have the opportunity of communicating with the memories of the past, in those historic walls where were displayed the comprehensive intellects, and the liberal, disinterested virtues of our fathers, who framed the Constitution of the Federal States, over which you have been called upon to preside."

Mr. Lincoln replied:

"*Mr. Mayor and Fellow-citizens of Philadelphia:* I appear before you to make no lengthy speech but to thank you for this reception. The reception you have given me to-night is not to me, the man, the individual, but to the man who temporarily represents, or should represent, the majesty of the nation. It is true, as your worthy Mayor has said, that there is anxiety among the citizens of the United States at this time. I deem it a happy circumstance that this dissatisfied portion of our fellow-citizens do not point us to any thing in which they are being injured, or are about to be injured; for which reason I have felt all the while justified in concluding that the crisis, the panic, the anxiety of the country at this time, is artificial. If there be those who differ with me upon this subject, they have not pointed out the substantial difficulty that exists. I do not mean to say that an artificial panic may not do considerable harm; that it has done such I do not deny. The hope that has been expressed by your Mayor, that I may be able to restore peace, harmony, and prosperity to the country, is most worthy of him; and happy indeed will I be if I shall be able to verify and fulfil that hope. I promise you, in all sincerity, that I bring to the work a sincere heart. Whether I will bring a head equal to that heart, will be for future times to determine. It were useless for me to speak of details of plans now; I shall speak officially next Monday week, if ever. If I should not speak then, it were useless for me to do so now. If I do speak then, it is useless for me to do so now. When I do speak, I shall take such ground as I deem best calculated to restore peace, harmony, and prosperity to the country, and tend to the perpetuity of the nation, and the liberty of these States and these people. Your worthy Mayor has expressed the wish, in which I join with him, that it were convenient for me to remain with your city long enough to consult your merchants and manufacturers; or, as it were, to listen to those breathings rising within the consecrated walls wherein the Constitution of the United States, and, I will add, the Declaration of Independence, were originally framed and adopted. I assure you and your Mayor, that I had hoped on this occasion, and upon all occasions during my life, that I shall do nothing inconsistent with the teachings of these holy and most sacred walls. I never asked any thing that does not breathe from those walls. All my political warfare has been in favor of the teachings that come forth from these sacred walls. May my right hand forget its cunning, and my tongue cleave to the roof of my mouth, if ever I prove false to those teachings. Fellow-citizens, now allow me to bid you good-night."

On the next morning, Mr. Lincoln visited the old "Independence Hall," for the purpose of raising the national flag over it. Here he was received with a warm welcome, and made the following address:

"I am filled with deep emotion at finding myself standing here, in this place, where were collected the wisdom, the patriotism, the devotion to principle, from which sprang the institutions under which we live. You have kindly suggested to me that in my hands is the task of restoring peace to the present distracted condition of the country. I can say in return, sir, that all the political sentiments I entertain have been drawn, so far as I have been able to draw them, from the sentiments which originated and were given to the world from this hall. I have never had a feeling politically that did not spring from the sentiments embodied in the Declaration of Independence. I have often pondered over the dangers which were incurred by the men who assembled here, and framed and adopted that Declaration of Independence. I have pondered over the toils that were endured by the officers and soldiers of the army who achieved that independence. I have often inquired of myself what great principle or idea it was that kept this Confederacy so long together. It was not the mere matter of the separation of the colonies from the mother-land, but that sentiment in the Declaration of Independence which gave liberty, not alone to the people of this country, but, I hope, to the world for all future time. It was that which gave promise that in due time the weight would be lifted from the shoulders of all men. This is a sentiment embodied in the Declaration of Independence. Now, my friends, can this country be saved upon this basis? If it can, I will consider myself one of the happiest men in the world if I can help to save it. If it cannot be saved upon that principle, it will be truly awful. But if this country cannot be saved without giving up that principle, I was about to say I would rather be assassinated on this spot than surrender it. Now, in my view of the present aspect of affairs, there need be no bloodshed or war. There is no necessity for it. I am not in favor of such a course, and I may say, in advance, that there will be no bloodshed unless it be forced upon the government, and then it will be compelled to act in self-defence.

"My friends, this is wholly an unexpected speech, and I did not expect to be called upon to say a word when I came here. I supposed it was merely to do something towards raising the flag. I may, therefore, have said something indiscreet. I have said nothing but what I am willing to live by, and, if it be the pleasure of Almighty God, to die by."

The party then proceeded to a platform erected in front of the State House, and Mr. Benton, of the Select Council, invited the President-elect to raise the flag. Mr. Lincoln responded in a brief speech, stating his cheerful compliance with the request, and alluded to the original flag of thirteen stars, saying that the number had increased as time rolled on, and we became a happy and a powerful people, each star adding to its prosperity. "The future," he added, "is in the hands of the people. It is on such an occasion as this that we can reason together, reaffirm our devotion to the country and the principles of the Declaration of Independence. Let us make up our mind, that when we do put a new star upon our banner, it shall be a fixed one, never to be dimmed by the horrors of war, but brightened by the contentment and prosperity of peace. Let us go on to extend the area of our usefulness, add star upon star, until their light shall shine upon five hundred millions of a free and happy people."

The President-elect then raised the flag to the top of the staff.

At half-past 9 o'clock the party left for Harrisburg. Both Houses of the Legislature were visited by Mr. Lincoln, and to an address of welcome he thus replied:

"I appear before you only for a very few brief remarks, in response to what has been said to me. I thank you most sincerely for this reception, and the generous words in which support has been promised me upon this occasion. I thank your great commonwealth for the overwhelming support it recently gave, not to me personally, but the cause, which I think a just one, in the late election. Allusion has been made to the fact—the interesting fact, perhaps we should say—that I, for the first time, appear at the Capital of the great Commonwealth of Pennsylvania upon the birthday of the Father of his Country, in connection with that beloved anniversary connected with the history of this country. I have already gone through one exceedingly interesting scene this morning in the ceremonies at Philadelphia. Under the high conduct of gentlemen there, I was, for the first time, allowed the privilege of standing in Old Independence Hall, to have a few words addressed to me there, and opening up to me an opportunity of expressing, with much regret, that I had not more time to express something of my own feelings, excited by the occasion, somewhat to harmonize and give shape to the feelings that had been really the feelings of my whole life. Besides this, our friends there had provided a magnificent flag of the country. They had arranged it so that I was given the honor of raising it to the head of its staff. And when it went up I was pleased that it went to its place by the strength of my own feeble arm; when, according to the arrangement, the cord was pulled, and it flaunted gloriously to the wind without an accident, in the bright glowing sunshine of the morning, I could not help hoping that there was in the entire success of that beautiful ceremony at least something of an omen of what is to come. Nor could I help feeling then, as I often have felt, in the whole of that proceeding, I was a very humble instrument. I had not provided the flag; I had not made the arrangements for elevating it to its place. I had applied but a very small portion of my feeble strength in raising it. In the whole transaction I was in the hands of the people who had arranged it, and if I can have the same generous coöperation of the people of the nation, I think the flag of our country may yet be kept flaunting gloriously. I recur for a moment but to repeat some words uttered at the hotel in regard to what has been said about the military support which the General Government may expect from the Commonwealth of Pennsylvania in a proper emergency. To guard against any possible mistake do I recur to this. It is not with any pleasure that I contemplate the possibility that a necessity may arise in this country for the use of the military arm. While I am exceedingly gratified to see the manifestation upon your streets of your military force here, and exceedingly gratified at your promise here to use that force upon a proper emergency—while I make these acknowledgments, I desire to repeat, in order to preclude any possible misconstruction, that I do most sincerely hope that we shall have no use for them; that it will never become their duty to shed blood, and most especially never to shed fraternal blood. I promise that, so far as I may have wisdom to direct, if so painful a result shall in any wise be brought about, it shall be through no fault of mine. Allusion has also been made by one of your honored speakers to some remark recently made by myself at Pittsburg, in regard to what is supposed to be the especial interests of this great Commonwealth of Pennsylvania. I now wish only to say, in regard to that matter, that the few remarks which I uttered on that occasion were rather carefully worded. I took pains that they should be so. I have seen no occasion since to add to them or subtract from them. I leave them precisely as they stand, adding only now, that I am pleased to have an expression from you, gentlemen of Pennsylvania, significant that they are satisfactory to you. And now, gentlemen of the General Assembly of the Commonwealth of Pennsylvania, allow me to return you again my most sincere thanks."

PLOT TO ASSASSINATE HIM—HOW IT WAS THWARTED.

Arrangements had been made for his departure from

Harrisburg on the following morning, but the discovery of a plot to assassinate him as he passed through Baltimore—a plot in which some of the principal residents of that city were interested, although their projects were to be accomplished by means of paid emissaries—caused a change in the schedule, and on the evening of the day that he had been received by the Legislature, he left in a special train for Philadelphia, and from thence proceeded in the sleeping-car attached to the regular midnight train to Washington, where he arrived at an early hour on the morning of the twenty-third.

The sudden departure of Mr. Lincoln from the Pennsylvania State Capital naturally astonished the people of the country; and while the loyal citizens exulted in the fact that he was safe in Washington, the traitors and their sympathizers were greatly exasperated at the failure of their nefarious designs, and pronouncing the movement an act of cowardice, solemnly declared that he should never be inaugurated.

IS WELCOMED TO WASHINGTON BY THE AUTHORITIES.

A few days after his arrival he was waited upon by the Mayor and other municipal authorities, who welcomed him to the city, and to whom he made the following reply:

"*Mr. Mayor:* I thank you, and through you the municipal authorities of this city who accompany you, for this welcome. And as it is the first time in my life since the present phase of politics has presented itself in this country, that I have said any thing publicly within a region of country where the institution of slavery exists, I will take this occasion to say that I think very much of the ill-feeling that has existed, and still exists, between the people in the sections from whence I came and the people here, is dependent upon a misunderstanding of one another. I therefore avail myself of this opportunity to assure you, Mr. Mayor, and all the gentleman present, that I have not now, and never have had, any other than as kindly feelings towards you as the people of my own section. I have not now, and never have had, any disposition to treat you in any respect otherwise than as my own neighbors. I have not now any purpose to withhold from you any of the benefits of the Constitution, under any circumstances, that I would not feel myself constrained to withhold from my neighbors; and I hope, in a word, that, when we shall become better acquainted, and I say it with great confidence, we shall like each other the more. I thank you for the kindness of this reception."

ADDRESSES THE REPUBLICAN ASSOCIATION.

On the following evening the Republican Association tendered him a delightful serenade, at the conclusion of which he made the following remarks to the assembled crowd:

"*My friends*: I suppose that I may take this as a compliment paid to me, and as such please accept my thanks for it. I have reached this city of Washington under circumstances considerably differing from those under which any other man has ever reached it. I am here for the purpose of taking an official position amongst the people, almost all of whom were politically opposed to me, and are yet opposed to me as I suppose. I propose no lengthy address to you. I only propose to say, as I did on yesterday, when your worthy Mayor and Board of Aldermen called upon me, that I thought much of the ill-feeling that has existed between you and the people of your surroundings and that people from amongst whom I came, has depended, and now depends, upon a misunderstanding.

"I hope that, if things shall go along as prosperously as I believe we all desire they may, I may have it in my power to remove something of this misunderstanding; that I may be enabled to convince you, and the people of your section of the country, that we regard you as in all things our equals, and in all things entitled to the same respect and the same treatment that we claim for ourselves; that we are in nowise disposed, if it were in our power, to oppress you, to deprive you of any of your rights under the Constitution of the United States, or even narrowly to split hairs with you in regard to those rights, but are determined to give you, as far as lies in our hands, all your rights under the Constitution—not grudgingly, but fully and fairly. I hope that, by thus dealing with you, we will become better acquainted, and be better friends. And now, my friends, with these few remarks, and again returning my thanks for this compliment, and expressing my desire to hear a little more of your good music, I bid you good-night."

IS INAUGURATED PRESIDENT OF THE UNITED STATES.

On the fourth of March, 1861, Abraham Lincoln was inaugurated the Sixteenth President of the United States, the ceremonies incident to the event being of the most imposing description. A large number of troops participated in the procession, and every arrangement was made to frustrate any movement the Secessionists or their friends might make to prevent the choice of a majority of the voters of the nation from taking the oath of office. From a platform erected in the usual position on the east front of the capitol, and in the presence of not less than ten thousand persons, Mr. Lincoln delivered the following Inaugural Address:

INAUGURAL ADDRESS OF ABRAHAM LINCOLN.

"*Fellow-citizens of the United States:*

"In compliance with a custom as old as the Government itself, I appear before you to address you briefly, and to take, in your presence, the oath prescribed by the Constitution of the United States to be taken by the President, before he enters on the execution of his office.

"I do not consider it necessary, at present, for me to discuss those matters of administration about which there is no special anxiety or excitement. Apprehension seems to exist among the people of the Southern States, that, by the accession of a Republican Administration, their property and their peace and personal security are to be endangered. There has never been any reasonable cause for such apprehension. Indeed, the most ample evidence to the contrary has all the while existed, and been open to their inspection. It is found in nearly all the published speeches of him who now addresses you. I do but quote from one of those speeches, when I declare that 'I have no purpose, directly or indirectly, to interfere with the institution of slavery in the States where it exists.' I believe I have no lawful right to do so; and I have no inclination to do so. Those who nominated and elected me, did so with the full knowledge that I had made this, and made many similar declarations, and had never recanted them. And more than this, they placed in the platform, for my acceptance, and as a law to themselves and to me, the clear and emphatic resolution which I now read:

"'*Resolved,* That the maintenance inviolate of the rights of the States, and especially the right of each State to order and control its own domestic institutions according to its own judgment exclusively, is essential to that balance of power on which the perfection and endurance of our political fabric depend; and we denounce the lawless invasion by armed force of the soil of any State or Territory, no matter under what pretext, as among the gravest of crimes.'

"I now reiterate these sentiments; and in doing so I only press upon the public attention the most conclusive evidence of which the case is susceptible, that the property, peace, and security of no section are to be in anywise endangered by the now incoming Administration.

"I add, too, that all the protection which, consistently with the Constitution and the laws, can be given, will be cheerfully given to all the States when lawfully demanded, for whatever cause, as cheerfully to one section as to another.

"There is much controversy about the delivering up of fugitives from service or labor. The clause I now read is as plainly written in the Constitution as any other of its provisions:

"'No person held to service or labor in one State under the laws thereof, escaping into another, shall, in consequence of any law or regulation therein, be discharged from such service or labor, but shall be delivered up on claim of the party to whom such service or labor may be due.'

"It is scarcely questioned that this provision was intended by those who made it for the reclaiming of what we call fugitive slaves; and the intention of the lawgiver is the law.

"All members of Congress swear their support to the whole Constitution—to this provision as well as any other. To the proposition, then, that slaves whose cases come within the terms of this clause 'shall be delivered up,' their oaths are unanimous. Now, if they would make the effort in good temper, could they not, with nearly equal unanimity, frame and pass a law by means of which to keep good that unanimous oath?

"There is some difference of opinion whether this clause should be enforced by national or by State authority; but surely that difference is not a very material one. If the slave is to be surrendered, it can be of but little consequence to him or to others by which authority it is done; and should any one, in any case, be content that this oath shall go unkept on a merely unsubstantial controversy as to how it shall be kept?

"Again, in any law upon this subject, ought not all the safeguards of liberty known in the civilized and humane jurisprudence to be introduced, so that a free man be not, in any case, surrendered as a slave? And might it not be well at the same time to provide by law for the enforcement of that clause in the Constitution, which guarantees that 'the citizens of each State shall be entitled to all the privileges and immunities of citizens in the several States?'

"I take the official oath to-day with no mental reservations, and with no purpose to construe the Constitution or laws by any hypercritical rules; and while I do not choose now to specify particular acts of Congress as proper to be enforced, I do suggest that it will be much safer for all, both in official and private stations, to conform to and abide by all those acts which stand unrepealed, than to violate any of them, trusting to find impunity in having them held to be unconstitutional.

"It is seventy-two years since the first inauguration of a President under our national Constitution. During that period fifteen different and very distinguished citizens have in succession administered the executive branch of the government. They have conducted it through many perils, and generally with great success. Yet, with all this scope for precedent, I now enter upon the same task, for the brief constitutional term of four years, under great and peculiar difficulties.

"A disruption of the Federal Union, heretofore only menaced, is now formidably attempted. I hold that in the contemplation of universal law and of the Constitution, the Union of these States is perpetual. Perpetuity is implied, if not expressed, in the fundamental law of all national governments. It is safe to assert that no government proper ever had a provision in its organic law for its own termination. Continue to execute all the express provisions of our national Constitution, and the Union will endure forever, it being impossible to destroy it except by some action not provided for in the instrument itself.

"Again, if the United States be not a government proper, but an association of States in the nature of a contract merely, can it, as a contract, be peaceably unmade by less than all the parties who made it? One party to a contract may violate it—break it, so to speak; but does it not require all to lawfully rescind it? Descending from these general principles, we find the proposition that in legal contemplation the Union is perpetual, confirmed by the history of the Union itself.

"The Union is much older than the Constitution. It was formed, in fact, by the Articles of Association in 1774. It was matured and continued in the Declaration of Independence in 1776. It was further matured, and the faith of all the then thirteen States expressly plighted and engaged that it should be perpetual, by the Articles of Confederation, in 1778; and, finally, in 1787, one of the declared objects for ordaining and establishing the Constitution was to form a more perfect Union. But if the destruction of the Union by one or by a part only of the States be lawfully possible, the Union is less than before, the Constitution having lost the vital element of perpetuity.

"It follows from these views that no State, upon its own mere motion, can lawfully get out of the Union; that resolves and ordinances to that effect are legally void; and that acts of vio lence within any State or States against the authority of the United States are insurrectionary or revolutionary, according to circumstances.

"I therefore consider that, in view of the Constitution and the laws, the Union is unbroken, and, to the extent of my ability, I shall take care, as the Constitution itself expressly enjoins upon me, that the laws of the Union shall be faithfully executed in all the States. Doing this, which I deem to be only a simple duty on my part, I shall perfectly perform it, so far as is practicable, unless my rightful masters, the American people, shall withhold the requisition, or, in some authoritative manner, direct the contrary.

"I trust this will not be regarded as a menace, but only as the declared purpose of the Union that it will constitutionally defend and maintain itself.

"In doing this there need be no bloodshed or violence, and there shall be none unless it is forced upon the national authority.

"The power confided to me *will be used to hold, occupy, and possess the property and places belonging to the government*, and collect the duties and imposts; but beyond what may be necessary for these objects there will be no invasion, no using of force against or among the people anywhere.

"Where hostility to the United States shall be so great and so universal as to prevent competent resident citizens from holding the Federal offices, there will be no attempt to force obnoxious strangers among the people that object. While strict legal right may exist of the government to enforce the exercise of these offices, the attempt to do so would be so irritating, and so nearly impracticable withal, that I deem it better to forego for the time the uses of such offices.

"The mails, unless repelled, will continue to be furnished to all parts of the Union.

"So far as possible, the people everywhere shall have that sense of perfect security which is most favorable to calm thought and reflection.

"The course here indicated will be followed, unless current events and experience shall show a modification or change to be proper; and in every case and exigency my best discretion will be exercised according to the circumstances actually existing, and with a view and hope of a peaceful solution of the national troubles, and the restoration of fraternal sympathies and affections.

"That there are persons, in one section or another, who seek to destroy the Union at all events, and are glad of any pretext to do it, I will neither affirm nor deny. But if there be such, I need address no word to them.

"To those, however, who really love the Union, may I not speak, before entering upon so grave a matter as the destruction of our national fabric, with all its benefits, its memories, and its hopes? Would it not be well to ascertain why we do it? Will you hazard so desperate a step, while any portion of the ills you fly from have no real existence? Will you, while the certain ills you fly to, are greater than all the real ones you fly from? Will you risk the commission of so fearful a mistake? All profess to be content in the Union if all constitutional rights can be maintained. Is it true, then, that any right, plainly written in the Constitution, has been denied? I think not. Happily the human mind is so constituted, that no party can reach to the audacity of doing this.

"Think, if you can, of a single instance in which a plainly-written provision of the Constitution has ever been denied. If, by the mere force of numbers, a majority should deprive a minority of any clearly-written constitutional right, it might, in a moral point of view, justify revolution; it certainly would, if such right were a vital one. But such is not our case.

"All the vital rights of minorities and of individuals are so plainly assured to them by affirmations and negations, guarantees and prohibitions in the Constitution, that controversies never rise concerning them. But no organic law can ever be framed with a provision specifically applicable to every question which may occur in practical administration. No foresight can anticipate, nor any document of reasonable length contain, express provisions for all possible questions. Shall fugitives from labor be surrendered by national or by State authorities? The Constitution does not expressly say. Must Congress protect slavery in the territories? The Constitution does not expressly say. From questions of this class spring all our constitutional controversies, and we divide upon them into majorities and minorities.

"If the minority will not acquiesce, the majority must, or the government must cease. There is no alternative for continuing the government but acquiescence on the one side or the other. If a minority in such a case will secede rather than acquiesce, they make a precedent which in turn will ruin and divide them, for a minority of their own will secede from them whenever a majority refuses to be controlled by such a minority. For instance, why not any portion of a new confederacy, a year or two hence, arbitrarily secede again, precisely as portions of the present Union now claim to secede from it? All who cherish disunion sentiments are now being educated to the exact temper of doing this. Is there such perfect identity of interests among the States to compose a new Union as to produce harmony only, and prevent renewed secession? Plainly, the central idea of secession is the essence of anarchy.

"A majority held in restraint by constitutional check and limitations, and always changing easily with deliberate changes of popular opinions and sentiments, is the only true sovereign of a free people. Whoever reject it, does, of necessity, fly to anarchy or to despotism. Unanimity is impossible; the rule of a majority, as a permanent arrangement, is wholly inadmissible. So that, rejecting the majority principle, anarchy or despotism in some form is all that is left.

"I do not forget the position assumed by some that constitutional questions are to be decided by the Supreme Court, nor do I deny that such decisions must be binding in any case upon the parties to a suit, as to the object of that suit, while they are also entitled to very high respect and consideration in all parallel cases by all other departments of the government: and while it is obviously possible that such decision may be erroneous in any given case, still the evil effect following it, being limited to that particular case, with the chance that it may be overruled and never become a precedent for other cases, can better be borne than could the evils of a different practice.

"At the same time, the candid citizen must confess that, if the policy of the government upon the vital questions affecting the whole people is to be irrevocably fixed by the decisions of the Supreme Court, the instant they are made, as in ordinary litigation between parties in personal actions, the people will have ceased to be their own masters, unless having to that extent practically resigned their government into the hands of that eminent tribunal.

"Nor is there in this view any assault upon the court or the judges. It is a duty from which they may not shrink, to decide cases properly brought before them; and it is no fault of theirs if others seek to turn their decisions to political purposes. One section of our country believes slavery is right, and ought to be extended, while the other believes it is wrong, and ought not to be extended; and this is the only substantial dispute; and the fugitive slave clause of the Constitution, and the law for the suppression of the foreign slave-trade, are each as well enforced, perhaps, as any law can ever be in a community where the moral sense of the people imperfectly supports the law itself. The great body of the people abide by the dry legal obligation in both cases, and a few break over in each. This, I think, cannot be perfectly cured, and it would be worse, in both cases, after the separation of the sections, than before. The foreign slave-trade, now imperfectly suppressed, would be ultimately revived, without restriction, in one section; while fugitive slaves, now only partially surrendered, would not be surrendered at all by the other.

"Physically speaking, we cannot separate—we cannot remove our respective sections from each other, nor build an impassable wall between them. A husband and wife may be divorced, and go out of the presence and beyond the reach of the other, but the different parts of our country cannot do that. They cannot but remain face to face; and intercourse, either amicable or hostile, must continue between them. Is it possible, then, to make that intercourse more advantageous or more satisfactory after separation than before? Can aliens make treaties easier than friends can make laws? Can treaties be more faithfully enforced between aliens than laws can among friends? Suppose you go to war, you cannot fight always; and when, after much loss on both sides, and no gain on either, you cease fighting, the identical questions as to terms of intercourse are again upon you.

"This country, with its institutions, belongs to the people who inhabit it. Whenever they shall grow weary of the existing government, they can exercise their constitutional right of amending, or their revolutionary right to dismember or overthrow it. I cannot be ignorant of the fact that many worthy and patriotic citizens are desirous of having the national Constitution amended. While I make no recommendation of amendment, I fully recognize the full authority of the people over the whole subject, to be exercised in either of the modes prescribed in the instrument itself, and I should, under existing circumstances, favor, rather than oppose, a fair opportunity being afforded the people to act upon it.

"I will venture to add that to me the convention mode seems preferable, in that it allows amendments to originate with the people themselves, instead of only permitting them to take or reject propositions originated by others not especially chosen for the purpose, and which might not be precisely such as they would wish either to accept or refuse. I understand that a proposed amendment to the Constitution (which amendment, however, I have not seen) has passed Congress, to the effect that the Federal Government shall never interfere with the domestic institutions of States, including that of persons held to service. To avoid misconstruction of what I have said, I depart from my purpose not to speak of particular amendments, so far as to say that, holding such a provision to now be implied constitutional law, I have no objections to its being made express and irrevocable.

"The chief magistrate derives all his authority from the people, and they have conferred none upon him to fix the terms for the separation of the States. The people themselves, also, can do this if they choose, but the Executive, as such, has nothing to do with it. His duty is to administer the present government as it came to his hands, and to transmit it, unimpaired by him, to his successor. Why should there not be a patient confidence in the ultimate justice of the people? Is there any better or equal hope in the world? In our present differences, is either party without faith of being in the right? If the Almighty Ruler of nations, with his eternal truth and justice, be on your side of the North, or on yours of the South, that truth and that justice will surely prevail by the judgment of this great tribunal, the American people. By the frame of the government under which we live, this same people have wisely given their public servants but little power for mischief, and have, with equal wisdom, provided for the return of that little to their own hands at very short intervals. While the people retain their virtue and vigilance, no administration, by any extreme wickedness or folly, can very seriously injure the government in the short space of four years.

"My countrymen, one and all, think calmly and well upon this whole subject. Nothing valuable can be lost by taking time.

"If there be an object to hurry any of you, in hot haste, to a step which you would never take deliberately, that object will be frustrated by taking time; but no good object can be frustrated by it.

"Such of you as are now dissatisfied still have the old Constitution unimpaired, and, on the sensitive point, the laws of your own framing under it; while the new administration will have no immediate power, if it would, to change either.

"If it were admitted that you who are dissatisfied hold the right side in the dispute, there is still no single reason for precipitate action. Intelligence, patriotism, Christianity, and a firm reliance on Him who has never yet forsaken this favored land, are still competent to adjust, in the best way, all our present difficulties.

"In your hands, my dissatisfied fellow-countrymen, and not in mine, is the momentous issue of civil war. The government will not assail you.

"You can have no conflict without being yourselves the aggressors. You have no oath registered in heaven to destroy the government; while I shall have the most solemn one to 'preserve, protect, and defend it.'

"I am loth to close. We are not enemies, but friends. We must not be enemies. Though passion may have strained, it must not break our bonds of affection.

"The mystic cords of memory, stretching from every battle-field and patriot grave to every living heart and hearthstone all over this broad land, will yet swell the chorus of the Union, when again touched, as surely they will be, by the better angels of our nature."

Chief Justice Taney then administered the oath of office, and President Lincoln left the Capitol for the White House, where he held a public reception.

PRESIDENT LINCOLN'S INTERVIEW WITH THE VIRGINIA COMMISSIONERS.

On the 13th of April, 1861, Messrs. Preston Stuart and

Randolph, a committee appointed by the Virginia Convention, were formally received by the President, and presented the resolutions under which they were appointed. In response, Mr. Lincoln made the following address :

"GENTLEMEN : As a committee of the Virginia Convention, now in session, you present me a preamble and resolution in these words :

"'*Whereas*, in the opinion of this Convention, the uncertainty which prevails in the public mind as to the policy which the Federal Executive intends to pursue towards the seceded States is extremely injurious to the industrial and commercial interests of the country, tends to keep up an excitement which is unfavorable to the adjustment of the pending difficulties, and threatens a disturbance of the public peace ; therefore,

"'*Resolved*, That a committee of three delegates be appointed to wait on the President of the United States, present to him this preamble, and respectfully ask him to communicate to this Convention the policy which the Federal Executive intends to pursue in regard to the Confederate States.'

"In answer I have to say, that having, at the beginning of my official term, expressed my intended policy as plainly as I was able, it is with deep regret and mortification I now learn there is great and injurious uncertainty in the public mind as to what that policy is, and what course I intend to pursue. Not having as yet seen occasion to change, it is now my purpose to pursue the course marked out in the inaugural address. I commend a careful consideration of the whole document as the best expression I can give to my purposes. As I then and therein said, I now repeat, 'The power confided in me will be used to hold, occupy, and possess property and places belonging to the Government, and to collect the duties and imports ; but beyond what is necessary for these objects there will be no invasion, no using of force against or among the people anywhere.' By the words 'property and places belonging to the Government,' I chiefly allude to the military posts and property which were in possession of the government when it came into my hands. But if, as now appears to be true, in pursuit of a purpose to drive the United States authority from these places, an unprovoked assault has been made upon Fort Sumter, I shall hold myself at liberty to repossess it, if I can, like places which had been seized before the Government was devolved upon me, and in any event I shall, to the best of my ability, repel force by force. In case it proves true that Fort Sumter has been assaulted, as is reported, I shall, perhaps, cause the United States mails to be withdrawn from all the States which claim to have seceded, believing that the commencement of actual war against the Government justifies and possibly demands it. I scarcely need to say that I consider the military posts and property situated within the States which claim to have seceded, as yet belonging to the Government of the United States as much as they did before the supposed secession. Whatever else I may do for the purpose, I shall not attempt to collect the duties and imposts by any armed invasion of any part of the country; not meaning by this, however, that I may not land a force deemed necessary to relieve a fort upon the border of the country. From the fact that I have quoted a part of the inaugural address, it must not be inferred that I repudiate any other part, the whole of which I reaffirm, except so far as what I now say of the mails may be regarded as a modification."

Two days later the following proclamation was issued:

THE FIRST CALL FOR TROOPS.---CONGRESS SUMMONED TO ASSEMBLE.

"*Whereas*, The laws of the United States have been for some time past, and now are opposed, and the execution thereof obstructed, in the States of South Carolina, Georgia, Alabama, Florida, Mississippi, Louisiana, and Texas, by combinations too powerful to be suppressed by the ordinary course of judicial proceedings, or by the powers vested in the marshals by law; now, therefore, I, Abraham Lincoln, President of the United States, in virtue of the power in me vested by the Constitution and the laws, have thought fit to call forth, and hereby do call forth, the militia of the several States of the Union to the aggregate number of 75,000, in order to suppress said combinations and to cause the laws to be duly executed.

"The details for this object will be immediately communicated to the State authorities through the War Department. I appeal to all loyal citizens to favor, facilitate, and aid this effort to maintain the honor, the integrity, and existence of our national Union, and the perpetuity of popular government, and to redress wrongs already long enough endured. I deem it proper to say that the first service assigned to the forces hereby called forth, will probably be to repossess the forts, places, and property which have been seized from the Union; and in every event the utmost care will be observed, consistently with the objects aforesaid, to avoid any devastation, any destruction of, or interference with property, or any disturbance of peaceful citizens of any part of the country; and I hereby command the persons composing the combinations aforesaid, to disperse and retire peaceably to their respective abodes, within twenty days from this date.

"Deeming that the present condition of public affairs presents an extraordinary occasion, I do hereby, in virtue of the power in me vested by the Constitution, convene both Houses of Congress. The Senators and Representatives are, therefore, summoned to assemble at their respective chambers at twelve o'clock, noon, on Thursday, the fourth day of July next, then and there to consider and determine such measures as, in their wisdom, the public safety and interest may seem to demand.

"In witness whereof, I have hereunto set my hand, and caused the seal of the United States to be affixed.

"Done at the City of Washington, this fifteenth day of April, in the year of our Lord, one thousand eight hundred and sixty-one, and of the independence of the United States the eighy-fifth.

"By the President: "ABRAHAM LINCOLN.

"WILLIAM H. SEWARD, *Secretary of State.*"

Within three days after the appeal had been made to the patriots of the North, six hundred of their number had arrived in Washington, prepared for active duty and ready to sacrifice their lives in defence of the capital. The avenues to the city of Washington were guarded night and day, and cannon were placed in position. The excitement was intense, but amid all the various apprehensions of the residents and the country, he, who really should have been more especially anxious and fearful, was always calm and collected. The murderous outbreak in Baltimore on the nineteenth only increased the excitement, but, as if indifferent to the scenes which were in progress immediately around him, the President issued the following Proclamation, ordering a blockade of the Southern ports:

A BLOCKADE OF SOUTHERN PORTS ORDERED.

"*Whereas*, An insurrection against the Government of the United States has broken out in the States of South Carolina, Georgia, Alabama, Florida, Mississippi, Louisiana, and Texas, and the laws of the United States for the collection of the revenue cannot be efficiently executed therein conformably to that provision of the Constitution which requires duties to be uniform throughout the United States.

"*And whereas*, A combination of persons, engaged in such insurrection, have threatened to grant pretended letters of marque to authorize the bearers thereof to commit assaults on the lives, vessels, and property of good citizens of the country lawfully engaged in commerce on the high seas, and in waters of the United States.

"*And whereas*, An Executive Proclamation has been already issued, requiring the persons engaged in these disorderly proceedings to desist therefrom, calling out a militia force for the purpose of repressing the same, and convening Congress in extraordinary session to deliberate and determine thereon.

"Now, therefore, I, ABRAHAM LINCOLN, President of the United States, with a view to the same purpose before mentioned, and to the protection of the public peace, and the lives and property of quiet and orderly citizens pursuing their lawful occupations, until Congress shall have assembled and deliberated on the said unlawful proceedings, or until the same shall have ceased, have further deemed it advisable to set on foot a blockade of the ports within the States aforesaid, in pursuance of the laws of the United States and of the laws of nations in such cases provided. For this purpose a competent force will be posted so as to prevent entrance and exit of vessels from the ports aforesaid. If, therefore, with a view to violate such blockade, a vessel shall approach, or shall attempt to leave any of the said ports, she will be duly warned by the commander of one of the blockading vessels, who will indorse on her register the fact and date of such warning; and if the same vessel shall again attempt to enter or leave the blockaded port, she will be captured and sent to the nearest convenient port, for such proceedings against her and her cargo as prize as may be deemed advisable.

"And I hereby proclaim and declare, that if any person, under the pretended authority of said States, or under any other pretence, shall molest a vessel of the United States, or the persons or cargo on board of her, such person will be held amenable to the laws of the United States for the prevention and punishment of piracy.

"By the President: "ABRAHAM LINCOLN.

"WILLIAM H. SEWARD, *Secretary of State.*

"*Washington, April 19th*, 1861."

THE PRESIDENT'S COMMUNICATION WITH THE MARYLAND AUTHORITIES.

On the twentieth of April, the President sent the following letter to the Governor of Maryland and also to the Mayor of Baltimore:

"WASHINGTON, *April 20th*, 1861.

"GOVERNOR HICKS AND MAYOR BROWN:

"GENTLEMEN:—Your letter by Messrs. Bond, Dobbin, and Brune, is received. I tender you both my sincere thanks for your efforts to keep the peace in the trying situation in which you are placed. For the future, troops *must* be brought here, but I make no point of bringing them *through* Baltimore.

"Without any military knowledge myself, of course I must leave details to General Scott. He hastily said this morning, in presence of those gentlemen, 'March them *around* Baltimore, and not through it.'

"I sincerely hope the general, on fuller reflection, will consider this practical and proper, and that you will not object to it. By this a collision of the people of Baltimore with the troops will be avoided, unless they go out of the way to seek it. I hope you will exert your influence to prevent this. Now and ever, I shall do all in my power for peace, consistently with the maintenance of government

"Your obedient servant,

"A. LINCOLN."

And on the twenty-first, he sent a despatch to Mayor Brown, requesting him to proceed immediately to Washington, a request that was obeyed, and upon arriving at the White House the invited guest was admitted to an interview with the Cabinet and General Scott. The President informed the Mayor, and three of the citizens of Baltimore who had accompanied him, that he recognized the good faith of the City and State authorities, but should insist upon a recognition of his own.

He admitted the excited state of feeling in Baltimore, and his desire and duty to avoid the fatal consequences of a collision with the people. He urged, on the other hand, the absolute, irresistible necessity of having a transit through the State for such troops as might be necessary for the protection of the Federal capital. The protection of Washington, he asseverated with great earnestness, was the sole object of concentrating troops there; and he protested that none of the troops brought through Maryland were intended for any purposes hostile to the State, or aggressive as against the Southern States. Being now unable to bring them up the Potomac in security, the Government must either bring them through Maryland or abandon the capital.

He called on General Scott for his opinion, which the General gave at length, to the effect that troops might be brought through Maryland, without going through Baltimore, by either carrying them from Perryville to Annapolis, and thence by rail to Washington, or by bringing them to the Relay House on the Northern Central railroad, and marching them to the Relay House on the Washington railroad, and thence by rail to the capital. If the people would permit them to go by either of these routes uninterruptedly, the necessity of their passing through Baltimore would be avoided. If the people would not permit them a transit thus remote from the city, they must select their own best route, and, if need be, fight their way through Baltimore, a result which the General earnestly deprecated.

The President expressed his hearty concurrence in the desire to avoid a collision, and said that no more troops should be ordered through Baltimore if they were permitted to go uninterrupted by either of the other routes suggested. In this disposition the Secretary of War expressed his participation.

About this same date a deputation of sympathizers visited the President, and demanded a cessation of hostilities until the convening of Congress, accompanying the demand with the assertion that seventy-five thousand Marylanders would contest the passage of troops over their soil. Mr. Lincoln, in refusing to accede to the truce, quietly replied that he presumed there was room enough on her soil to bury seventy-five thousand men.

BLOCKADING OF VIRGINIA AND NORTH CAROLINA.

On the twenty-seventh of April, the following additional proclamation, extending the blockade, was issued :

"*Whereas*, For the reasons assigned in my proclamation of the 19th instant, a blockade of the ports of the States of South Carolina, Georgia, Florida, Alabama, Louisiana, Mississippi, and Texas, was ordered to be established; *And whereas*, Since that date public property of the United States has been seized, the collection of the revenue obstructed, and duly commissioned officers of the United States, while engaged in executing the orders of their superiors, have been arrested and held in custody as prisoners, or have been impeded in the discharge of their official duties, without due legal process, by persons claiming to act under authority of the States of Virginia and North Carolina, an efficient blockade of the ports of these States will therefore also be established.

"In witness whereof, I have hereunto set my hand, and caused the seal of the United States to be affixed.

"Done at the City of Washington, this 27th day of April, in the year of our Lord one thousand eight hundred and sixty-one, and of the Independence of the United States the eighty-fifth.

"By the President: "ABRAHAM LINCOLN.

"WILLIAM H. SEWARD, *Secretary of State.*"

Although the first call for troops had been responded to in the most gratifying manner by the outraged citizens of the free States, it was early ascertained that the number asked was totally insufficient for the existing exigencies, and on the third of May the following proclamation was issued:

A CALL FOR ADDITIONAL TROOPS.

"WASHINGTON, FRIDAY, *May 3d*, 1861.

"*Whereas*, Existing exigencies demand immediate and adequate measures for the protection of the national Constitution and the preservation of the national Union by the suppression of the insurrectionary combinations now existing in several States for opposing the laws of the Union and obstructing the execution thereof, to which end a military force, in addition to that called forth by my Proclamation of the fifteenth day of April, in the present year, appears to be indispensably necessary, now, therefore, I, Abraham Lincoln, President of the United States, and Commander-in-Chief of the Army and Navy thereof, and of the militia of the several States, when called into actual service, do hereby call into the service of the United States forty-two thousand and thirty-four volunteers, to serve for a period of three years, unless sooner discharged, and to be mustered into service as infantry and cavalry. The proportions of each arm and the details of enrolment and organization will be made known through the Department of War; and I also direct that the regular army of the United States be increased by the addition of eight regiments of infantry, one regiment of cavalry, and one regiment of artillery, making altogether a maximum aggregate increase of 22,714 officers and enlisted men, the details of which increase will also be made known through the Department of War; and I further direct the enlistment, for not less than one nor more than three years, of 18,000 seamen, in addition to the present force, for the naval service of the United States. The details of the enlistment and organization will be made known through the Department of the Navy. The call for volunteers, hereby made, and the direction of the increase of the regular army, and for the enlistment of seamen hereby given, together with the plan of organization adopted for the volunteers and for the regular forces hereby authorized, will be submitted to Congress as soon as assembled.

"In the meantime, I earnestly invoke the co-operation of all good citizens in the measures hereby adopted for the effectual suppression of unlawful violence, for the impartial enforcement of constitutional laws, and for the speediest possible restoration of peace and order, and with those of happiness and prosperity throughout our country.

"In testimony whereof, I have hereunto set my hand, and caused the seal of the United States to be affixed.

"Done at the City of Washington, this third day of May, in the year of our Lord one thousand eight hundred and sixty-one, and of the Independence of the United States the eighty-fifth.

"By the President: "ABRAHAM LINCOLN.

"WILLIAM H. SEWARD, *Secretary of State.*"

AN INTERVIEW WITH THE MARYLAND LEGISLATURE.

On the following day, the President had an interview with a Committee of the Maryland Legislature, who admitted the right of the Government to transport troops through Baltimore or Maryland, but expressed their belief that no immediate efforts would be made by the State authorities at secession or resistance, and asked that the State might be spared military occupation, or a mere revengeful chastisement for former transgressions. The President, in reply, promised to give their suggestions a respectful consideration, and stated that whatever measures might be adopted, would be actuated entirely by the public interests and not by any spirit of revenge.

A SPECIAL ORDER FOR FLORIDA.

On the tenth of May, 1861, the following proclamation was promulgated:

"*Whereas*, An insurrection exists in the State of Florida, by which the lives, liberty, and property of loyal citizens of the United States are endangered.

"*And whereas*, It is deemed proper that all needful measures should be taken for the protection of such citizens and all officers of the United States in the discharge of their public duties in the State aforesaid.

"Now, therefore, be it known that I, Abraham Lincoln, President of the United States, do hereby direct the Commander of the forces of the United States on the Florida coast to permit no person to exercise any office or authority upon the Islands of Key West, the Tortugas, and Santa Rosa, which may be inconsistent with the laws and Constitution of the United States, authorizing him at the same time, if he shall find it necessary, to suspend there the writ of *habeas corpus*, and to remove from the vicinity of the United States fortresses all dangerous or suspected persons.

"In witness whereof, I have hereunto set my hand, and caused the seal of the United States to be affixed.

"Done at the City of Washington, this tenth day of May, in the year of our Lord one thousand eight hundred and sixty-one, and of the Independence of the United States the eighty-fifth.

"By the President: "ABRAHAM LINCOLN.

"WILLIAM H. SEWARD, *Secretary of State.*"

PRESIDENT LINCOLN'S FIRST MESSAGE TO CONGRESS.

On the fourth of July, 1861, Congress assembled, in pursuance to the call of the President, and received from the Executive the following Message:

"FELLOW-CITIZENS OF THE SENATE AND HOUSE OF REPRESENTATIVES:—Having been convened on an extraordinary occasion, as authorized by the Constitution, your attention is not called to any ordinary subject of legislation. At the beginning of the present Presidential term, four months ago, the functions of the Federal Government were found to be generally suspended within the several States of South Carolina, Georgia, Alabama, Mississippi, Louisiana, and Florida, excepting only those of the Post-Office Department.

"Within these States all the Forts, Arsenals, Dock-Yards, Custom-Houses, and the like, including the movable and stationary property in and about them, had been seized, and were held in open hostility to this Government, excepting only Forts Pickens, Taylor, and Jefferson, on and near the Florida coast, and Fort Sumter in Charleston harbor, South Carolina. The forts thus seized had been put in improved condition, new ones had been built, and armed forces had been organized, and were organizing, all avowedly for the same hostile purpose.

"The forts remaining in possession of the Federal Government in and near these States were either besieged or menaced by warlike preparations, and especially Fort Sumter was nearly surrounded by well-protected hostile batteries, with guns equal in quality to the best of its own, and outnumbering the latter as, perhaps, ten to one—a disproportionate share of the Federal muskets and rifles had somehow found their way into these States, and had been seized to be used against the Government.

"Accumulations of the public revenue lying within them had been seized for the same object. The navy was scattered in distant seas, leaving but a very small part of it within the immediate reach of the Government.

"Officers of the Federal army had resigned in great numbers, and of those resigning a large proportion had taken up arms against the Government.

"Simultaneously, and in connection with all this, the purpose to sever the Federal Union was openly avowed. In accordance with this purpose an ordinance had been adopted in each of these States, declaring the States respectively to be separated from the National Union. A formula for instituting a combined Government of these States had been promulgated, and this illegal organization, in the character of the 'Confederate States,' was already invoking recognition, aid, and intervention from foreign Powers.

"Finding this condition of things, and believing it to be an imperative duty upon the incoming Executive to prevent, if possible, the consummation of such attempt to destroy the Federal Union, a choice of means to that end became indispensable. This choice was made and was declared in the Inaugural Address.

"The policy chosen looked to the exhaustion of all peaceful measures before a resort to any stronger ones. It sought only to hold the public places and property not already wrested from the Government, and to collect the revenue, relying for the rest on time, discussion, and the ballot-box. It promised a continuance of the mails, at Government expense, to the very people who were resisting the Government, and it gave repeated pledges against any disturbances to any of the people, or any of their rights, of all that which a President might constitutionally and justifiably do in such a case; every thing was forborne, without which it was believed possible to keep the Government on foot.

"On the 5th of March, the present incumbent's first full day in office, a letter from Major Anderson, commanding at Fort Sumter, written on the 28th of February and received at the War Department on the 4th of March, was by that Department placed in his hands. This letter expressed the professional opinion of the writer, that reinforcements could not be thrown into that fort within the time for its relief rendered necessary by the limited supply of provisions, and with a view of holding possession of the same, with a force less than 20,000 good and well-disciplined men. This opinion was concurred in by all the officers of his command, and their memoranda on the subject were made inclosures of Major Anderson's letter. The whole was immediately laid before Lieutenant-General Scott, who at once concurred with Major Anderson in his opinion. On reflection, however, he took full time, consulting with other officers both of the army and navy, and at the end of four days came reluctantly but decidedly to the same conclusion as before. He also stated at the same time that no such sufficient force was then at the control of the Government, or could be raised and brought to the ground, within the time when the provisions in the fort would be exhausted. In a purely military point of view, this reduced the duty of the Administration in the case to the mere matter of getting the garrison safely out of the fort.

"It was believed, however, that to so abandon that position, under the circumstances, would be utterly ruinous; that the necessity under which it was to be done would not be fully understood; that by many it would be construed as a part of a voluntary policy; that at home it would discourage the friends of the Union, embolden its adversaries, aud go far to insure to the latter a recognition abroad; that, in fact, it would be our national destruction consummated. This could not be allowed. Starvation was not yet upon the garrison, and ere it would be reached, Fort Pickens might be reinforced. This last would be a clear indication of policy, and would better enable the country to accept the evacuation of Fort Sumter as a military necessity. An order was at once directed to be sent for the landing of the troops from the steamship Brooklyn into Fort Pickens. This order could not go by land, but must take the longer and slower route by sea. The first return news from the order was received just one week before the fall of Sumter. The news itself was that the officer commanding the Sabine, to which vessel the troops had been transferred from the Brooklyn, acting upon some quasi armistice of the late Administration, and of the existence of which the present Administration, up to the time the order was despatched, had only too vague and uncertain rumors to fix attention, had refused to land the troops. To now reinforce Fort Pickens before a crisis would be reached at Fort Sumter was impossible, rendered so by the near exhaustion of provisions at the latter named fort. In precaution against such a conjuncture the Government had a few days before commenced preparing an expedition, as well adapted as might be, to relieve Fort Sumter, which expedition was intended to be ultimately used or not, according to circumstances. The strongest anticipated case for using it was now presented, and it was resolved to send it forward as had been intended. In this contingency it was also resolved to notify the Governor of South Carolina that he might expect an attempt would be made to provision the fort, and that if the attempt should not be resisted, there would be no attempt to throw in men, arms, or ammunition, without further notice or in case of an attack upon the fort. This notice was accordingly given, whereupon the fort was attacked and bombarded to its fall, without even awaiting the arrival of the provisioning expedition.

"It is thus seen that the assault upon, and reduction of Fort Sumter, was, in no sense, a matter of self-defence on the part of the assailants. They well knew that the garrison in the fort could by no possibility commit aggression upon them; they knew they were expressly notified that the giving of bread to the few brave and hungry men of the garrison was all which would on that occasion be attempted, unless themselves, by resisting so much, should provoke more. They knew that this Government desired to keep the garrison in the fort, not to assail them, but merely to maintain visible possession, and thus to preserve the Union from actual and immediate dissolution; trusting, as hereinbefore stated, to time, discussion, and the ballot-box for final adjustment, and they assailed and reduced the fort, for precisely the reverse object, to drive out the visible authority of the Federal Union, and thus force it to immediate dissolution; that this was their object the Executive well understood, having said to them in the Inaugural Address, 'you can have no conflict without being yourselves the aggressors.' He took pains not only to keep this declaration good, but also to keep the case so far from ingenious sophistry as that the world should not misunderstand it. By the affair at Fort Sumter, with its surrounding circumstances, that point was reached. Then and thereby the assailants of the Government began the conflict of arms,—without a gun in sight or in expectancy to return their fire, save only the few in the fort sent to that harbor years before, for their own protection, and still ready to give that protection in whatever was lawful. In this act, discarding all else, they have forced upon the country the distinct issue, immediate dissolution or blood, and this issue embraces more than the fate of these United States. It presents to the whole family of man the question whether a Constitutional Republic or Democracy, a Government of the people, by the same people, can or cannot maintain its territorial integrity against its own domestic foes. It presents the question whether discontented individuals, too few in numbers to control the Administration according to the organic law in any case, can always, upon the pretences made in this case, or any other pretences or arbitrarily without any pretence, break up their Government, and thus practically put an end to free government upon the earth. It forces us to ask, 'Is there in all republics this inherent and fatal weakness?' Must a Government of necessity be too strong for the liberties of its own people, or too weak to maintain its own existence? So viewing the issue, no choice was left but to call out the war power of the Government, and so to resist the force employed for its destruction by force for its preservation. The call was made, and the response of the country was most gratifying, surpassing, in unanimity and spirit, the most sanguine expectation. Yet none of the States, commonly called slave States, except Delaware, gave a regiment through the regular State organization. A few regiments have been organized within some others of those States by individual enterprise, and received into the Government service. Of course the seceded States, so called, and to which Texas had been joined about the time of the inauguration, gave no troops to the cause of the Union. The Border States, so called, were not uniform in their action, some of them being almost for the Union, while in others as in Virginia, North Carolina, Tennessee, and Arkansas, the Union sentiment was nearly repressed and silenced. The course taken in Virginia was the most remarkable, perhaps the most important. A convention, elected by the people of that State to consider this very question of disrupting the Federal Union, was in session at the capital of Virginia when Fort Sumter fell.

"To this body the people had chosen a large majority of professed Union men. Almost immediately after the fall of Sumter many members of that majority went over to the original disunion minority, and with them adopted an ordinance for withdrawing the State from the Union. Whether this change was wrought by their great approval of the assault upon Sumter, or their great resentment at the Government's resistance to that assault, is not definitely known. Although they submitted the ordinance for ratification to a vote of the people, to be taken on a day then somewhat more than a month distant, the Convention and the Legislature, which was also in session at the same time and place, with leading men of the State, not members of either, immediately commenced acting as if the State was already out of the Union. They pushed military preparations vigorously forward all over the State. They seized the United States Armory at Harper's Ferry, and the Navy-Yard at Gosport, near Norfolk. They received, perhaps invited into their State large bodies of troops, with their warlike appointments, from the so-called seceded States.

"They formally entered into a treaty of temporary alliance with the so-called Confederate States, and sent members to their

Congress at Montgomery, and finally they permitted the insurrectionary Government to be transferred to their capitol at Richmond. The people of Virginia have thus allowed this giant insurrection to make its nest within her borders, and this Government has no choice left but to deal with it where it finds it, and it has the less to regret as the loyal citizens have in due form claimed its protection. Those loyal citizens this Government is bound to recognize and protect as being in Virginia. In the Border States, so called, in fact the middle States, there are those who favor a policy which they call armed neutrality, that is, an arming of those States to prevent the Union forces passing one way or the disunion forces the other over their soil. This would be disunion completed. Figuratively speaking, it would be the building of an impassable wall along the line of separation, and yet not quite an impassable one, for under the guise of neutrality it would tie the hands of the Union men, and freely pass supplies from among them to the insurrectionists, which it could not do as an open enemy. At a stroke it would take all the trouble off the hands of secession, except only what proceeds from the external blockade. It would do for the disunionists that which of all things they most desire, feed them well and give them disunion without a struggle of their own. It recognizes no fidelity to the Constitution, no obligation to maintain the Union, and while very many who have favored it are doubtless loyal citizens, it is nevertheless very injurious in effect.

"Recurring to the action of the Government it may be stated that at first a call was made for 75,000 militia, and rapidly following this a proclamation was issued for closing the ports of the insurrectionary districts by proceedings in the nature of a blockade. So far all was believed to be strictly legal.

"At this point the insurrectionists announced their purpose to enter upon the practice of privateering.

"Other calls were made for volunteers, to serve three years, unless sooner discharged, and also for large additions to the regular army and navy. These measures, whether strictly legal or not, were ventured upon under what appeared to be a popular demand and a public necessity, trusting then, as now, that Congress would ratify them.

"It is believed that nothing has been done beyond the constitutional competency of Congress. Soon after the first call for militia it was considered a duty to authorize the commanding general, in proper cases, according to his discretion, to suspend the privilege of the writ of habeas corpus; or, in other words, to arrest and detain, without resort to the ordinary processes and forms of law, such individuals as he might deem dangerous to the public safety. This authority has purposely been exercised but very sparingly. Nevertheless the legality and propriety of what has been done under it are questioned, and the attention of the country has been called to the proposition that one who is sworn to take care that the laws be faithfully executed, should not himself violate them. Of course some consideration was given to the questions of power and propriety before this matter was acted upon. The whole of the laws which were required to be faithfully executed were being resisted, and failing of execution in nearly one-third of the States. Must they be allowed to finally fail of execution, even had it been perfectly clear that by use of the means necessary to their execution, some single law, made in such extreme tenderness of the citizen's liberty that practically it relieves more of the guilty than the innocent, should to a very great extent be violated? To state the question more directly, are all the laws but one to go unexecuted, and the Government itself to go to pieces lest that one be violated? Even in such a case would not the official oath be broken if the Government should be overthrown when it was believed that disregarding the single law would tend to preserve it.

"But it was not believed that this question was presented. It was not believed that any law was violated. The provision of the Constitution, that the privilege of the writ of habeas corpus shall not be suspended, unless when, in cases of rebellion or invasion, the public safety may require it, is equivalent to a provision that such privilege may be suspended when, in cases of rebellion or invasion, the public safety does require it. It was decided that we have a case of rebellion, and that the public safety does require the qualified suspension of the privilege of the writ, which was authorized to be made. Now, it is insisted that Congress, and not the Executive, is vested with this power. But the Constitution itself is silent as to which or who is to exercise the power; and as the provision was plainly made for a dangerous emergency, it cannot be believed that the framers of the instrument intended that in every case the danger should run its course until Congress could be called together, the very assembling of which might be prevented, as was intended in this case by the rebellion. No more extended argument is now afforded, as an opinion at some length will probably be presented by the Attorney-General. Whether there shall be any legislation on the subject, and if so what, is submitted entirely to the better judgment of Congress. The forbearance of this Government had been so extraordinary, and so long continued, as to lead some foreign nations to shape their action as if they supposed the early destruction of our national Union was probable. While this, on discovery, gave the Executive some concern, he is now happy to say that the sovereignty and rights of the United States are now everywhere practically respected by foreign Powers, and a general sympathy with the country is manifested throughout the world.

"The reports of the Secretaries of the Treasury, War, and

the Navy, will give the information in detail deemed necessary and convenient for your deliberation and action, while the Executive and all the departments will stand ready to supply omissions or to communicate new facts considered important for you to know.

"It is now recommended that you give the legal means for making this contest a short and decisive one; that you place at the control of the Government for the work at least 400,000 men and $400,000,000; that number of men is about one-tenth of those of proper ages within the regions where apparently all are willing to engage, and the sum is less than a twenty-third part of the money value owned by the men who seem ready to devote the whole. A debt of $600,000,000 now is a less sum per head than was the debt of our Revolution when we came out of that struggle, and the money value in the country bears even a greater proportion to what it was then than does the population. Surely each man has as strong a motive now to preserve our liberties as each had then to establish them.

"A right result at this time will be worth more to the world than ten times the men and ten times the money. The evidence reaching us from the country leaves no doubt that the material for the work is abundant, and that it needs only the hand of legislation to give it legal sanction, and the hand of the Executive to give it practical shape and efficiency. One of the greatest perplexities of the Government is to avoid receiving troops faster than it can provide for them; in a word, the people will save their Government if the Government will do its part only indifferently well. It might seem at first thought to be of little difference whether the present movement at the South be called secession or rebellion. The movers, however, well understand the difference. At the beginning they knew that they could never raise their treason to any respectable magnitude by any name which implies violation of law; they knew their people possessed as much of moral sense, as much of devotion to law and order, and as much pride in its reverence for the history and Government of their common country, as any other civilized and patriotic people. They knew they could make no advancement directly in the teeth of these strong and noble sentiments. Accordingly they commenced by an insidious debauching of the public mind; they invented an ingenious sophism, which, if conceded, was followed by perfectly logical steps through all the incidents of the complete destruction of the Union. The sophism itself is that any State of the Union may, consistently with the nation's Constitution, and therefore lawfully and peacefully, withdraw from the Union without the consent of the Union or of any other State.

"The little disguise that the supposed right is to be exercised only for just cause, themselves to be the sole judge of its justice, is too thin to merit any notice with rebellion. Thus sugar coated, they have been drugging the public mind of their section for more than thirty years, and until at length they have brought many good men to a willingness to take up arms against the Government the day after some assemblage of men have enacted the farcical pretence of taking their State out of the Union, who could have been brought to no such thing the day before. This sophism derives much, perhaps the whole of its currency, from the assumption that there is some omnipotent and sacred supremacy pertaining to a State, to each State of our Federal Union. Our States have neither more nor less power than that reserved to them in the Union by the Constitution, no one of them ever having been a State out of the Union. The original ones passed into the Union before they cast off their British Colonial dependence, and the new ones came into the Union directly from a condition of dependence, excepting Texas, and even Texas, in its temporary independence, was never designated as a State. The new ones only took the designation of States on coming into the Union, while that name was first adopted for the old ones in and by the Declaration of Independence. Therein the United Colonies were declared to be *free* and *independent* States. But even then the object plainly was not to declare their independence of one another of the Union, but directly the contrary, as their mutual pledge and their mutual action before, at the time, and afterward, abundantly show. The express plight of faith by each and all of the original thirteen States in the Articles of Confederation two years later that the Union shall be perpetuated, is most conclusive. Having never been States either in substance or in name outside of the Union, whence this magical omnipotence of State rights, asserting a claim of power to lawfully destroy the Union itself. Much is said about the sovereignty of the States, but the word even is not in the National Constitution, nor, as is believed, in any of the State constitutions. What is sovereignty in the political sense of the word? Would it be far wrong to define it a political community without a political superior? Tested by this, no one of our States, except Texas, was a sovereignty, and even Texas gave up the character on coming into the Union, by which act she acknowledged the Constitution of the United States; and the laws and treaties of the United States, made in pursuance of States, have their status in the Union, made in pursuance of the Constitution, to be for her the supreme law. The States have their status in the Union, and they have no other legal status. If they break from this, they can only do so against law and by revolution. The Union, and not themselves separately, procured their independence and their liberty by conquest or purchase. The Union gave each of them whatever of independence and liberty it has. The Union is older than any of the States, and, in fact, it created them, as States. Originally, some dependent Colonies made the Union, and in turn the

Union threw off their old dependence for them and made them States, such as they are. Not one of them ever had a State constitution independent of the Union. Of course it is not forgotten that all the new States formed their constitutions before they entered the Union; nevertheless, dependent upon, and preparatory to coming into the Union. Unquestionably, the States have the powers and rights reserved to them in and by the National Constitution.

"But among these surely are not included all conceivable powers, however mischievous or destructive, but at most such only as were known in the world at the time as governmental powers, and certainly a power to destroy the Government itself had never been known as a governmental, as a merely administrative power. This relative matter of national power and State rights as a principle, is no other than the principle of generality and locality. Whatever concerns the whole should be conferred to the whole General Government, while whatever concerns only the State should be left exclusively to the State. This is all there is of original principle about it. Whether the National Constitution, in defining boundaries between the two, has applied the principle with exact accuracy, is not to be questioned. We are all bound by that defining without question. What is now combated, is the position that secession is consistent with the Constitution, is lawful and peaceful. It is not contended that there is any express law for it, and nothing should ever be implied as law which leads to unjust or absurd consequences. The nation purchased with money the countries out of which several of those States were formed. Is it just that they shall go off without leave and without refunding? The nation paid very large sums in the aggregate, I believe nearly a hundred millions, to relieve Florida of the aboriginal tribes. Is it just that she shall now be off without consent or without any return? The nation is now in debt for money applied to the benefit of these so-called seceding States, in common with the rest. Is it just, either that creditors shall go unpaid, or the remaining States pay the whole? A part of the present national debt was contracted to pay the old debt of Texas. Is it just that she shall leave and pay no part of this herself? Again, if one State may secede so may another, and when all shall have seceded none is left to pay the debts. Is this quite just to creditors? Did we notify them of this sage view of ours when we borrowed their money? If we now recognize this doctrine by allowing the seceders to go in peace, it is difficult to see what we can do if others choose to go, or to extort terms upon which they will promise to remain. The seceders insist that our Constitution admits of secession. They have assumed to make a National Constitution of their own, in which, of necessity, they have either discarded or retained the right of secession, as they insist exists in ours. If they have discarded it, they thereby admit that on principle it ought not to exist in ours; if they have retained it, by their own construction of ours that shows that to be consistent, they must secede from one another whenever they shall find it the easiest way of settling their debts, or effecting any other selfish or unjust object. The principle itself is one of disintegration, and upon which no Government can possibly endure. If all the States save one should assert the power to drive that one out of the Union, it is presumed the whole class of seceder politicians would at once deny the power, and denounce the act as the greatest outrage upon State rights. But suppose that precisely the same act, instead of being called driving the one out, should be called the seceding of the others from that one, it would be exactly what the seceders claim to do, unless, indeed, they made the point that the one, because it is a minority, may rightfully do what the others, because they are a majority, may not rightfully do. These politicians are subtle, and profound in the rights of minorities. They are not partial to that power which made the Constitution, and speaks from the preamble, calling itself, 'We, the people.' It may be well questioned whether there is to-day a majority of the legally-qualified voters of any State, except, perhaps, South Carolina, in favor of disunion. There is much reason to believe that the Union men are the majority in many, if not in every one of the so-called seceded States. The contrary has not been demonstrated in any one of them. It is ventured to affirm this, even of Virginia and Tennessee, for the result of an election held in military camps, where the bayonets are all on one side of the question voted upon, can scarcely be considered as demonstrating popular sentiment. At such an election all that large class who are at once for the Union and against coercion, would be coerced to vote against the Union. It may be affirmed, without extravagance, that the free institutions we enjoy have developed the powers and improved the condition of our whole people beyond any example in the world. Of this we now have a striking and impressive illustration. So large an army as the Government has now on foot was never before known, without a soldier in it but who has taken his place there of his own free choice. But more than this, there are many single regiments whose members, one and another, possess full practical knowledge of all the arts, sciences, professions, and whatever else, whether useful or elegant, is known in the whole world, and there is scarcely one from which there could not be selected a President, a Cabinet, a Congress, and perhaps a Court, abundantly competent to administer the Government itself. Nor do I say this is not true also in the army of our late friends, now adversaries, in this contest. But it is so much better the reason why the Government which has conferred such benefits on both them and us should not be broken up. Whoever in any section proposes to abandon such a Government, would do well to consider in deference to what prin ciple it is that he does it. What better he is likely to get in its stead, whether the substitute will give, or be intended to give so much of good to the people. There are some foreshadowings on this subject. Our adversaries have adopted some declarations of independence in which, unlike the good old one penned by Jefferson, they omit the words, 'all men are created equal.' Why? They have adopted a temporary National Constitution, in the preamble of which, unlike our good old one signed by Washington, they omit 'We the people,' and substitute 'We, the deputies of the sovereign and independent States.' Why? Why this deliberate pressing out of view the rights of men and the authority of the people? This is essentially a people's contest. On the side of the Union it is a struggle for maintaining in the world that form and substance of Government whose leading object is to elevate the condition of men, to lift artificial weights from all shoulders, to clear the paths of laudable pursuit for all, to afford all an unfettered start and a fair chance in the race of life, yielding to partial and temporary departures from necessity. This is the leading object of the Government, for whose existence we contend.

"I am most happy to believe that the plain people understand and appreciate this. It is worthy of note that while in this, the Government's hour of trial, large numbers of those in the army and navy who have been favored with the offices, have resigned and proved false to the hand which pampered them, not one common soldier or common sailor is known to have deserted his flag. Great honor is due to those officers who remained true despite the example of their treacherous associates, but the greatest honor and the most important fact of all, is the unanimous firmness of the common soldiers and common sailors. To the last man, so far as known, they have successfully resisted the traitorous efforts of those whose commands but an hour before they obeyed as absolute law. This is the patriotic instinct of plain people. They understand without an argument that the destroying the Government which was made by Washington means no good to them. Our popular Government has often been called an experiment. Two points in it our people have settled: the successful establishing and the successful administering of it. One still remains. Its successful maintenance against a formidable internal attempt to overthrow it. It is now for them to demonstrate to the world that those who can fairly carry an election can also suppress a rebellion; that ballots are the rightful and peaceful successors of bullets, and that when ballots have fairly and constitutionally decided, there can be no successful appeal back to bullets; that there can be no successful appeal except to ballots themselves at succeeding elections. Such will be a great lesson of peace, teaching men that what they cannot take by an election, neither can they take by a war, teaching all the folly of being the beginners of a war.

"Lest there be some uneasiness in the minds of candid men

as to what is to be the course of the government toward the Southern States after the rebellion shall have been suppressed, the Executive deems it proper to say it will be his purpose, then, as ever, to be guided by the Constitution and the laws, and that he probably will have no different understanding of the powers and duties of the Federal Government relatively to the rights of the States and the people under the Constitution than that expressed in the inaugural address. He desires to preserve the government, that it may be administered for all, as it was administered by the men who made it. Loyal citizens everywhere have the right to claim this of their government, and the government has no right to withhold or neglect it. It is not perceived that, in giving it, there is any coercion, any conquest, or any subjugation in any sense of these terms.

"The Constitution provided, and all the States have accepted the provision, 'that the United States shall guarantee to every State in this Union a Republican form of government;' but if a State may lawfully go out of the Union, having done so, it may also discard the Republican form of government. So that to prevent its going out is an indispensable means to the end of maintaining the guarantee mentioned; and, when an end is lawful and obligatory, the indispensable means to it are also lawful and obligatory.

"It was with the deepest regret that the Executive found the duty of employing the war power forced upon him. In defence of the government he could but perform this duty or surrender the existence of the government. No compromise by public servants could, in this case, be a cure; not that compromises are not often proper, but that no popular government can long survive a marked precedent, that those who carry an election can only save the government from immediate destruction by giving up the main point upon which the people gave the election. The people themselves and not their servants can safely reverse their own deliberate decisions.

"As a private citizen, the Executive could not have consented that these institutions shall perish, much less could he in betrayal of so vast and so sacred a trust as these free people had confided to him. He felt that he had no moral right to shrink, nor even to count the chances of his own life in what might follow.

"In full view of his great responsibility, he has so far done what he has deemed his duty. You will now, according to your own judgment, perform yours. He sincerely hopes that your views and your actions may so accord with his as to assure all faithful citizens who have been disturbed in their rights of a certain and speedy restoration to them under the Constitution and laws; and, having thus chosen our cause without guile, and with pure purpose, let us renew our trust in God, and go forward without fear and with manly hearts.

"ABRAHAM LINCOLN."

A DAY OF FASTING AND PRAYER APPOINTED.

On the twelfth of August, the following proclamation, appointing a day of fasting and prayer, was issued:

"*Whereas*, A joint committee of both Houses of Congress has waited on the President of the United States, and requested him to 'recommend a day of public humiliation, prayer, and fasting, to be observed by the people of the United States with religious solemnities, and the offering of fervent supplications to Almighty God for the safety and welfare of these States, His blessings on their arms, and a speedy restoration of peace.'

"*And whereas*, It is fit and becoming in all people, at all times, to acknowledge and revere the Supreme Government of God; to bow in humble submission to his chastisements; to confess and deplore their sins and transgressions, in the full conviction that the fear of the Lord is the beginning of wisdom, and to pray, with all fervency and contrition, for the pardon of their past offences, and for a blessing upon their present and prospective action.

"*And whereas*, When our own beloved country, once, by the blessing of God, united, prosperous, and happy, is now afflicted with faction and civil war, it is peculiarly fit for us to recognize the hand of God in this terrible visitation, and, in sorrowful remembrance of our own faults and crimes as a nation, and as individuals, to humble ourselves before Him, and to pray for His mercy—to pray that we may be spared further punishment, though most justly deserved; that our arms may be blessed and made effectual for the re-establishment of law, order, and peace throughout the wide extent of our country; and that the inestimable boon of civil and religious liberty, earned under His guidance and blessing by the labors and sufferings of our fathers, may be restored in all its original excellence;

"Therefore I, Abraham Lincoln, President of the United States, do appoint the last Thursday in September next as a day of humiliation, prayer and fasting for all the people of the nation. And I do earnestly recommend to all the people, and especially to all ministers and teachers of religion, of all denominations, and to all heads of families, to observe and keep that day, according to their several creeds and modes of worship, in all humility, and with all religious solemnity, to the end that the united prayer of the nation may ascend to the Throne of Grace, and bring down plentiful blessings upon our country.

"In testimony whereof, I have hereunto set my hand, and caused the seal of the United States to be affixed, this [L. S.] 12th day of August, A. D. 1861, and of the Independence of the United States of America the eighty-sixth.

'By the President: "ABRAHAM LINCOLN.

"WILLIAM H. SEWARD, *Secretary of State*."

COMMERCIAL INTERCOURSE WITH THE REBELLIOUS STATES PROHIBITED.

Four days later he also promulgated the following :

"*Whereas*, On the 15th day of April, the President of the United States, in view of an insurrection against the laws, Constitution, and Government of the United States, which had broken out within the States of South Carolina, Georgia, Alabama, Florida, Mississippi, Louisiana, and Texas, and in pursuance of the provisions of the act entitled an act to provide for calling forth the militia to execute the laws of the Union, suppress insurrections, and repel invasions, and to repeal the act now in force for that purpose, approved February 28th, 1795, did call forth the militia to suppress said insurrection and cause the laws of the Union to be duly executed—and the insurgents have failed to disperse by the time directed by the President; *and whereas*, such insurrection has since broken out and yet exists within the States of Virginia, North Carolina, Tennessee, and Arkansas; *and whereas*, the insurgents in all the said States claim to act under authority thereof, and such claim is not disclaimed or repudiated by the persons exercising the functions of government in such State or States, or in the part or parts thereof, in which such combinations exist, nor has such insurrection been suppressed by said States.

"Now, therefore, I, Abraham Lincoln, President of the United States, in pursuance of the act of Congress approved July 13th, 1861, do hereby declare that the inhabitants of the said States of Georgia, South Carolina, Tennessee, Alabama, Louisiana, Texas, Arkansas, Mississippi, and Florida, except the inhabitants of that part of the State of Virginia lying west of the Alleghany Mountains, and of such other parts of that State and the other States hereinbefore named as may maintain a loyal adhesion to the Union and the Constitution, or may be, from time to time occupied and controlled by the forces of the United States engaged in the dispersion of said insurgents, as are in a state of insurrection against the United States, and that all commercial intercourse between the same and the inhabitants thereof, with the exception aforesaid, and the citizens of other States and other parts of the United States, is unlawful and will remain unlawful until such insurrection shall cease or has been suppressed ; that all goods and chattels, wares and merchandize, coming from any of the said States, with the exceptions aforesaid, into other parts of the United States, without the special license and permission of the President, through the Secretary of the Treasury, or proceeding to any of the said States, with the exception aforesaid, by land or water, together with the vessel or vehicle conveying the same or conveying persons to and from the said States, with the said exceptions, will be forfeited to the United States; and that, from and after fifteen days from the issuing of this proclamation, all ships and vessels belonging, in whole or in part, to any citizen or inhabitant of any of the said States, with the said exceptions, found at sea in any part of the United States, will be forfeited to the United States; and I hereby enjoin upon all district attorneys, marshals, and officers of the revenue of the military and naval forces of the United States to be vigilant in the execution of the said act, and in the enforcement of the penalties and forfeitures imposed or declared by it, leaving any party who may think himself aggrieved thereby to his application to the Secretary of the Treasury for the remission of any penalty or forfeiture, which the said Secretary is authorized by law to grant if, in his judgment, the special circumstances of any case shall require such a remission.

"In witness whereof, I have hereunto set my hand, and caused the seal of the United States to be affixed.

"Done in the city of Washington, this, the 16th day of August, in the year of our Lord one thousand eight hundred and sixty-one, and of the Independence of the United States of America the eighty-sixth.

"By the President: "ABRAHAM LINCOLN.

"WILLIAM H. SEWARD."

HE MODIFIES AN ORDER OF GENERAL FREMONT.

In the latter part of August, General Fremont declared martial law throughout the State of Missouri, and at the same time ordered that the property of all persons within the limits of his Department who had been disloyal, should be confiscated, and their slaves declared free men, but the President promptly issued an order modifying that clause of the proclamation in relation to the confiscation of property and the liberation of slaves, so as to conform with, and not transcend the provisions on the same subject contained in the Act of Congress approved August 6th, 1861.

HIS SECOND MESSAGE TO CONGRESS.

On the 3d of December, 1861, Congress having convened on the preceding day, the President sent in his Message, a document which was eminently conservative and which was received with great satisfaction by the loyal men of the country. No general scheme of emancipation was urged, and in alluding to the policy to be adopted to ensure the suppression of the rebellion, he stated that he had been anxious and careful that the inevitable conflict necessary for that purpose should not degenerate into a violent and remorseless revolutionary struggle. "I have, therefore," he continued, "in every case, thought it proper to keep the integrity of the Union prominent as the primary object of the contest on our part, leaving all questions which are not of vital military importance to the more deliberate action of the Legislature."

There can never be any difficulty in ascertaining Mr. Lincoln's views upon the exciting and absorbing topics of the day. His messages, proclamations, and correspondence all evince the same spirit of independence and determination, while his language is so explicit that there can be no doubt of his meaning. In his letter to Governor Magoffin, of Kentucky, declining to remove the Union troops from that State, and rebuking that official for his indifference to the cause of his country—in the one to General Fremont, in reference to the modification of his proclamation, and in fact in all his correspondence on matters connected with political movements, his views have been of such a force and exalted character that they could not fail to receive the hearty approbation of his fellow-countrymen.

On the nineteenth of February, 1862, he issued a proclamation requesting the people of the United States to assemble on the twenty-second of the same month and celebrate the day by reading the Farewell Address of the "Father of his Country."

THE PRESIDENT'S MESSAGE RECOMMENDING GRADUAL EMANCIPATION.

On the sixth of March, 1862. the President sent into

Congress the following Message, recommending the adoption of measures looking to "gradual, and not sudden" emancipation:

"*Fellow-Citizens of the Senate and House of Representatives:*

"I recommend the adoption of a joint resolution by your honorable bodies which shall be substantially as follows:

"'*Resolved,* That the United States ought to coöperate with any State which may adopt a gradual abolishment of slavery, giving to such State pecuniary aid to be used by such State in its discretion, to compensate for the inconveniences, public and private, produced by such change of system.'

"If the proposition contained in the resolution does not meet the approval of Congress and the country, there is the end; but if it does command such approval, I deem it of importance that the States and people immediately interested should be at once distinctly notified of the fact, so that they may begin to consider whether to accept or reject it. The Federal Government would find its highest interest in such a measure as one of the most efficient means of self-preservation. The leaders of the existing insurrection entertain the hope that the Government will ultimately be forced to acknowledge the independence of some part of the disaffected region, and that all the slave States north of such parts will then say: 'The Union for which we have struggled being already gone, we now choose to go with the southern section.' To deprive them of this hope, substantially ends the rebellion, and the initiation of emancipation completely deprives them of it as to all the States initiating it.

"The point is not that all the States tolerating slavery would very soon, if at all, initiate emancipation, but that while the offer is equally made to all, the more northern shall, by such initiation, make it certain to the more southern that in no event will the former ever join the latter in their proposed confederacy. I say 'initiation,' because, in my judgment, gradual and not sudden emancipation is better for all. In the mere financial or pecuniary view, any member of Congress, with the census tables and the treasury report before him, can readily see for himself how very soon the current expenditures of this war would purchase, at a fair valuation, all the slaves in any named State.

"Such a proposition on the part of the general Government sets up no claim of a right by Federal authority to interfere with slavery within State limits, referring as it does the absolute control of the subject in each case to the State and its people immediately interested. It is proposed as a matter of perfectly free choice with them.

"In the annual message last December I thought fit to say:

'The Union must be preserved, and hence all indispensable means must be employed.' I said this not hastily, but deliberately. War has been, and continues to be an indispensable means to this end. A practical re-acknowledgment of the national authority would render the war unnecessary, and it would at once cease. If, however, resistance continues, the war must also continue, and it is impossible to foresee all the incidents which may attend, and all the ruin which may follow it. Such as may seem indispensable, or may obviously promise great efficiency toward ending the struggle, must and will come. The proposition now made is an offer only, and I hope it may be esteemed no offence to ask whether the pecuniary consideration tendered would not be of more value to the States and private persons concerned than are the institution and property in it, in the present aspect of affairs. While it is true that the adoption of the proposed resolution would be merely initiatory, and not within itself a practical measure, it is recommended in the hope that it would soon lead to important results. In full view of my great responsibility to my God and to my country, I earnestly beg the attention of Congress and the people to the subject. "ABRAHAM LINCOLN."

This important recommendation was received with the most unbounded satisfaction in all sections of the great North and West, and the leading loyal journals vied with each other in the laudatory notices bestowed upon its illustrious author. The English press favorable to the preservation of the Union, were equally complimentary, and pronounced it a fair, moderate, and magnanimous policy, greatly in contrast with that adopted by the rebel authorities.

ASSUMES ACTIVE COMMAND OF THE ARMY AND NAVY.

On the eleventh of March, 1862, the President gave an additional evidence of his independence and fearlessness by promulgating, for the information of the service and the country, three important military orders, assuming the active duties of Commander-in-Chief of the Army and Navy of the United States; ordering a general and combined movement of the land and naval forces; requiring the Army of the Potomac to be organized into Corps; confining General McClellan to the command of the Department of the Potomac; and organizing the Department of the Mississippi and the Mountain Department.

THANKSGIVING FOR SIGNAL VICTORIES.

The triumphant success of our arms in the South and West during the early spring months of that year of conflict and carnage, prompted Mr. Lincoln to call upon the patriots of the nation to offer up their thanks to the Almighty for his manifold kindnesses, and for the inestimable blessings he had showered upon them in their hour of need. The recommendation was scrupulously observed, and from almost every place of public worship arose upon the following Sabbath songs of thanksgiving, mingled with invocations for a continuance of the Divine guidance.

SLAVERY ABOLISHED IN THE DISTRICT OF COLUMBIA.

On the sixteenth of April, 1862, Mr. Lincoln consummated an act which had for many years been one of his most favorite projects, by sending into Congress the following Message:

"*Fellow-Citizens of the Senate and House of Representatives:*

"The act entitled 'An act for the release of certain persons held to service or labor in the District of Columbia,' has this day been approved and signed.

"I have never doubted the constitutional authority of Congress to abolish slavery in this District, and I have ever desired to see the national capital freed from the institution in some satisfactory way. Hence there has never been in my mind any question upon the subject except the one of expediency, arising in view of all the circumstances. If there be matters within and about this act, which might have taken a course or shape more satisfactory to my judgment, I do not attempt to specify them. I am gratified that the two principles of compensation and colonization are both recognized and practically applied in the act.

"In the matter of compensation, it is provided that claims may be presented within ninety days from the passage of the act, but not thereafter, and there is no saving for minors, *femmes coverts*, insane, or absent persons. I presume this is an omission by mere oversight, and I recommend that it be supplied by an amendatory or supplemental act. "ABRAHAM LINCOLN."

RE-OPENING OF SOUTHERN PORTS.

During the month of May, 1862, two important proclamations were published—one on the twelfth, declaring the ports of Beaufort, Port Royal, and New Orleans open for trade; and the second, a week later, repudiating an emancipation order of Major-General Hunter. This last document is too important a part of the history of the rebellion to be omitted here, and we therefore give it in full. It is as follows:

" *Whereas*, There appears in the public prints what purports to be a proclamation of Major-General Hunter, in the words and figures following, to wit:

"'HEAD-QUARTERS, DEPARTMENT OF THE SOUTH,
"'HILTON HEAD, S. C., *May 9th*, 1862.

"'GENERAL ORDERS NO. 11.

"'The three States of Georgia, Florida, and South Carolina, comprising the Military Department of the South, having deliberately declared themselves no longer under the protection of the United States of America, and having taken up arms against the said United States, it becomes a military necessity to declare them under martial law. This was accordingly done on the twenty-fifth day of April, 1862. Slavery and martial law in a free country are altogether incompatible. The persons in these three States, Georgia, Florida, and South Carolina, heretofore held as slaves, are therefore declared forever free.

"'DAVID HUNTER, *Major-General Commanding.*

"'Official:

"'ED. W. SMITH, *Acting Assistant Adjutant-General.*'

"*And whereas*, The same is producing some excitement and misunderstanding,

"*Therefore*, I, Abraham Lincoln, President of the United States, proclaim and declare that the government of the United States had no knowledge or belief of an intention, on the part of General Hunter, to issue such a proclamation, nor has it yet any authentic information that the document is genuine; and further, that neither General Hunter nor any other commander or person has been authorized by the government of the United States to make proclamation declaring the slaves of any State free, and that the supposed proclamation now in question, whether genuine or false, is altogether void, so far as respects such declaration.

"I further make known, that whether it be competent for me as commander-in-chief of the army and navy to declare the slaves of any State or States free, and whether at any time, or in any case, it shall have become a necessity indispensable to the maintenance of the government to exercise such supposed power, are questions which, under my responsibility, I reserve to myself, and which I cannot feel justified in leaving to the decision of commanders in the field. These are totally different questions from those of police regulations in armies and camps.

"On the sixth day of March last, by a special message, I recommended to Congress the adoption of a joint resolution, to be substantially as follows:

"'*Resolved*, That the United States ought to co-operate with any State which may adopt a gradual abolishment of slavery, giving to such State in its discretion to compensate for the inconveniences, public and private, produced by such change of system.'

"The resolution, in the language above quoted, was adopted by large majorities in both branches of Congress, and now stands an authentic, definite and solemn proposal of the nation to the States and people most immediately interested in the subject matter. To the people of these States I now earnestly appeal. I do not argue; I beseech you to make the arguments for yourselves. You cannot, if you would, be blind to the signs of the times. I beg of you a calm and enlarged consideration of them, ranging, if it may be, far above personal and partisan politics. This proposal makes common cause for a common object, casting no reproaches upon any. It acts not the Pharisee. The change it contemplates would come gently as the dews of Heaven, not rending or wrecking any thing. Will you not embrace it? So much good has not been done by one effort in all past time, as in the Providence of God it is now your high privilege to do. May the vast future not have to lament that you have neglected it.

"In witness whereof, I have hereunto set my hand, and caused the seal of the United States to be affixed.

"Done at the City of Washington, this nineteenth day of May, in the year of our Lord one thousand eight hundred and sixty-two, and of the Independence of the United States the eighty-sixth.

"By the President: "ABRAHAM LINCOLN.

"WM. H. SEWARD, *Secretary of State*."

THE PRESIDENT'S CONFERENCE WITH THE LOYAL GOVERNORS—HIS INTERVIEW WITH THE BORDER CONGRESSMEN.

On the first of July, 1862, the President, in accordance with the Act for the collection of direct taxes in the insurrectionary districts, issued a proclamation declaring in what States and in what counties of Virginia insurrection existed; and on the same day addressed a letter to the Governors of the loyal States, in reply to one received from them, asking that for the purpose of following up recent signal successes by measures which would ensure the speedy restoration of the Union, a sufficient number of men from each State to fill up existing regiments and to form new organizations, might be called for. Mr. Lincoln fully concurred in the views of the Executives and expressed his intention to call for an additional force of three hundred thousand men.

On the twelfth of July, an interesting interview took place at the White House, the Senators and Representatives of the Border States having assembled there by invitation of the President, who wished to converse with them upon the important topic of gradual emancipation. During an extended conversation, he expressed his views clearly and explicitly, requesting their calm consideration of the subject, and charging them to commend his suggestions to their constituents, and to prevent all doubt of his meaning, read to them the following appeal:

"*Gentlemen:* After the adjournment of Congress, now near, I shall have no opportunity of seeing you for several months. Believing that you of the border States hold more power for good than any other equal number of members, I feel it a duty, which I cannot justifiably waive, to make this appeal to you.

"I intend no reproach or complaint when I assure you that, in my opinion, if you all had voted for the resolution in the gradual emancipation message of last March, the war would now be substantially ended. And the plan therein proposed is yet one of the most potent and swift means of ending it. Let the States which are in rebellion see definitely and certainly that, in no event, will the States you represent ever join their proposed confederacy, and they cannot much longer maintain the contest. But you cannot divest them of their hope to ultimately have you with them so long as you show a determination to perpetuate the institutions within your own States. Beat them at elections, as you have overwhelmingly done, and, nothing daunted, they still claim you as their own. You and I know what the lever of their power is. Break that lever before their faces, and they can shake you no more forever.

"Most of you have treated me with kindness and consideration, and I trust you will not now think I improperly touch what is exclusively your own, when, for the sake of the whole country, I ask, 'Can you, for your States, do better than to take the course I urge?' Discarding *punctilio* and maxims adapted to more manageable times, and looking only to the unprecedentedly stern facts of our case, can you do better in any possible event? You prefer that the constitutional relation of the States to the nation shall be practically restored without disturbance of the institution; and, if this were done, my whole duty, in this respect, under the Constitution and my oath of office, would be performed. But it is not done, and we are trying to accomplish it by war. The incidents of the war cannot be avoided. If the war continues long, as it must if the object be not sooner attained, the institution in your States will be extinguished by mere friction and abrasion—by the mere incidents of the war. It will be gone, and you will have nothing valuable in lieu of it. Much of its value is gone already. How much better for you and for your people to take the step which at once shortens the war, and secures substantial compensation for that which is sure to be wholly lost in any other event! How much better to thus save the money which else we sink forever in the war! How much better to do it while we can, lest the war, ere long, render us pecuniarily unable to do it! How much better for you, as seller, and the nation, as buyer, to sell out and buy out that without which the war could never have been, than to sink both the thing to be sold and the price of it in cutting one another's throats.

"I do not speak of emancipation *at once*, but of a *decision* at once to emancipate *gradually*. Room in South America for colonization can be obtained cheaply and in abundance; and, when numbers shall be large enough to be company and encouragement for one another, the freed people will not be so reluctant to go.

"I am pressed with a difficulty not yet mentioned—one which threatens division among those who, united, are none too strong. An instance of it is known to you. General Hunter is an honest man. He was, and I hope still is, my friend. I valued him none the less for his agreeing with me in the general wish that all men everywhere could be freed. He proclaimed all men free within certain States, and I repudiated the proclamation. He expected more good and less harm from the measure than I could believe would follow. Yet, in repudiating it, I gave dissatisfaction, if not offence, to many whose support the country cannot afford to lose. And this is not the end of it. The pressure in this direction is still upon me, and is increasing. By conceding what I now ask, you can relieve me, and, much more, can relieve the country in this important point.

"Upon these considerations I have again begged your attention to the message of March last. Before leaving the capital, consider and discuss it among yourselves. You are patriots and statesmen, and, as such, I pray you consider this proposition, and, at the least, commend it to the consideration of your States and people. As you would perpetuate popular government for the best people in the world, I beseech you that you do in nowise omit this. Our common country is in great peril, demanding the loftiest views and boldest action to bring a speedy relief. Once relieved, its form of government is saved to the world, its beloved history and cherished memories are vindicated, and its happy future fully assured and rendered inconceivably grand. To you, more than to any others, the privilege is given to assure that happiness and swell that grandeur, and to link your own names therewith forever."

INSTRUCTIONS TO MILITARY AND NAVAL COMMANDERS.

On the twenty-second of July, he issued the following order:

"WAR DEPARTMENT, WASHINGTON, *July 22d*, 1862.

"*First*. Ordered that military commanders within the States of Virginia, North Carolina, Georgia, Florida, Alabama, Mississippi, Louisiana, Texas, and Arkansas, in an ordinary manner seize and use any property, real or personal, which may be necessary or convenient for their several commands, for supplies, or for other military purposes; and that while property may be destroyed for proper military objects, none shall be destroyed in wantonness or malice.

"*Second*. That military and naval commanders shall employ as laborers, within and from said States, so many persons of African descent as can be advantageously used for military or naval purposes, giving them reasonable wages for their labor.

"*Third*. That, as to both property, and persons of African descent, accounts shall be kept sufficiently accurate and in detail to show quantities and amounts, and from whom both property and such persons shall have come, as a basis upon which compensation can be made in proper cases; and the several departments of this government shall attend to and perform their appropriate parts toward the execution of these orders.

"By order of the President.

"EDWIN M. STANTON,
"*Secretary of War*."

And on the twenty-fifth of July, by proclamation, he warned all persons to cease participating in aiding, countenancing, or abetting the rebellion, and to return to their allegiance under penalty of the forfeitures and seizures provided by an Act "to suppress insurrection, to punish treason and rebellion, to seize and confiscate the property of rebels, and for other purposes," approved on the seventeenth of July, 1862.

A DRAFT FOR THREE HUNDRED THOUSAND MEN ORDERED.

On the fourth of August, 1862, the following order for a draft was issued:

"ORDERED: *First*, that a draft of three hundred thousand militia be immediately called into the service of the United States, *to serve for nine months, unless sooner discharged.* The Secretary of War will assign the quotas to the States and establish regulations for the draft.

"*Second*, that if any State shall not, by the fifteenth of August, furnish its quota of the additional three hundred thousand volunteers authorized by law, the deficiency of volunteers in that State will also be made up by a special draft from the militia. The Secretary of War will establish regulations for this purpose.

"*Third*, regulations will be prepared by the War Department, and presented to the President, with the object of securing the promotion of officers of the army and volunteers for meritorious and distinguished services, and of preventing the nomination and appointment in the military service of incompetent or unworthy officers.

"The regulations will also provide for ridding the service of such incompetent persons as now hold commissions.

"By order of the President.

"EDWIN M. STANTON,
"*Secretary of War.*"

THE PRESIDENT SPEAKS AT A WAR MEETING.

On the sixth of August, 1862, a large and enthusiastic Union meeting was held in Washington, at which a series of patriotic resolutions was adopted, and numerous eloquent speeches delivered, among others the following characteristic one by the Chief Magistrate of the nation:

"*Fellow-citizens:* I believe there is no precedent for my appearing before you on this occasion, [applause,] but it is also true that there is no precedent for your being here yourselves, [applause and laughter,] and I offer, in justification of myself and of you, that, upon examination, I have found nothing in the Constitution against it. [Renewed applause.] I, however, have an impression that there are younger gentlemen who will entertain you better, [voices—'No, no! none can do better than yourself. Go on!'] and better address your understanding than I will or could, and therefo e I propose but to detain you a moment longer. [Cries—'Go on! Tar and feather the rebels!']

"I am very little inclined on any occasion to say any thing unless I hope to produce some good by it. [A voice—'You do that; go on.'] The only thing I think of just now not likely to be better said by some one else is a matter in which we have heard some other persons blamed for what I did myself. [Voices—'What is it?'] There has been a very wide-spread attempt to have a quarrel between General McClellan and the Secretary of War. Now, I occupy a position that enables me to observe, at least these two gentlemen are not nearly so deep in the quarrel as some pretending to be their friends. [Cries of 'Good.'] General McClellan's attitude is such that, in the very selfishness of his nature, he cannot but wish to be successful, and I hope he will—and the Secretary of War is in precisely the same situation. If the military commanders in the field cannot be successful, not only the Secretary of War, but myself, for the time being the master of them both, cannot be but failures. [Laughter and applause.] I know General McClellan wishes to be successful, and I know he does not wish it any more than the Secretary of War for him, and both of them together no more than I wish it. [Applause and cries of 'Good.'] Sometimes we have a dispute about how many men General McClellan has had, and those who would disparage him say that he has had a very large number, and those who would disparage the Secretary of War insist that General McClellan has had a very small number. The basis for this is, there is always a wide difference, and on this occasion perhaps a wider one, between the grand total on McClellan's rolls and the men actually fit for duty; and those who would disparage him talk of the grand total on paper, and those who would disparage the Secretary of War talk of those at present fit for duty. General McClellan has sometimes asked for things that the Secretary of War did not give him. General McClellan is not to blame for asking what he wanted and needed, and the Secretary of War is not to blame for not giving when he had none to give. [Applause, laughter, and cries of 'Good, good.'] And I say here, as far as I know, the Secretary of War has withheld no one thing at any time in my power to give him. [Wild applause, and a voice—'Give him enough now!'] I have no accusation against him. I believe he is a brave and able man, [applause,] and I stand here, as justice requires me to do, to take upon myself what has been charged on the Secretary of War, as withholding from him.

"I have talked longer than I expected to, [cries of 'No, no—go on,'] and now I avail myself of my privilege of saying no more."

THE EMANCIPATION PROCLAMATIONS OF SEPTEMBER, 1862, AND JANUARY, 1863.

On the twenty-second of September, 1862, Mr. Lincoln issued one of the two most important proclamations ever penned by a President of the United States: that which announced to the negroes held as slaves in the rebellious States that on and after the first day of the new year, they should be forever released from bondage. This great document, which was read with joy by the loyal residents of the North, and which was a source of such infinite happiness to the unfortunate class of beings who were to be more particularly affected by its provisions, was as follows:

"I, Abraham Lincoln, President of the United States of America, and Commander-in-Chief of the Army and Navy thereof, do hereby proclaim and declare that hereafter as heretofore the war will be prosecuted for the object of practically restoring the constitutional relation between the United States and the people thereof in those States in which that relation is, or may be, suspended or disturbed; that it is my purpose upon the next meeting of Congress to again recommend the adoption of a practical measure tendering pecuniary aid to the free acceptance or rejection of all the slave States, so-called, the people whereof may not then be in rebellion against the United States, and which States may then have voluntarily adopted, or thereafter may voluntarily adopt, the immediate or gradual abolishment of slavery within their respective limits, and that the effort to colonize persons of African descent, with their consent, upon the continent or elsewhere, with the previously obtained consent of the government existing there, will be continued; that on the first day of January, in the year of our Lord one thousand eight hundred and sixty-three, all persons held as slaves within any State, or any designated part of a State, the people whereof shall then be in rebellion against the United States, shall be then, thenceforward and forever, free, and the executive government of the United States, including the military and naval authority thereof, will recognize and maintain the freedom of such persons, and will do no act or acts to repress such persons, or any of them, in any efforts they may make for their actual freedom; that the Executive will, on the first day of January aforesaid, by proclamation, designate the States and parts of States, if any, in which the people thereof respectively shall then be in rebellion against the United States; and the fact that any State, or the people thereof, shall on that day be in good faith represented in the Congress of the United States by members chosen thereto, at elections wherein a majority of the qualified voters of such State shall have participated, shall, in the absence of strong countervailing testimony, be deemed conclusive evidence that such State and the people thereof have not been in rebellion against the United States.

"That attention is hereby called to an act of Congress entitled, 'An act to make an additional article of war,' approved March 13, 1862, and which act is in the words and figures following:

"'*Be it enacted by the Senate and House of Representatives of the United States of America, in Congress assembled*, That hereafter the following shall be promulgated as an additional article of war for the government of the army of the United States, and shall be observed and obeyed as such.

"'*Article* —. All officers or persons of the military or naval service of the United States are prohibited from employing any of the forces under their respective commands for the purpose of returning fugitives from service or labor who may have escaped from any persons to whom such service or labor is claimed to be due, and any officer who shall be found guilty by a court-martial of violating this article, shall be dismissed from the service.

"'*Sec.* 2. And be it further enacted, That this act shall take effect from and after its passage.'

'Also to the ninth and tenth sections of an act entitled, 'An act to suppress insurrection, to punish treason and rebellion, to seize and confiscate property of rebels, and for other purposes,' approved July 17, 1862, and which sections are in the words and figures following:

"'*Sec.* 9. And be it further enacted, That all slaves of persons who shall hereafter be engaged in rebellion against the government of the United States, or who shall in any way give aid or comfort thereto, escaping from such persons and taking refuge within the lines of the army; and all slaves captured from such persons or deserted by them, and coming under the control of the government of the United States, and all slaves of such persons found on (or being within) any place occupied by rebel forces and afterwards occupied by the forces of the United States, shall be deemed captives of war, and shall be forever free of their servitude and not again held as slaves.

"'*Sec.* 10. And be it further enacted, That no slave escaping into any State, Territory, or the District of Columbia, from any of the States, shall be delivered up, or in any way impeded or hindered of his liberty, except for crime, or some offence against the laws, unless the person claiming said fugitive shall first make oath that the person to whom the labor or service of such fugitive is alleged to be due, is his lawful owner, and has not been in arms against the United States in the present rebellion, nor in any way given aid and comfort thereto; and no person engaged in the military or naval service of the United States shall, under any pretence whatever, assume to decide on the validity of the claim of any person to the service or labor of any other person, or surrender up any such person to the claimant, on pain of being dismissed from the service.'

"And I do hereby enjoin upon, and order all persons engaged in the military and naval service of the United States to observe, obey and enforce within their respective spheres of service the act and sections above recited.

"And the executive will in due time recommend that all citizens of the United States who shall have remained loyal thereto throughout the rebellion, shall (upon the restoration of the constitutional relation between the United States and their respective States and people, if the relation shall have been suspended or disturbed) be compensated for all losses by acts of the United States, including the loss of slaves.

"In witness whereof, I have hereunto set my hand and caused the seal of the United States to be affixed.

"Done at the city of Washington, this twenty-second day of September, in the year of our Lord one thousand eight hundred and sixty-two, and of the Independence of the United States the eighty-seventh.

"By the President: "ABRAHAM LINCOLN.

"WM. H. SEWARD, *Secretary of State*."

Such a bold movement was necessarily distasteful to the traitors, and while the Southern journals pronounced it to be a bid for the slaves to rise in insurrection, a bid which none but a barbarian would devise, it was denounced in the Richmond Congress, and a resolution was there offered, exhorting the people to slay every Union soldier and raider found within their borders, and offering a reward to every negro, who would, after the first of January, 1863, kill a Unionist.

The other important proclamation was issued on the first of January, 1863, and was worded as follows:

"*Whereas*, on the twenty-second day of September, in year of our Lord one thousand eight hundred and sixty-two, a proclamation was issued by the President of the United States containing among other things the following, to wit:

"That on the first day of January, in the year of our Lord one thousand eight hundred and sixty-three, all persons held as slaves within any State, or designated part of a State, the people whereof shall then be in rebellion against the United States, shall be then, thenceforth and forever free, and the Executive Government of the United States, including the military and naval authorities thereof, will recognize and maintain the freedom of such persons, and will do no act or acts to repress such persons, or any of them, in any efforts they may make for their actual freedom.

"That the Executive will, on the first day of January aforesaid, by proclamation, designate the States and parts of States, if any, in which the people therein respectively shall then be in rebellion against the United States, and the fact that any State or the people thereof, shall on that day be in good faith represented in the Congress of the United States by members chosen thereto, at elections wherein a majority of the qualified voters of such States shall have participated, shall, in the absence of strong countervailing testimony, be deemed conclusive evidence that such State and the people thereof are not then in rebellion against the United States.

"Now, therefore, I, Abraham Lincoln, President of the United States, by virtue of the power in me vested as Commander-in-chief of the Army and Navy of the United States in time of actual armed rebellion against the authority and Government of the United States, and as a fit and necessary war measure for suppressing said rebellion, do, on this first day of January, in the year of our Lord one thousand eight hundred and sixty-three, and in accordance with my purpose so to do, publicly proclaimed for the full period of one hundred days from the day of the first above-mentioned order, and designate, as the States and parts of States wherein the people thereof respectively are this day in rebellion against the United States, the following to wit: Arkansas, Texas, Louisiana, except the parishes of St. Bernard, Plaquemines, Jefferson, St. John, St. Charles, St. James, Ascension, Assumption, Terre Bonne, Lafourche, St. Mary, St. Martin, and Orleans, including the City of New Orleans. Mississippi, Alabama, Florida, Georgia, South Carolina, North Carolina, and Virginia, except the forty-eight counties designated as West Virginia, and also the counties of Berkeley, Accomac, Northampton, Elizabeth City, York, Princess Ann, and Norfolk, including the cities of Norfolk and Portsmouth, and which excepted parts are, for the present, left precisely as if this proclamation were not issued.

"And by virtue of the power and for the purpose aforesaid, I do order and declare that all persons held as slaves within said designated States and parts of States are, and henceforward shall be free; and that the Executive Government of the United States, including the Military and Naval authorities thereof, will recognize and maintain the freedom of said persons.

"And I hereby enjoin upon the people so declared to be free, to abstain from all violence, unless in necessary self-defence, and I recommend to them, that in all cases, when allowed, they labor faithfully for reasonable wages.

"And I further declare and make known that such persons of suitable condition will be received into the armed service of the United States to garrison forts, positions, stations, and other places, and to man vessels of all sorts in said service.

"And upon this, sincerely believed to be an act of justice, warranted by the Constitution, upon military necessity, I invoke the considerate judgment of mankind and the gracious favor of Almighty God.

"In witness whereof, I have hereunto set my hand and caused the seal of the United States to be affixed.

[L. S.] "Done at the City of Washington, this first day of January, in the year of our Lord one thousand eight hundred and sixty-three, and of the Independence of the United States of America the eighty-seventh.

"By the President: "ABRAHAM LINCOLN.

"WILLIAM H. SEWARD, *Secretary of State.*"

SUSPENSION OF THE WRIT OF HABEAS CORPUS.

On the twenty-fourth of September, 1862, two days after the promulgation of the renowned Emancipation Proclamation, the following order was published:

" *Whereas*, It has become necessary to call into service, not only volunteers, but also portions of the militia of the State by draft, in order to suppress the insurrection existing in the United States, and disloyal persons are not adequately restrained by the ordinary processes of law from hindering this measure, and from giving aid and comfort in various ways to the insurrection:

" Now, therefore, be it ordered:

" *First*. That during the existing insurrection, and as a necessary measure for suppressing the same, all rebels and insurgents, their aiders and abettors, within the United States, and all persons discouraging volunteer enlistments, resisting militia drafts, or guilty of any disloyal practice affording aid and comfort to the rebels against the authority of the United States, shall be subject to martial law, and liable to trial and punishment by courts-martial or military commissions.

" *Third*. That the writ of *habeas corpus* is suspended in respect to all persons arrested, or who are now, or hereafter during the rebellion shall be imprisoned in any fort, camp, arsenal, military prison, or other place of confinement, by any military authority or by the sentence of any court-martial or military commission.

"In witness whereof, I have hereunto set my hand, and caused the seal of the United States to be affixed.

"Done at the City of Washington, this twenty-fourth day of September, in the year of our Lord one thousand eight hundred and sixty-two, and of the Independence of the United States the eighty-seventh.

"By the President. "ABRAHAM LINCOLN.

"WM. H. SEWARD, *Secretary of State.*"

The suspension of the Writ of Habeas Corpus was naturally obnoxious to Northern sympathizers with treason, and for some time their newspaper organs were daily filled with editorial and other articles, teeming with invidious criticism and abuse. The act placed more power in the hands of the President than was acceptable to men who, by their voice and pen, if not by their pecuniary means, were aiding and abetting the enemies of the country, and as they were not aware what moment they might be arrested and imprisoned for their despicable crimes, in their regard for their personal safety, they forgot their prudence, and abused the Executive. The beneficial effects of the order were not over-estimated by Mr. Lincoln, and with its promulgation almost entirely ceased the inteference with enlistments, which had too often before that date delayed the organization of regiments in some of the loyal States.

THE SABBATH TO BE OBSERVED.

On the sixteenth of November, 1862, the following order was issued to the soldiers and sailors of the Union :

"The President, Commander-in-Chief of the Army and Navy, desires and enjoins the orderly observance of the Sabbath by the officers and men in the military and naval service. The importance for man and beast of the prescribed weekly rest, the sacred rights of Christian soldiers and sailors, a becoming deference to the best sentiment of a Christian people, and a due regard for the Divine will, demand that Sunday labor in the Army and Navy be reduced to the measure of strict necessity.

"The discipline and character of the National forces should not suffer, nor the cause they defend be imperilled, by the profanation of the day or name of the Most High. 'At this time of public distress' adopting the words of Washington in 1776, 'men may find enough to do in the service of God and their country without abandoning themselves to vice and immorality.' The first general order issued by the Father of his Country after the Declaration of Independence indicates the spirit in which our institutions were founded and should ever be defended: 'The General hopes and trusts that every officer and man will endeavor to live and act as becomes a Christian soldier defending the dearest rights and liberties of his country.'

"ABRAHAM LINCOLN."

HIS ANNUAL MESSAGE.—IMPORTANT RECOMMENDATIONS TO CONGRESS.

On the first of December, 1862, Mr. Lincoln sent in to Congress his annual message; giving a satisfactory resumé of the events of the previous twelve months; calling the attention of the Senators and Representatives to important matters which should receive their notice; recommending the organization of national banking associations, under the hope and belief that they would be the means of promoting the early resumption of specie payments; re-impressed upon them the importance of his plan of "compensated emancipation;" repeated at length his views upon the slavery question, and recommended the adoption of the following resolutions and articles amendatory to the Constitution:

"*Resolved*, By the Senate and House of Representatives of the United States of America in Congress assembled, two-thirds of both houses concurring, that the following articles be proposed to the Legislatures or Conventions of the several States, as amendments to the Constitution of the United States, all or any of which articles, when ratified by three-fourths of the said Legislatures or Conventions, to be valid as part or parts of the said Constitution, namely:

"ARTICLE —. Every State wherein slavery now exists, which shall abolish the same therein at any time or times before the first day of January, in the year of our Lord one thousand nine hundred, shall receive compensation from the United States as follows, to wit:

"The President of the United States shall deliver to every such State, bonds of the United States, bearing interest at the rate of ——, for each slave shown to have been therein, by the eighth census of the United States; said bonds to be delivered to such State by instalments, or in one parcel at the completion of the abolishment, according as the same shall have been gradual or at one time within such State; and interest shall begin to run upon any such bond only from the proper time of its delivery as aforesaid, and afterward. Any State having received bonds as aforesaid, and afterward introducing or tolerating slavery therein, shall refund to the United States the bonds so received, or the value thereof, and all interest paid thereon.

"ARTICLE —. All slaves who shall have enjoyed actual freedom, by the chances of the war at any time, before the end of the rebellion, shall be forever free; but all owners of such, who shall not have been disloyal, shall be compensated for them at the same rates as is provided for States adopting abolishment of slavery—but in such a way that no slave shall be twice accounted for.

"ARTICLE —. Congress may appropriate money, and otherwise provide for colonizing free colored persons with their own consent, at any place or places without the United States."

The message and its recommendations were received with the same *eclat* which has attended all the official documents penned by the illustrious statesman. The proclamation of September had awakened the people of the Union to the vast advantages to be derived from the adoption of his views and suggestions on every thing relating to slavery, and as the day on which the unfortunate blacks were to be rescued from a life of degradation approached, thousands, who had hitherto protested against interference with the "peculiar institution," united with their old political opponents, and awaited anxiously the hour when the order of emancipation was to go into effect. Residents of foreign lands were no less eager for the time to arrive when the Federal Government should strike off the fetters of the slave, and among other complimentary addresses sent to the President, was one from Manchester, England, from which we make the following extracts:

"As citizens of Manchester, assembled at the Free-Trade Hall, we beg to express our fraternal sentiments toward you and your country. We rejoice in your greatness as an outgrowth of England, whose blood and language you share, whose orderly and legal freedom you have applied to new circumstances, over a region immeasurably greater than our own. We honor your Free States, as a singularly happy abode for the working millions where industry is honored. One thing alone has, in the past, lessened our sympathy with your country and our confidence in it—we mean the ascendency of politicians who not merely maintained negro slavery, but desired to extend and root it more firmly. We joyfully honor you, as the President, and the Congress with you, for many decisive steps toward practically exemplifying your belief in the words of your great founders: 'All men are created free and equal.' You have procured the liberation of the slaves in the district around Washington, and thereby made the centre of your Federation visibly free. You have enforced the laws against the slave-trade, and kept up your fleet against it, even while every ship was wanted for service in your terrible war. You have nobly decided to receive embassadors from the negro republics of Hayti and Liberia, thus forever renouncing that unworthy prejudice which refuses the rights of humanity to men and women on account of their color. In order more effectually to stop the slave-trade, you have made with our Queen a treaty, which your Senate has ratified, for the right of mutual search. Your Congress has decreed freedom as the law forever in the vast unoccupied or half unsettled Territories which are directly subject to its legislative power. It has offered pecuniary aid to all States which will enact emancipation locally, and has forbidden your generals to restore fugitive slaves who seek their protection. You have entreated the slave-masters to accept these moderate offers; and after long and patient waiting, you, as Commander-in-chief of the Army, have appointed to-morrow, the first of January, 1863, as the day of unconditional freedom for the slaves of the rebel States. We implore you, for your own honor and welfare, not to faint in your providential mission. While your enthusiasm is aflame, and the tide of events runs high, let the work be finished effectually. Leave no root of bitterness to spring up and work fresh misery to your children. It is a mighty task, indeed, to reorganize the industry not only of four millions of the colored race, but of five millions of whites. Nevertheless, the vast progress you have made in the short space of twenty months, fill us with hope that every stain on your freedom will shortly be removed, and that the erasure of that foul blot upon civilization and Christianity—chattle slavery—during your Presidency, will cause the name of Abraham Lincoln to be honored and revered by posterity."

In answer to this flattering letter, Mr. Lincoln sent a happy response, in which he explained the motive which had prompted him to the undeviating course he has pursued since his inauguration. He had, he said, considered the duty of maintaining and preserving the Constitution and the integrity of the Federal Republic paramount to all others, and as a conscientious purpose to perform that duty was the key to all the measures of his administration, he could not, if he would, under his oath and our frame of government, depart from that purpose.

THE PRESIDENT VISITS THE ARMY OF THE POTOMAC.

Early in April, 1863, the President left Washington on a visit to the Army of the Potomac. He had in the previous year, when the same noble troops were resting at Harrison's Landing, after their campaign before Richmond, gone thither to observe for himself their true condition, and upon other occasions has visited their camping-grounds, where he has been always received with great enthusiasm. Upon the visit to which we now refer, he was accompanied by Mrs. Lincoln and one of his sons, and an eye-witness thus describes the proceedings incident to the entertainment of such distinguished guests:

On the morning of April seventh, 1863, a reception was had in General Hooker's tent, the members of the staff passing in and being introduced to the President by the Chief of Staff. Mr. Lincoln was in unusual good humor, and completely banished the constraint felt by all by his sociability and shafts of wit. The interview lasted some time, much to the enjoyment of all, until finally the officers one by one dropped out, and the hour designated for the review arrived. Early in the morning the several cavalry brigades commenced moving towards the field selected for the review, and during the forenoon were engaged forming the lines and stationing guards to keep off the crowd. At noon the roar of artillery announced that the cortege had arrived. President Lincoln, mounted on a magnificent bay, adorned with heavy trappings, rode steadily and rapidly along the line, with Generals Hooker and Stoneman at his side, and followed by an imposing cavalcade of general officers, aides-de-camp and orderlies. Having returned to the right of the line, a position was selected for the President upon a slight eminence, while the cavalry at a walk passed in review before him, the bands playing and the bugles sounding merrily. Mrs. Lincoln occupied a carriage at the right of the President while the regiments passed in review, surrounded by major-generals and stars of lesser magnitude. After the cavalry had moved off the field, the lancers, in splendid order, wheeled around into line fronting the President, while the light artillery dashed at a gallop through the avenue thus formed, the guns and caissons bounding over the irregularities as though the wheels were of India rubber. The cannon were soon off the field, the lancers filed in behind the cavalcade of generals, spectators vanished, and the plateau, torn and trodden by the squadrons, was left to the scattering working parties engaged in preparing the ground for the grand review of infantry. The President also rode over to the head-quarters of several commanding officers, and during the day reviewed the reserve artillery.

Doubtless the lady readers are anxious to know in what dress the wife of the Chief Magistrate visited the army, how she appeared, what she said, and how she liked the contrast—the Executive mansion, with its costly furniture, and the bare floor, cot and camp stools of the field. Mrs. Lincoln's attire was exceedingly simple—of that peculiar style of simplicity which creates at the time no impression upon the mind, and prevents one from remembering any article of dress. In this case there was nothing to attract attention, and after she had entered the tent there was not one in twenty of those gathered about who

9

could tell what she wore. A rich black silk dress, with narrow flounces; a black cape, with a broad trimming of velvet around the border, and a plain hat of the same hue, composed her costume. A shade of weariness, doubtless the result of her labors in behalf of the sick and wounded in Washington, rested upon her countenance; but the change seemed pleasant to her, and the scenes of camp were noted with evident interest. The President wore a dark sack overcoat and a fur muffler, while Master Lincoln sported a suit of gray, and rambled about among the tents, examining the quarters of the staff, and watched by the orderlies and sentries with a curiosity somewhat amusing.

THE ENROLMENT ACT AND THE RIGHTS OF ALIENS.

To enumerate all the proclamations which the President issued during the year 1863, would be impossible in this work, and we must therefore restrict ourselves to those which were of more than usual interest. The one in regard to the rights of aliens, under the act calling out the national forces, was one of these, and reads as follows:

"*Whereas,* The Congress of the United States at its last session enacted a law entitled, 'An act for enrolling and calling out the national forces and for other purposes,' which was approved on the third day of March last, and,

"*Whereas,* It is recited in the said act that there now exists in the United States an insurrection and rebellion against the authority thereof, and it is, under the Constitution of the United States, the duty of the Government to suppress insurrection and rebellion, to guarantee to each State a republican form of government, and to preserve the public tranquility, and

"*Whereas,* For these high purposes a military force is indispensable, to raise and support which all persons ought willingly to contribute; and

"*Whereas,* No service can be more praiseworthy and honorable than that which is rendered for the maintenance of the Constitution and the Union, and the consequent preservation of the Government; and

"*Whereas,* For the reasons thus recited, it was enacted by the said statute that all able-bodied male citizens of the United States and persons of foreign birth, who shall have declared on oath their intentions to become citizens, under and in pursuance of the laws thereof, between the ages of twenty and forty-five years, with certain exceptions not necessary to be here mentioned, are declared to constitute the national forces, and shall be liable to perform military duty in the service of the United States, when called out by the President for that purpose; and

"*Whereas*, It is claimed, and in behalf of persons of foreign birth within the ages specified in said act who have heretofore declared on oath their intentions to become citizens under and in pursuance of the laws of the United States, and who have not exercised the right of suffrage or any other political franchise under the laws of the United States, or any of the States thereof, are not absolutely precluded by their aforesaid declaration of intention from renouncing their purpose to become citizens, and that, on the contrary, such persons under treaties or the law of nations, retain a right to renounce that purpose and to forego the privilege of citizenship and residence within the United States under the obligations imposed by the aforesaid act of Congress.

"Now, therefore, to avoid all misapprehensions concerning the liability of persons concerned to perform the service required by such enactment, and to give it full effect, I do hereby order and proclaim that no plea of alienage will be received or allowed to exempt from the obligations imposed by the aforesaid act of Congress, any person of foreign birth who shall have declared, on oath, his intention to become a citizen of the United States under the laws thereof, and who shall be found within the United States at any time during the continuance of the present insurrection and rebellion, at or after the expiration of the sixty-five days from the date of this proclamation, nor shall any such plea of alienage be allowed in favor of any such person who has so as aforesaid declared his intention to become a citizen of the United States, and shall have exercised at any time the right of suffrage or any other political franchise within the United States, under the laws thereof, or under the laws of any of the several States.

"In witness whereof I have hereunto set my hand and caused the seal of the United States to be affixed.

"Done at the city of Washington, this eighth day of May, in the year of our Lord 1863, and of the independence of the United States the eighty-seventh.

"By the President, "ABRAHAM LINCOLN.

"WILLIAM H SEWARD, *Secretary of State*."

A NATIONAL THANKSGIVING ORDERED.

On the fifteenth day of July, 1863, the President ordered the sixth of the following month to be set apart as a day of National Thanksgiving. Victories had crowned our arms on land and sea, and no greater cause for offering thanks to the Almighty ever prompted the Chief Magistrate of a country to call the people together, and few proclamations were ever written more chaste and beautiful than the following:

"It has pleased Almighty God to hearken to the supplications and prayers of an afflicted people, and to vouchsafe to the army and the navy of the United States, on the land and on the sea, victories so signal and so effective as to furnish reasonable grounds for augmented confidence that the union of these States will be maintained, their constitutions preserved, and their peace and prosperity permanently preserved.

"But these victories have been accorded not without sacrifice of life, limb and liberty, incurred by the brave, patriotic and loyal citizens. Domestic affliction in every part of the country follows in the train of these fearful bereavements. It is meet and right to recognize and confess the presence of the Almighty Father, and the power of His hand equally in these triumphs and these sorrows.

"Now, therefore, be it known, that I do set apart Thursday, the sixth day of August next, to be observed as a day for national Thanksgiving, praise, and prayer, and I invite the people of the United States to assemble on that occasion in their customary places of worship, and in the forms approved by their own conscience, render the homage due to the Divine Majesty for the wonderful things He has done in the nation's behalf, and invoke the influence of His Holy Spirit to subdue the anger which has produced and so long sustained a needless and cruel rebellion; to change the hearts of the insurgents, to guide the counsels of the government with wisdom adequate to so great a national emergency, and to visit with tender care and consolation throughout the length and breadth of our land all those who through the vicissitudes of marches, voyages, battles and sieges, have been brought to suffer in mind, body or estate and family, to lead the whole nation through paths of repentance and submission to the Divine Will, back to the perfect enjoyment of Union and fraternal peace.

"In witness whereof, I have hereunto set my hand and caused the seal of the United States to be affixed.

"Done at the city of Washington, this 15th day of July, in the year of our Lord one thousand eight hundred aud sixty-three, and of the independence of the United States of America the eighty-eighth. "ABRAHAM LINCOLN.

"By the President:

"WILLIAM H. SEWARD, *Secretary of State.*"

LETTER FROM THE PRESIDENT ON THE EMANCIPATION PROCLAMATION.

The following letter, written in August, 1863, in answer to an invitation to attend a meeting of unconditional Union men held in Illinois, gives at length the President's views at that time on his Emancipation proclamation:

"EXECUTIVE MANSION, WASHINGTON, *August 26th*, 1863.

"MY DEAR SIR:—Your letter inviting me to attend a mass meeting of unconditional Union men, to be held at the capitol of Illinois on the third day of September, has been received. It would be very agreeable to me thus to meet my old friends at my own home; but I cannot just now be absent from this city so long as a visit there would require. The meeting is to be of all those who maintain unconditional devotion to the Union; and I am sure that my old political friends will thank me for tendering, as I do, the nation's gratitude to those other noble men whom no partisan malice or partisan hope can make false to the nation's life. There are those who are dissatisfied with me. To such I would say:—You desire peace, and you blame me that we do not have it. But how can we attain it? There are but three conceivable ways:—First, to suppress the rebellion by force of arms. This I am trying to do. Are you for it? If you are, so far we are agreed. If you are not for it, a second way is to give up the Union. I am against this. If you are, you should say so, plainly. If you are not for force, nor yet for dissolution, there only remains some imaginable compromise. I do not believe that any compromise embracing the maintenance of the Union is now possible. All that I learn leads to a directly opposite belief. The strength of the rebellion is its military—its army. That army dominates all the country and all the people within its range. Any offer of any terms made by any man or men within that range in opposition to that army is simply nothing for the present, because such man or men have no power whatever to enforce their side of a compromise, if one were made with them. To illustrate: Suppose refugees from the South and peace men of the North get together in convention, and frame and proclaim a compromise embracing the restoration of the Union. In what way can that compromise be used to keep General Lee's army out of Pennsylvania? General Meade's army can keep Lee's army out of Pennsylvania, and I think can ultimately drive it out of existence. But no paper compromise to which the controllers of General Lee's army are not agreed, can at all affect that army. In an effort at such compromise we would waste time which the enemy would improve to our disadvantage, and that would be all. A compromise, to be effective, must be made either with those who control the rebel army, or with the people, first liberated from the domination of that army by the success of our army. Now, allow me to assure you that no word or intimation from the rebel army, or from any of the men controlling it, in relation to any peace compromise, has ever come to my knowledge or belief. All charges and intimations to the contrary are deceptive and groundless. And I promise you that if any such proposition shall hereafter come, it shall not be rejected and kept secret from you. I freely acknowledge myself to be the servant of the people, according to the bond of service, the United States constitution; and that, as such, I am responsible to them. But, to be plain. You are dissatisfied with me about the negro. Quite likely there is a difference of opinion between you and myself upon that subject. I certainly wish that all men could be free, while you, I suppose, do not. Yet I have neither adopted nor proposed any measure which is not consistent with even your view, provided you are for the Union. I suggested compensated emancipation, to which you replied that you wished not to be taxed to buy negroes. But I have not asked you to be taxed to buy negroes, except in such way as to save you from greater taxation, to save the Union exclusively by other means.

"You dislike the emancipation proclamation, and perhaps would have it retracted. You say it is unconstitutional. I think differently. I think that the constitution invests its commander-in-chief with the law of war in time of war. The most that can be said, if so much, is, that the slaves are property. Is there, has there ever been, any question that by the law of war, property, both of enemies and friends, may be taken when needed? And is it not needed whenever taking it helps us or hurts the enemy? Armies, the world over, destroy enemies' property when they cannot use it; and even destroy their own to keep it from the enemy. Civilized belligerents do all in their power to help themselves or hurt the enemy, except a few things regarded as barbarous or cruel. Among the exceptions are the massacre of vanquished foes and non-combatants, male and female. But the proclamation, as law, is valid or is not valid. If it is not valid it needs no retraction. If it is valid it cannot be retracted, any more than the dead can be brought to life. Some of you profess to think that its retraction would operate favorably for the Union. Why better after the retraction than before the issue? There was more than a year and a half of trial to suppress the rebellion before the proclamation was issued, the last one hundred days of which passed under an explicit notice, that it was coming unless averted by those in revolt returning to their allegiance. The war has certainly progressed as favorably for us since the issue of the proclamation as before. I know as fully as one can know the opinions of others, that some of the commanders of our armies in the field, who have given us our most important victories, believe the emancipation policy and the aid of colored troops constitute the heaviest blows yet dealt to the rebellion, and that at least one of those important successes could not have been achieved when it was but for the aid of black soldiers. Among the commanders holding these views are some who have never had any affinity with what is called abolitionism or with 'republican party politics.'—But who hold them purely as military opinions. I submit their opinions as being entitled to some weight against the objections often urged that emancipation and arming the blacks are unwise as military measures, and were not adopted as such in good faith. You say that you will not fight to free negroes. Some of them seem to be willing to fight for you—but no matter. Fight you, then, exclusively to save the Union. I issued the proclamation on purpose to aid you in saving the Union. Whenever you shall have conquered all resistance to the Union, if I shall urge you to continue fighting, it will be an apt time then for you to declare that you will not fight to free negroes. I thought that in your struggle for the Union, to whatever extent the negroes should cease helping the enemy, to that extent it weakened the enemy in his resistance to you. Do you think differently? I thought that whatever negroes can be got to do as soldiers, leaves just so much less for white soldiers to do in saving the Union. Does it appear otherwise to you? But negroes, like other people, act upon motives. Why should they do any thing for us if we will do nothing for them? If they stake their lives for us they must be prompted by the strongest motive, even the promise of freedom. And the promise, being made, must be kept. The signs look better. The Father of Waters again goes unvexed to the sea. Thanks to the great North-west for it. Not yet wholly to them. Three hundred miles up they met New England, Empire, Keystone and Jersey, hewing their way right and left. The Sunny South, too, in more colors than one, also lent a hand. On the spot their part of the history was jotted down in black and white. The job was a great national one, and let none be banned who bore an honorable part in it; and, while those who have cleared the great river may well be proud, even that is not all. It is hard to say that any thing has been more bravely and better done than at Antietam, Murfreesboro, Gettysburg, and on many fields of less note. Nor must Uncle Sam's webfleet be forgotten. At all the waters' margins they have been present:—not only on the deep sea, the broad bay and the rapid river, but also up the narrow, muddy bayou; and wherever the ground was a little damp they have been and made their tracks. Thanks to all. For the great republic—for the principles by which it lives and keeps alive—for man's vast future—thanks to all. Peace does not appear so far distant as it did. I hope it will come soon, and come to stay: and so come as to be worth the keeping in all future time. It will then have been proved that among freemen there can be no successful appeal from the ballot to the bullet, and that they who take such appeal are sure to lose their case and pay the cost. And then there will be some black men who can remember that, with silent tongue, and clenched teeth, and steady eye, and well poised bayonet, they have helped mankind on to this great consummation; while I fear that there will be some white men unable to forget that with malignant heart and deceitful speech they have striven to hinder it. Still let us not be over sanguine of a speedy final triumph. Let us be quite sober. Let us diligently apply the means, never doubting that a just God, in his own good time, will give us the rightful result. Yours very truly, "A. LINCOLN."

During September and October, 1863, the following proclamations were published:

SUSPENSION OF THE WRIT OF HABEAS CORPUS IN CERTAIN CASES.

"WASHINGTON, *Sept.* 15*th*, 1863.

"*Whereas*, the Constitution of the United States has ordained that 'the privilege of the writ of habeas corpus shall not be suspended, unless when in cases of rebellion or invasion the public safety may require it;' and

"*Whereas*, a rebellion was existing on the third day of March, 1863, which rebellion is still existing; and

"*Whereas*, by a statute which was approved on that day, it was enacted by the Senate and House of Representatives of the United States in Congress assembled, that during the present insurrection the President of the United States, whenever in his judgment the public safety may require, is authorized to suspend the privilege of the writ of habeas corpus in any case throughout the United States, or any part thereof; and

"*Whereas*, in the judgment of the President the public safety does require that the privilege of the said writ shall now be suspended throughout the United States in cases where, by the authority of the President of the United States, military, naval and civil officers of the United States, or any of them, hold persons under their command or in their custody, either as prisoners of war, spies, or aiders or abettors of the enemy, or officers, soldiers, or seamen enrolled, drafted or mustered or enlisted in or belonging to the land or naval forces of the United States, or as deserters therefrom, or otherwise amenable to military law, or to the Rules and Articles of War, or to the rules and regulations prescribed for the military or naval service by the authority of the President of the United States, or for resisting a draft, or for any other offence against the military or naval service:

"Now, therefore, I, Abraham Lincoln, President of the United States, do hereby proclaim and make known to all whom it may concern, that the privilege of the writ of habeas corpus is suspended throughout the United States in the several cases before mentioned, and that the suspension will continue throughout the duration of the said rebellion; or until this proclamation shall by a subsequent one, to be issued by the President of the United States, be modified and revoked. And I do hereby require all magistrates, attorneys and other civil officers within the United States, and all officers and others in the military and naval services of the United States, to take distinct notice of this suspension, and give it full effect; and all citizens of the United States to conduct and govern themselves accordingly and in conformity with the Constitution of the United States and the laws of Congress in such cases made and provided.

"In testimony whereof I have hereunto set my hand and caused the seal of the United States to be affixed, this fifteenth day of September, in the year of our Lord one thousand eight hundred and sixty-three, and of the Independence of the United States of America the eighty-eighth.

"Abraham Lincoln.

"By the President:

"William H. Seward, *Secretary of State.*"

NATIONAL THANKSGIVING PROCLAMATION.

"The year that is drawing towards its close has been filled with the blessings of fruitful fields and healthful skies. To these bounties, which are so constantly enjoyed that we are prone to forget the source from which they come, others have been added, which are of so extraordinary a nature, that they cannot fail to penetrate and soften even the heart which is habitually insensible to the ever watchful providence of Almighty God.

"In the midst of a civil war of unequalled magnitude and severity, which has sometimes seemed to invite and provoke the aggression of foreign States, peace has been preserved with all nations, order has been maintained, the laws have been respected and obeyed, and harmony has prevailed everywhere, except in the theatre of military conflict; while that theatre has been greatly contracted by the advancing armies and navies of the Union.

"The needful diversions of wealth and strength from the fields of peaceful industry to the national defence have not arrested the plough, the shuttle or the ship. The axe has enlarged the borders of our settlements, and the mines, as well of iron and coal as of the precious metals, have yielded even more abundantly than heretofore. Population has steadily increased, notwithstanding the waste that has been made in the camp, the siege and the battle-field; and the country, rejoicing in the consequences of augmented strength and vigor, is permitted to expect continuance of years with large increase of freedom.

"No human counsel hath devised, nor hath any mortal hand worked out these great things. They are the gracious gifts of the Most High God, who, while dealing with us in anger for our sins, hath nevertheless remembered mercy.

"It has seemed to me fit and proper that they should be solemnly, reverently and gratefully acknowledged as with one heart and voice by the whole American people; I do, therefore, invite my fellow-citizens in every part of the United States, and also those who are at sea and those who are sojourning in foreign lands, to set apart and observe the last Thursday of November next as a Day of Thanksgiving and Prayer to our beneficent Father, who dwelleth in the heavens. And I recommend to them that, while offering up the ascriptions justly due to him for such singular deliverances and blessings; they do also, with humble penitence for our national perverseness and disobedience, commend to his tender care all those who have become widows, orphans, mourners or sufferers in the lamentable civil strife in which we are unavoidably engaged, and fervently implore the interposition of the Almighty hand to heal the wounds of the nation and to restore it, as soon as may be consistent with the Divine purposes, to the full enjoyment of peace, harmony, tranquillity, and union.

"In testimony whereof I have hereunto set my hand and caused the seal of the United States to be affixed.

"Done at the city of Washington this third day of October, in the year of our Lord one thousand eight hundred and sixty-three, and of the Independence of the United States the eighty-eighth.

"ABRAHAM LINCOLN.

"By the President:

"WILLIAM H. SEWARD, *Secretary of State.*"

We have shown, in the first pages of this volume, that the early instruction of Abraham Lincoln was of that religious character which could not fail to have a proper effect upon his after life, and it is not therefore surprising that during his Presidential career he has embraced every opportunity to publicly acknowledge the source from whence have come all the blessings the people of the Union have received during the progress of the civil war; and the unanimity with which his numerous requests for a general Thanksgiving have been acquiesced in, can but be gratifying to their author.

THREE HUNDRED THOUSAND MORE MEN CALLED FOR.

"*Whereas*, The term of service of part of the volunteer forces of the United States will expire during the coming year; and *whereas*, in addition to the men raised by the present draft, it is deemed expedient to call out three hundred thousand volunteers, to serve for three years or the war—not, however, exceeding three years.

"Now, therefore, I, Abraham Lincoln, President of the United States and Commander-in-Chief of the Army and Navy thereof, and of the militia of the several States when called into actual service, do issue this my proclamation, calling upon the Governors of the different States to raise and have enlisted into the United States service, for the various companies and regiments in the field from their respective States, their quotas of three hundred thousand men.

"I further proclaim that all the volunteers thus called out and duly enlisted shall receive advance pay, premium and bounty, as heretofore communicated to the Governors of States by the War Department, through the Provost Marshal General's office, by special letters.

"I further proclaim that all volunteers received under this call, as well as all others not heretofore credited, shall be duly credited and deducted from the quotas established for the next draft.

"I further proclaim that, if any State shall fail to raise the quota assigned to it by the War Department under this call; then a draft for the deficiency in said quota shall be made in said State, or on the districts of said State, for their due proportion of said quota, and the said draft shall commence on the fifth day of January, 1864.

"And I further proclaim that nothing in this proclamation shall interfere with existing orders, or with those which may be issued for the present draft in the States where it is now in progress or where it has not yet been commenced.

"The quotas of the States and districts will be assigned by the War Department, through the Provost Marshal General's office, due regard being had for the men heretofore furnished, whether by volunteering or drafting, and the recruiting will be conducted in accordance with such instructions as have been or may be issued by that department.

"In issuing this proclamation I address myself not only to the Governors of the several States, but also to the good and loyal people thereof, invoking them to lend their cheerful, willing and effective aid to the measures thus adopted, with a view to reinforce our victorious armies now in the field and bring our needful military operations to a prosperous end, thus closing forever the fountains of sedition and civil war.

"In witness whereof I have hereunto set my hand and caused the seal of the United States to be affixed.

"Done at the city of Washington, this seventeenth day of October, in the year of our Lord one thousand eight hundred and sixty-three, and of the independence of the United States the eighty-eighth. "ABRAHAM LINCOLN.

"By the President:

"WM. H. SEWARD, *Secretary of State*."

THE PRESIDENT'S DEDICATORY ADDRESS AT GETTYSBURG.

On the nineteenth of November, 1863, the President participated in the solemn and imposing ceremonies incident to the consecration of the National Cemetery at Gettysburg. Arriving in the town on the previous evening, he was the recipient of a delightful serenade, which he acknowledged in a brief speech. On the next day he delivered the following beautiful Dedicatory Address:

"Fourscore and seven years ago our fathers brought forth upon this continent a new nation, conceived in Liberty, and dedicated to the proposition that all men are created equal. Now we are engaged in a great civil war, testing whether that nation, or any nation so conceived and so dedicated, can long endure. We are met on a great battle-field of that war. We are met to dedicate a portion of it as the final resting-place of those who here gave their lives that that nation might live. It is altogether fitting and proper that we should do this.

"But in a larger sense we cannot dedicate, we cannot consecrate, we cannot hallow this ground. The brave men, living and dead, who struggled here, have consecrated it far above our power to add or detract. The world will little note, nor long remember what we say here, but it can never forget what they did here. It is for us, the living, rather to be dedicated here to the unfinished work that they have thus far so nobly carried on. It is rather for us to be here dedicated to the great task remaining before us—that from these honored dead we take increased devotion to the cause for which they here gave the last full measure of devotion,—that we here highly resolve that the dead shall not have died in vain, that the nation shall, under God, have a new birth of freedom, and that the government of the people, by the people, and for the people, shall not perish from the earth."

THANKSGIVING PROCLAMATION.

On the seventh of December, 1863, the following recommendation was made to the people of the country:

"EXECUTIVE MANSION, WASHINGTON, *Dec. 7th*, 1863.—Reliable information being received that the insurgent force is retreating from East Tennessee, under circumstances rendering it probable that the Union forces cannot hereafter be dislodged from that important position, and esteeming this to be of high National consequence, I recommend that all loyal people do, on the receipt of this, informally assemble at their places of worship, and render special homage and gratitude to Almighty God for this great advancement of the National cause. "A. LINCOLN."

THE ANNUAL MESSAGE OF 1863—FULL PARDON OFFERED TO THE REBELS.

On the ninth of December, 1863, President Lincoln sent into Congress his Annual Message, and never were his wisdom and moderation more satisfactorily exhibited than in this document. His review of our foreign relations and the operations of the various departments of the Government was comprehensive and clear, while on the subject of the rebellion he re-affirmed all that he had written in his previous messages, and in referring to the success which had attended the proclamation of emancipation, he said: "While I remain in my present position, I shall not attempt to retract or modify the emancipation proclamation; nor shall I return to slavery any person who is free by the terms of that proclamation, or by any of the acts of Congress."

Accompanying the Message, was a proclamation offering for the acceptance of the traitors a fair and practicable mode, by which they might return to their allegiance, and once again become loyal citizens. It was worded as follows:

"*Whereas*, In and by the Constitution of the United States, it is provided that the President 'shall have power to grant reprieves and pardons for offences against the United States, except in cases of impeachment;" and

"*Whereas*, A rebellion now exists whereby the loyal State governments of several States have for a long time been subverted, and many persons have committed and are now guilty of treason against the United States; and

"*Whereas*, With reference to said rebellion and treason, laws have been enacted by Congress, declaring forfeitures and confiscations of property and liberation of slaves, all upon terms and conditions therein stated, and also declaring that the President was thereby authorized at any time thereafter, by proclamation, to extend to persons who may have participated in the existing rebellion in any State, or part thereof, pardon and amnesty, with such exceptions and at such times and on such conditions as he may deem expedient for the public welfare; and

"*Whereas*, The Congressional declaration for limited and conditional pardon accords with well-established judicial exposition of the pardoning power; and

"*Whereas*, With reference to said rebellion, the President of the United States has issued several proclamations, with provisions in regard to the liberation of slaves; and

"*Whereas*, It is now desired by some persons heretofore engaged in said rebellion to resume their allegiance to the United States, and to re-inaugurate loyal State governments within and for their respective States;

"Therefore, I, Abraham Lincoln, President of the United States, do proclaim, declare, and make known to all persons who have, directly or by implication, participated in the existing rebellion, except as hereinafter excepted, that a FULL PARDON is hereby granted to them and each of them, with restoration of all rights of property, except as to slaves, and in property cases where rights of third parties shall have intervened, and upon the condition that every such person shall take and subscribe an oath, and thenceforward keep and maintain said oath inviolate; and which oath shall be registered for permanent preservation, and shall be of the tenor and effect following, to wit:

"'I ——, do solemnly swear, in presence of Almighty God, that I will henceforth faithfully support, protect, and defend the Constitution of the United States, and the Union of the States thereunder; and that I will, in like manner, abide by and faithfully support all acts of Congress passed during the existing rebellion with reference to slaves, so long and so far as not repealed, modified, or held void by Congress, or by decision of the Supreme Court; and that I will, in like manner, abide by and faithfully support all proclamations of the President made during the existing rebellion having reference to slaves, so long and so far as not modified or declared void by decision of the Supreme Court. So help me God.'

"The persons excepted from the benefits of the foregoing provisions are all who are or shall have been civil or diplomatic officers or agents of the so-called Confederate Government; all who have left judicial stations under the United States to aid the rebellion; all who are or shall have been military or naval officers of said Confederate Government above the rank of Colonel in the army or of Lieutenant in the navy; all who left seats in the United States Congress to aid the rebellion; all who resigned their commissions in the army or navy of the United

States, and afterwards aided the rebellion, and all who have engaged in any way, in treating colored persons or white persons, in charge of such, otherwise than lawfully, as prisoners of war, and which persons may be found in the United States service, as soldiers, seamen, or in any other capacity.

"And I do further proclaim, declare, and make known, that whenever, in any of the States of Arkansas, Texas, Louisiana, Mississippi, Tennessee, Alabama, Georgia, Florida, South Carolina, and North Carolina, a number of persons, not less than one-tenth in number of the votes cast in such State at the Presidential election of the year of our Lord 1860, each having taken the oath aforesaid and not having since violated it, and being a qualified voter by the election law of the State existing immediately before the so-called act of secession, and excluding all others, shall re-establish a State government which shall be Republican, and in nowise contravening said oath, such shall be recognized as the true government of the State, and the State shall receive thereunder the benefits of the constitutional provision, which declares that 'the United States shall guarantee to every State in this Union a Republican form of government, and shall protect each of them against invasion; and, on application of the Legislature, or the executive (when the Legislature cannot be convened), against domestic violence.'

"And I do further proclaim, declare, and make known, that any provision which may be adopted by such State Government in relation to the freed people of such State, which shall recognize and declare their permanent freedom, provide for their education, and which may yet be consistent, as a temporary arrangement, with their present condition as a laboring, landless, and homeless class, will not be objected to by the National Executive. And it is suggested as not improper, that, in constructing a loyal State government in any State, the name of the State, the boundary, the subdivisions, the Constitution, and the general code of laws, as before the rebellion, be maintained, subject only to the modifications made necessary by the conditions hereinbefore stated. and such others, if any, not contravening said conditions, and which may be deemed expedient by those framing the new State Government.

"To avoid misunderstanding, it may be proper to say that this proclamation, so far as it relates to State Governments, has no reference to States wherein loyal State Governments have all the while been maintained. And for the same reason, it may be proper to further say, that whether members sent to Congress from any State shall be admitted to seats constitutionally, rests exclusively with the respective Houses, and not to any extent with the Executive. And still further, that this proclamation is intended to present the people of the States wherein the National authority has been suspended, and loyal State Governments have been subverted, a mode in and by which the National authority and loyal State Governments may be re-established within said States, or in any of them; and, while the mode presented is the best the Executive can suggest, with his present impressions, it must not be understood that no other possible mode would be acceptable.

"Given under my hand at the City of Washington, the eighth day of December, A. D. one thousand eight hundred and sixty-three, and of the Independence of the United States of America the eighty-eighth.

"By the President: "ABRAHAM LINCOLN.

"WM. H. SEWARD, *Secretary of State*."

CALLS MADE FOR SEVEN HUNDRED THOUSAND MEN.

Since the beginning of the present year, 1864, two orders have been issued by the President, with a view of augmenting the armies of the Union to correspond with the requirements of the service. The first, dated February first, is as follows:

"EXECUTIVE MANSION, WASHINGTON, *February 1st*, 1864.—Ordered, that a draft for five hundred thousand men, to serve three years or during the war, be made on the tenth of March next, for the military service of the United States, crediting and deducting therefrom so many as have been enlisted or drafted into the service prior to the first day of March, and not heretofore credited.

"(Signed) "ABRAHAM LINCOLN."

The other, dated March fourteenth, was worded as follows:

"EXECUTIVE MANSION, WASHINGTON, *March 14th*, 1864.—In order to supply the force required to be drafted for the navy, and to provide an adequate reserve force for all contingencies, in addition to the five hundred thousand men called for February 1st, 1864, the call is hereby made, and a draft ordered for two hundred thousand men, for the military service of the army, navy, and marine corps of the United States. The proportionate quotas for the different wards, towns, townships, precincts, election districts, or counties will be made known through the Provost Marshal General's bureau, and account will be taken of the credits and deficiencies on former quotas. The 15th day of April, 1864, is designated as the time up to which the numbers required in each ward of a city, town, etc., may be raised by voluntary enlistment; and drafts will be made in each ward of a city, town, etc., which shall not have filled the quota assigned to it within the time designated for the number required to fill the said quotas. The draft will be commenced as soon after the 15th of April as practicable. The Government bounties, as now paid, will be continued until April 15th, 1864, at which time the additional bounties cease. On and after that date, one hundred dollars only will be paid, as provided by the act approved July 22nd, 1861. "ABRAHAM LINCOLN.

"Official. "E. D. TOWNSEND, *A. A. G.*"

EXPLANATORY PROCLAMATION.

On the twenty-sixth of March, 1864, the following proclamation, explanatory of the one issued on the eighth of December, 1863, was published:

"*Whereas*, It has become necessary to define the cases in which insurgent enemies are entitled to the benefits of the Proclamation of the President of the United States, which was made on the 8th day of December, 1863, and the manner in which they shall proceed to avail themselves of these benefits;

"*And whereas*, The object of that proclamation were to suppress the insurrection and to restore the authority of the United States;

"*And whereas*, The amnesty therein proposed by the President was offered with reference to these objects alone;

"Now, therefore, I, Abraham Lincoln, President of the United States, do hereby proclaim and declare that the said proclamation does not apply to the cases of persons who, at the time when they seek to obtain the benefits thereof, by taking the oath thereby prescribed, are in military, naval or civil confinement or custody, or under bonds or on parole of the civil, military or naval authorities or agents of the United States, as prisoners of war, or persons detained for offences of any kind, either before or after conviction; and that on the contrary, it does apply only to those persons who, being at large and free from any arrest, confinement or duress, shall voluntarily come forward and take the said oath, with the purpose of restoring peace and establishing the national authority.

"Prisoners excluded from the amnesty offered in the said proclamation may apply to the President for clemency, like all other offenders, and their application will receive due consideration.

"I do further declare and proclaim that the oath prescribed in the aforesaid proclamation of the 8th of December, 1863, may be taken and subscribed to before any commanding officer, civil, military or naval, in the service of the United States, or any civil or military officer of a State or territory not in insurrection, who, by the laws thereof, may be qualified for administering oaths.

"All officers who receive such oaths are hereby authorized to give certificates thereon to the persons respectively by whom they are made, and such officers are hereby required to transmit the original records of such oaths at as early a day as may be convenient to the Department of State, where they will be deposited and remain in the archives of the government.

"The Secretary of State will keep a register thereof, and will, on application, in proper cases, issue certificates of such records in the customary form of official certificates.

"In testimony whereof, I have hereunto set my hand, and caused the seal of the United States to be affixed.

"Done at the City of Washington, the twenty-sixth day of March, in the year of our Lord one thousand eight hundred and sixty-four, and of the Independence of the United States the eighty-eighth.

"By the President: "ABRAHAM LINCOLN.

"WM. H. SEWARD, *Secretary of State.*"

REVIEW OF THE PRESIDENT'S POLICY.

In the number of the *North American Review* for January, 1864, a most able article was published, reviewing the policy of President Lincoln, and from it we make the following extracts:

"'Bare is back,' says the Norse proverb, 'without brother behind it;' and this is, by analogy, true of an elective magistracy. The hereditary ruler in any critical emergency may reckon on the inexhaustible resources of *prestige*, of sentiment, of superstition, of dependent interest, while the new man must slowly and painfully create all these out of the unwilling material around him, by superiority of character, by patient singleness of purpose, by sagacious presentiment of popular tendencies and instinctive sympathy with the national character. Mr. Lincoln's task was one of peculiar and exceptional difficulty. Long habit had accustomed the American people to the notion of a party in power, and of a President as its creature and organ, while the more vital fact, that the executive for the time being represents the abstract idea of government as a permanent principle superior to all party and all private interest, had gradually become unfamiliar. They had so long seen the public policy more or less directed by views of party, and often even of personal advantage, as to be ready to suspect the motives of a chief magistrate compelled, for the first time in our history, to feel himself the head and hand of a great nation, and to act upon the fundamental maxim, laid down by all publicists, that the first duty of a government is to defend and maintain its own existence. Accordingly, a powerful weapon seemed to be put into the hands of the opposition by the necessity under which the administration found itself of applying this old truth to new relations. They were not slow in turning it to use, but the patriotism and common-sense of the people were more than a match for any sophistry of mere party. The radical mistake of the leaders of the opposition was in forgetting that they had a country, and expecting a similar obliviousness on the part of the people. In the undisturbed possession of office for so many years, they had come to consider the government as a kind of public Gift Enterprise conducted by themselves, and whose profits were nominally to be shared among the holders of their tickets, though all the prizes had a trick of falling to the lot of the managers. Amid the tumult of war, when the life of the nation was at stake, when the principles of despotism and freedom were grappling in deadly conflict, they had no higher conception of the crisis than such as would serve the purpose of a contested election; no thought but of advertising the tickets for the next drawing of that private speculation which they miscalled the Democratic party. But they were too little in sympathy with the American people to understand them, or the motives by which they were governed. It became more and more clear that, in embarrassing the administration, their design was to cripple the country; that, by a strict construction of the Constitution, they meant nothing more than the locking up of the only arsenal whence effective arms could be drawn to defend the nation Fortunately, insincerity by its very nature, by its necessary want of conviction, must ere long betray itself by its inconsistencies. It was hard to believe that men had any real horror of sectional war, who were busy in fomenting jealousies between East and West; that they could be in favor of a war for the Union as it was, who were for accepting the violent amendments of Rebellion; that they could be heartily opposed to insurrection in the South, who threatened government with forcible resistance in the North; or that they were humanely anxious to stay the effusion of blood, who did not scruple to stir up the mob of our chief city to murder and arson, and to compliment the patriotism of assassins with arms in their hands. Believers, if they believed any thing, in the divine right of Sham, they brought the petty engineering of the caucus to cope with the resistless march of events, and hoped to stay the steady drift of the nation's purpose, always setting deeper and stronger in one direction, with the scoop-nets that had served their turn so well in dipping fish from the turbid eddies of politics. They have given an example of the shortest and easiest way of reducing a great party to an inconsiderable faction.

"The change which three years have brought about, is too remarkable to be passed over without comment—too weighty in its lesson not to be laid to heart. Never did a President enter upon office with less means at his command, outside his own strength of heart and steadiness of understanding, for inspiring confidence in the people, and so winning it for himself, than Mr. Lincoln. All that was known of him was that he was a good stump-speaker, nominated for his *availability*—that is, because he had no history—and chosen by a party with whose more extreme opinions he was not in sympathy. It might well be feared that a man past fifty, against whom the ingenuity of hostile partisans could rake up no accusation, must be lacking in manliness of character, in decision of principle, in strength of will,—that a man who was at best only the representative of a party, and who yet did not fairly represent even that—would fail of political, much more of popular support. And certainly no one ever entered upon office with so few resources of power in the past, and so many materials of weakness in the present, as Mr. Lincoln. Even in that half of the Union which acknowledged him as President, there was a large, and at that time dangerous minority, that hardly admitted his claim to the office, and even in the party that elected him there was also a large minority that suspected him of being secretly a communicant with the church of Laodicea. All that he did was sure to be virulently attacked as ultra by one side; all that he left undone, to be stigmatized as proof of lukewarmness and backsliding by the other. Meanwhile he was to carry on a truly colossal war by means of both; he was to disengage the country from diplomatic entanglements of unprecedented peril undisturbed by the help or the hinderance of either, and to win from the crowning dangers of his administration, in the confidence of the people, the means of his safety and their own. He has contrived to do it, and perhaps none of our Presidents since Washington has stood so firm in the confidence of the people as he does after three years of stormy administration.

"Mr. Lincoln's policy was a tentative one, and rightly so. He laid down no programme which must compel him to be either inconsistent or unwise—no cast-iron theorem to which circumstances must be fitted as they rose, or else be useless to his ends. He seemed to have chosen Mazarin's motto, *Le temps et moi.* The *moi*, to be sure, was not very prominent at first; but it has grown more and more so, till the world is beginning to be persuaded that it stands for a character of marked individuality and capacity for affairs. Time was his prime-minister, and, we began to think at one period, his general-in-chief also. At first he was so slow that he tired out all those who see no evidence of progress but in blowing up the engine; then he was so fast, that he took the breath away from those who think there is no getting on safely while there is a spark of fire under the boilers. God is the only being who has time enough; but a prudent man, who knows how to seize occasion, can commonly make a shift to find as much as he needs. Mr. Lincoln, as it seems to us in reviewing his career, though we have sometimes in our impatience thought otherwise, has always waited, as a wise man should, till the right moment brought up all his reserves. *Semper nocuit differre paratis* is a sound axiom, but the really efficacious man will also be sure to know when he is *not* ready, and be firm against all persuasion and reproach till he is.

" One would be apt to think, from some of the criticisms made on Mr. Lincoln's course by those who mainly agree with him in principle, that the chief object of a statesman should be rather to proclaim his adhesion to certain doctrines than to achieve their triumph by quietly accomplishing his ends. In our opinion, there is no more unsafe politician than a conscientiously rigid *doctrinaire*, nothing more sure to end in disaster than a theoretic scheme of policy that admits of no pliability for contingencies. True, there is a popular image of an impossible He, in whose plastic hands the submissive destinies of mankind become as wax, and to whose commanding necessity the toughest facts yield with the graceful pliancy of fiction; but in real life we commonly find that the men who control circumstances, as it is called, are those who have learned to allow for the influence of their eddies, and have the nerve to turn them to account at the happy instant. Mr. Lincoln's perilous task has been to carry a rather shackly raft through the rapids, making fast the unrulier logs as he could snatch opportunity; and the country is to be congratulated that he did not think it his duty to run straight at all hazards, but cautiously to assure himself with his setting-pole where the main current was, and keep steadily to that. He is still in wild water, but we have faith that his skill and sureness of eye will bring him out right at last.

"A curious, and, as we think, not inapt parallel might be drawn between Mr. Lincoln and one of the most striking figures in modern history—Henry IV. of France. The career of the latter may be more picturesque, as that of a daring captain always is; but, in all its vicissitudes, there is nothing more romantic than that sudden change, as by a rub of Aladdin's lamp, from the attorney's office in a country town of Illinois to the helm of a great nation in times like these. The analogy between the characters and circumstances of the two men is, in many respects, singularly close. Succeeding to a rebellion rather than a crown, Henry's chief material dependence was the Huguenot party, whose doctrines sat upon him with a looseness distasteful certainly, if not suspicious, to the more fanatical among them. King only in name over the greater part of France, and with his capital barred against him, it yet gradually became clear to the more far-seeing even of the Catholic party, that he was the only centre of order and legitimate authority round which France could reorganize itself. While preachers who held the divine right of kings made the churches of Paris ring with declamations in favor of democracy rather than submit to the heretic dog of a Béarnois—much as our *soi-disant* Democrats have lately been preaching the divine right of slavery, and denouncing the heresies of the Declaration of Independence—Henry bore both parties in hand till he was convinced that only one course of action could possibly combine his own interests and those of France

Meanwhile the Protestants believed somewhat doubtfully that he was theirs, the Catholics hoped somewhat doubtfully that he would be theirs, and Henry himself turned aside remonstrance, advice, and curiosity alike with a jest or a proverb, (if a little *high*, he liked them none the worse,) joking continually, as his manner was. We have seen Mr. Lincoln contemptuously compared to Sancho Panza by persons incapable of appreciating one of the deepest pieces of wisdom in the profoundest romance ever written—namely, that, while Don Quixote was incomparable in theoretic and ideal statesmanship, Sancho, with his stock of proverbs, the ready-money of human experience, made the best possible practical governor. Henry IV. was as full of wise saws and modern instances as Mr. Lincoln, but beneath all this was the thoughtful, practical, humane, and thoroughly earnest man, around whom the fragments of France were to gather themselves till she took her place again as a planet of the first magnitude in the European system. In one respect Mr. Lincoln was more fortunate than Henry. However some may think him wanting in zeal, the most fanatical can find no taint of apostasy in any measure of his, nor can the most bitter charge him with being influenced by motives of personal interest. The leading distinction between the policies of the two is one of circumstances. Henry went over to the nation; Mr. Lincoln has steadily drawn the nation over to him. One left a united France; the other, we hope and believe, will leave a re-united America. We leave our readers to trace the further points of difference and resemblance for themselves, merely suggesting a general similarity which has often occurred to us. One only point of melancholy interest we will allow ourselves to touch upon. That Mr. Lincoln is not handsome nor elegant, we learn from certain English tourists who would consider similar revelations in regard to Queen Victoria as thoroughly American in their want of *bienséance*. It is no concern of ours, nor does it affect his fitness for the high place he so worthily occupies; but he is certainly as fortunate as Henry in the matter of good looks, if we may trust contemporary evidence. Mr. Lincoln has also been reproached with Americanism by some not unfriendly British critics; but, with all deference, we cannot say that we like him any the worse for it, or see in it any reason why he should govern Americans the less wisely.

"The most perplexing complications that Mr. Lincoln's government has had to deal with have been the danger of rupture with the two leading commercial countries of Europe, and the treatment of the slavery question. In regard to the former, the peril may be considered as nearly past, and the latter has been withdrawing steadily, ever since the war began, from the noisy debating-ground of faction to the quieter region of practical solution by convincingness of facts and consequent advance of opinion which we are content to call Fate.

"Even so long ago as when Mr. Lincoln, not yet convinced of the danger and magnitude of the crisis, was endeavoring to persuade himself of Union majorities at the South, and to carry on a war that was half peace in the hope of a peace that would have been all war,—while he was still enforcing the Fugitive Slave Law, under some theory that Secession, however it might absolve States from their obligations, could not escheat them of their claims under the Constitution, and that slaveholders in rebellion had alone among mortals the privilege of having their cake and eating it at the same time,—the enemies of free government were striving to persuade the people that the war was an Abolition crusade. To rebel without reason was proclaimed as one of the rights of man, while it was carefully kept out of sight that to suppress rebellion is the first duty of government. All the evils that have come upon the country have been attributed to the Abolitionists, though it is hard to see how any party can become permanently powerful except in one of two ways,—either by the greater truth of its principles, or the extravagance of the party opposed to it. To fancy the ship of state, riding safe at her constitutional moorings, suddenly engulfed by a huge kraken of Abolitionism, rising from unknown depths and grasping it with slimy tentacles, is to look at the natural history of the matter with the eyes of Pontoppidan. To believe that the leaders in the Southern treason feared any danger from Abolitionism, would be to deny them ordinary intelligence, though there can be little doubt that they made use of it to stir the passions and excite the fears of their deluded accomplices. They rebelled, not because they thought slavery weak, but because they believed it strong enough, not to overthrow the government, but to get possession of it; for it becomes daily clearer that they used rebellion only as a means of revolution, and if they got revolution, though not in the shape they looked for, is the American people to save them from its consequences at the cost of its own existence? The election of Mr. Lincoln, which it was clearly in their power to prevent had they wished, was the occasion merely, and not the cause, of their revolt. Abolitionism, till within a year or two, was the despised heresy of a few earnest persons, without political weight enough to carry the election of a parish constable; and their cardinal principle was disunion, because they were convinced that within the Union the position of slavery was impregnable. In spite of the proverb, great effects do not follow from small causes,—that is, disproportionately small,—but from adequate causes acting under certain required conditions. To contrast the size of the oak with that of the parent acorn, as if the poor seed had paid all costs from its slender strong box, may serve for a child's wonder; but the real miracle lies in that divine league which bound all the forces of nature to the service of the tiny germ in fulfilling its destiny. Every thing has been at work for the past ten years in the cause of antislavery, but Garrison and Phillips have been far less successful propagandists than the slaveholders themselves, with the constantly-growing arrogance of their pretensions and encroachments. They have forced the question upon the attention of every voter in the Free States, by defiantly putting freedom and democracy on the defensive. But, even after the Kansas outrages, there was no wide-spread desire on the part of the North to commit aggressions, though there was a growing determination to resist them. The popular unanimity in favor of the war three years ago was but in small measure the result of antislavery sentiment, far less of any zeal for abolition. But every month of the war, every movement of the allies of slavery in the Free States, has been making Abolitionists by the thousands. The masses of any people, however intelligent, are very little moved by abstract principles of humanity and justice, until those principles are interpreted for them by the stinging commentary of some infringement upon their own rights, and then their instincts and passions, once aroused, do indeed derive an incalculable reinforcement of impulse and intensity from those higher ideas, those sublime traditions, which have no motive political force till they are allied with a sense of immediate personal wrong or imminent peril. Then at last the stars in their courses begin to fight against Sisera. Had any one doubted before that the rights of human nature are unitary, that oppression is of one hue the world over, no matter what the color of the oppressed,—had any one failed to see what the real essence of the contest was,—the efforts of the advocates of slavery among ourselves to throw discredit upon the fundamental axioms of the Declaration of Independence and the radical doctrines of Christianity, could not fail to sharpen his eyes. This quarrel, it is plain, is not between Northern fanaticism and Southern institutions, but between downright slavery and upright freedom, between despotism and democracy, between the Old World and the New.

"The progress of three years has outstripped the expectation of the most sanguine, and that of our arms, great as it undoubtedly is, is trifling in comparison with the advance of opinion. The great strength of slavery was a superstition, which is fast losing its hold on the public mind. When it was first proposed to raise negro regiments, there were many even patriotic men who felt as the West Saxons did at seeing their high priest hurl his lance against the temple of their idol. They were sure something terrible, they knew not what, would follow. But the earth stood firm, the heavens gave no sign, and presently they joined in making a bonfire of their bugbear. That we should employ the material of the rebellion for its own destruction, seems now the merest truism. In the same way men's minds are growing wonted to the thought of emancipation; and great as are the difficulties which must necessarily accompany and follow so vast a measure, we have no doubt that they will be successfully overcome. The point of interest and importance is, that the feeling of our country in regard to slavery is no whim of sentiment, but a settled conviction, and that the tendency of opinion is unmistakably and irrevocably in one direction, no less in the Border Slave States than in the Free. The chances of the war, which at one time seemed against us, are now greatly in our favor. The nation is more thoroughly united against any shameful or illusory peace than it ever was on any other question, and the very extent of the territory to be subdued, which was the most serious cause of misgiving, is no longer an element of strength, but of disintegration, to the conspiracy. The Rebel leaders can make no concessions; the country is unanimously resolved that the war shall be prosecuted, at whatever cost; and if the war go on, will it leave slavery with any formidable strength in the South? and without that, need there be any fear of effective opposition in the North?

"While every day was bringing the people nearer to the conclusion which all thinking men saw to be inevitable from the beginning, it was wise in Mr. Lincoln to leave the shaping of his policy to events. In this country, where the rough and ready understanding of the people is sure at last to be the controlling power, a profound common-sense is the best genius for statesmanship. Hitherto the wisdom of the President's measures has been justified by the fact that they have always resulted in more firmly uniting public opinion. It is a curious comment on the sincerity of political professions, that the party calling itself Democratic should have been the last to recognize the real movement and tendency of the popular mind. The same gentlemen who two years ago were introducing resolutions in Congress against coercion, are introducing them now in favor of the war, but against subjugation. Next year they may be in favor of emancipation, but against abolition. It does not seem to have occurred to them that the one point of difference between a civil and a foreign war is, that in the former, one of the parties must by the very nature of the case be put down, and the other left in possession of the government. Unless the country is to be divided, no compromise is possible, and, if one side must yield, shall it be the nation or the conspirators? A government may make, and any wise government would make, concessions to men who have risen against real grievances; but to make them in favor of a rebellion that had no juster cause than the personal ambition of a few bad men, would be to abdicate. Southern politicians, however, have always been so dexterous in drawing nice distinctions, that they may find some consolation inappreciable by obtuser minds in being coerced instead of subjugated.

"If Mr. Lincoln continue to act with the firmness and prudence which have hitherto distinguished him, we think he has little to fear from the efforts of the opposition. Men without sincere convictions are hardly likely to have a well-defined and settled policy, and the blunders they have hitherto committed must make them cautious. If their personal hostility to the President be unabated, we may safely count on their leniency to the opinion of majorities, and the drift of public sentiment is too strong to be mistaken. They have at last discovered that there is such a thing as Country, which has a meaning for men's minds and a hold upon their hearts; they may make the further discovery, that this is a revolution that has been forced on us, and not merely a civil war. In any event, an opposition is a wholesome thing; and we are only sorry that this is not a more wholesome opposition.

"We believe it is the general judgment of the country on the acts of the present administration, that they have been, in the main, judicious and well-timed. The only doubt about some of them seems to be as to their constitutionality. It has been sometimes objected to our form of government, that it was faulty in having a written constitution which could not adapt itself to the needs of the time as they arose. But we think it rather a theoretic than a practical objection; for in point of fact there has been hardly a leading measure of any administration that has not been attacked as unconstitutional, and which was not carried nevertheless. Purchase of Louisiana, Embargo, Removal of the Deposits, Annexation of Texas, not to speak of others less important,—on the unconstitutionality of all these, powerful parties have appealed to the country, and invariably the decision has been against them. The will of the people for the time being has always carried it. In the present instance, we purposely refrain from any allusion to the moral aspects of the question. We prefer to leave the issue to experience and common-sense. Has any sane man ever doubted on which side the chances were in this contest? Can any sane man who has watched the steady advances of opinion, forced onward slowly by the immitigable logic of facts, doubt what the decision of the people will be in this matter? The Southern conspirators have played a desperate stake, and, if they had won, would have bent the whole policy of the country to the interests of slavery. Filibustering would have been nationalized, and the slave-trade re-established as the most beneficent form of missionary enterprise. But if they lose? They have, of their own choice, put the chance into our hands of making this continent the empire of a great homogeneous population, substantially one in race, language, and religion,—the most prosperous and powerful of nations. Is there a doubt what the decision of a victorious people will be? If we were base enough to decline the great commission which Destiny lays on us, should we not deserve to be ranked with those dastards whom the stern Florentine condemns as hateful alike to God and God's enemies?

"We would not be understood as speaking lightly of the respect due to constitutional forms, all the more essential under a government like ours and in times like these. But where undue respect for the form will lose us the substance, and where the substance, as in this case, is nothing less than the country itself, to be over-scrupulous would be unwise. Who are most tender in their solicitude that we keep sacred the letter of the law, in order that its spirit may not keep us alive? Mr. Jefferson Davis and those who, in the Free States, would have been his associates, but must content themselves with being his political *guerilleros.* If Davis had succeeded, would he have had any scruples of constitutional delicacy? And if he has not succeeded, is it not mainly owing to measures which his disappointed partisans denounce as unconstitutional?

"We cannot bring ourselves to think that Mr. Lincoln has done any thing that would furnish a precedent dangerous to our liberties, or in any way overstepped the just limits of his constitutional discretion. If his course has been unusual, it was because the danger was equally so. It cannot be so truly said that he has strained his prerogative, as that the imperious necessity has exercised its own. Surely the framers of the Constitution never dreamed that they were making a strait waistcoat, in which the nation was to lie helpless while traitors were left free to do their will. In times like these, men seldom settle precisely the principles on which they *shall* act, but rather adjust those on which they *have* acted to the lines of precedent as well as they can after the event. This is what the English Parliament did in the Act of Settlement. Congress, after all, will only be called on for the official draft of an enactment, the terms of which have been already decided by agencies beyond their control. Even while they are debating, the current is sweeping them onward toward new relations of policy. At worst, a new precedent is pretty sure of pardon, if it successfully meet a new occasion. It is a harmless pleasantry to call Mr. Lincoln 'Abraham the First,'—we remember when a similar title was applied to President Jackson; and it will not be easy, we suspect, to persuade a people who have more liberty than they know what to do with, that they are the victims of despotic tyranny.

"Mr. Lincoln probably thought it more convenient, to say the least, to have a country left without a constitution, than a constitution without a country. We have no doubt we shall save both; for if we take care of the one, the other will take care of itself. Sensible men, and it is the sensible men in any country who at last shape its policy, will be apt to doubt whether it is true conservatism, after the fire is got under, to insist on keeping up the flaw in the chimney by which it made its way into the house. Radicalism may be a very dangerous thing, and so is calomel, but not when it is the only means of saving the life of the patient. Names are of great influence in ordinary times, when they are backed by the *vis inertiæ* of life-long prejudice, but they have little power in comparison with a sense of interest; and though, in peaceful times, it may be highly respectable to be conservative merely for the sake of being so, though without very clear notions of any thing in particular to be conserved, what we want now is the prompt decision that will not hesitate between the bale of silk and the ship when a leak is to be stopped. If we succeed in saving the great landmarks of freedom, there will be no difficulty in settling our constitutional boundaries again. We have no sympathy to spare for the pretended anxieties of men who, only two years gone, were willing that Jefferson Davis should break all the ten commandments together, and would now impeach Mr. Lincoln for a scratch on the surface of the tables where they are engraved."

As soon as the publication was received and read by the President, he sent to the publishers the following letter:

"EXECUTIVE MANSION, WASHINGTON, *January* 16*th*, 1864.

"*Messrs. Crosby & Nichols:*

"GENTLEMEN: The number for this month and year of the *North American Review* was duly received and for which please accept my thanks. Of course I am not the most impartial judge; yet, with due allowance for this, I venture to hope that the article entitled 'The President's Policy' will be of value to the country. I fear I am not quite worthy of all which is therein kindly said of me personally.

"The sentence of twelve lines, commencing at the top of page 252, (which in this book is on page 165,) I could wish to be not exactly as it is. In what is there expressed the writer has not correctly understood me. I have never had a theory that secession could absolve States or people from their obligations. Precisely the contrary is asserted in the inaugural address; and it was because of my belief in the continuation of those *obligations* that I was puzzled, for a time, as to denying the legal *rights* of those citizens who remained individually innocent of treason or rebellion. But I mean no more now than to merely call attention to this point.

"Yours respectfully,

"A. LINCOLN."

The sentence referred to by Mr. Lincoln, is as follows:

"Even so long ago as when Mr. Lincoln, not yet convinced of the danger and magnitude of the crisis, was endeavoring to persuade himself of Union majorities at the South, and to carry on a war that was half peace, in the hope of a peace that would have been all war, while he was still enforcing the Fugitive Slave law, under some theory that secession, however it might absolve States from their obligations, could not escheat them of their claims under the constitution, and that slaveholders in rebellion had alone among mortals, the privilege of having their cake and eating it at the same time,—the enemies of free government were striving to persuade the people that the war was an abolition crusade. To rebel without reason was proclaimed as one of the rights of man, while it was carefully kept out of sight that to suppress rebellion is the first duty of government."

RECENT ADDRESSES OF MR. LINCOLN.

On the night of the eighteenth of March, 1864, at the close of the successful fair held in the Patent Office at Washington, Mr. Lincoln spoke as follows:

"*Ladies and Gentlemen:*—I appear, to say but a word. This

extraordinary war in which we are engaged falls heavily upon all classes of people, but the most heavily upon the soldier. For it has been said, all that a man hath will he give for his life; and, while all contribute of their substance, the soldier puts his life at stake, and often yields it up in his country's cause. The highest merit, then, is due to the soldier.

"In this extraordinary war, extraordinary developments have manifested themselves, such as have not been seen in former wars; and among these manifestations nothing has been more remarkable than these fairs for the relief of suffering soldiers and their families. And the chief agents in these fairs are the women of America. I am not accustomed to the use of the language of eulogy; I have never studied the art of paying compliments to women; but I must say that, if all that has been said by orators and poets, since the creation of the world, in praise of women were applied to the women of America, it would not do them justice for their conduct during this war. I will close by saying, God bless the women of America!" (Great applause.)

Three days later, a committee appointed by the Workingmen's Democratic Republican Association of New York waited on the President, and presented him with an address informing him that he had been elected a member of that organization. After the chairman had stated the object of the visit, Mr. Lincoln made the following reply:

"*Gentlemen of the Committee*:—The honorary membership in your Association so generously tendered is gratefully accepted. You comprehend, as your address shows, that the existing rebellion means more and tends to more than the perpetuation of African slavery—that it *is*, in fact, a war upon the rights of all working people. Partly to show that the view has not escaped my attention, and partly that I cannot better express myself, I read a passage from the message to Congress in December, 1861:

"'It continues to develop that the insurrection is largely, if not exclusively, a war upon the first principle of popular Government—the rights of the people. Conclusive evidence of this is found in the most grave and maturely-considered public documents, as well as in the general tone of the insurgents. In those documents we find the abridgement of the existing right of suffrage, and the denial to the people of all right to participate in the selection of public officers, except the legislative body, boldly advocated with labored arguments, to prove that large control of the people in government is the source of all political evil. Monarchy is sometimes hinted at as a possible refuge from the power of the people. In my present position, I could scarcely be justified were I to omit raising my voice against this approach of returning despotism.

"'It is not needed or fitting here that a general argument should be made in favor of popular institutions; but there is one point, with its connections, not so hackneyed as most others, to which I ask a brief attention. It is the effort to place *capital* on an equal footing with, if not above, *labor* in the structure of the Government. It is assumed that labor is available only in connection with capital; that nobody labors unless somebody else owning capital somehow, by use of it, induces him to labor.

"'This assumed, it is next considered whether it is best that capital shall *hire* laborers, and thus induce them to work by their own consent, or *buy them* and drive them to it without their consent. Having proceeded so far, it is naturally concluded that all laborers are either hired laborers or what we call slaves. And, further, it is assumed that whoever is once a hired laborer is fixed in that condition for life. Now there is no such relation between capital and labor as assumed, nor is there any such thing as a free man being fixed for life in the condition of a hired laborer. Both of these assumptions are false, and all inferences from them are groundless.

"'Labor is prior to and independent of capital. Capital is only the fruit of labor, and never could have existed if labor had not first existed. Labor is the support of capital, and deserves much the higher consideration. Capital has its rights, which are as worthy of protection as any other rights. Nor is it denied that there is, and probably always will be, a relation between labor and capital producing mutual benefits. The error is in assuming that the whole labor of a community exists within that relation. A few men own capital, and that few avoid labor themselves, and with that capital hire or buy another few to labor for them.

"'A large majority belong to neither class—neither work for others nor have others working for them. In most of the Southern States a majority of the whole people, of all colors, are neither slaves nor masters, while, in the Northern States, a large majority are neither hirers nor hired. Men with their families—wives, sons, and daughters—work for themselves on their farms, in their houses, and in their shops, taking the whole product to themselves, and asking no favors of capital on the one hand nor of hired laborers or slaves on the other. It is not forgotten that a considerable number of persons mingle their own labor with capital—that is, they labor with their own hands and also buy or hire others to labor for them; but this is only a mixed and not a distinct class. No principle stated is disturbed by the existence of this mixed class.

"'Again. As has already been said, there is not of necessity any such thing as the free hired laborer being fixed to that condition for life. Many independent men everywhere in these

States, a few years back in their lives, were hired laborers. The prudent, penniless beginner in the world labors for wages a while, saves a surplus with which to buy tools or lands for himself, then labors on his own account another while, and at length hires another new beginner to help him. This is the just, and generous, and prosperous system which opens the way to all—gives hope to all, and consequent energy, and progress, and improvement to all. No men living are more worthy to be trusted than those who toil up from poverty—none less inclined to take or touch aught with which they have not honestly earned. Let them beware of surrendering a political power which they already possess, and which, if surrendered, will surely be used to close the door of advancement against such as they, and to fix new disabilities and burdens upon them till all of liberty shall be lost.'

"The views then expressed remain unchanged—nor have I much to add. None are so deeply interested to resist the present rebellion as the working people. Let them beware of prejudices working disunion and hostility among themselves. The most notable feature of a disturbance in your city last summer was the hanging of some working people by other working people. It should never be so. The strongest bond of human sympathy, outside of the family relation, should be one uniting all working people, of all nations, tongues, and kindreds. Nor should this lead to a war upon property or the owners of property. Property is the fruit of labor; property is desirable; is a positive good in the world. That some should be rich, shows that others may become rich, and hence is just encouragement to industry and enterprise. Let not him who is houseless pull down the house of another, but let him labor diligently and build one for himself; thus, by example, assuring that his own shall be safe from violence when built."

ABRAHAM LINCOLN THE CHOICE OF THE PEOPLE FOR ANOTHER TERM.

Within the past few months, a movement has been in progress throughout the North and West, which can but be as gratifying to Abraham Lincoln as it is pleasing to the great mass of the loyal voters of the country.

No President ever encountered the same difficulties which have met the present incumbent of the "White House" at every step he has taken since the day of his inauguration. The traitors in the South have naturally opposed every important order he has issued; have ridiculed every proclamation he has promulgated; have criticised and sneered at every message he has written; and have vilified and maligned the character of their author. This was to be expected; but there have been traitors at the North who have been no less bitter, no less strenuous in their opposition; but, under the guidance of Divine Providence, he has been able to repel the assaults of both of these classes of unprincipled advocates of treason; and, strong in his holy purpose to rescue the country from the machinations of its enemies, he has continued steadfast in the path of official duty. He may have made some mistakes, but they have been few, and it must be remembered that even those which have been more particularly referred to by his opponents were caused, not by ignorance, but by the exigencies of the occasion, which compelled him to give an important answer, or issue an important order, without being allowed the time for reflection which the magnitude of the subject demanded.

The importance, indeed the absolute necessity, of retaining Mr. Lincoln in his present exalted position, is now the popular belief, and from every loyal Commonwealth come tidings, pronouncing in language which cannot be mistaken, that he alone is deemed the proper person to rescue the country from its present danger. The Legislatures of fifteen States have declared that he is their choice and the choice of their constituents. Union Leagues, Conventions, and public assemblies of different political characters, have indorsed the decision of their legislative bodies; and the loyal people almost unanimously approve of the action which has again brought Mr. Lincoln prominently forward as the best and only man to nominate and elect to the Presidency. He has been tried, and not found wanting, and no better return for the perils encountered, the labors accomplished, and the benefits derived to the country, could be offered, than his re-nomination and re-election, both of which are now almost as certain as that the Union Convention will assemble at Baltimore in June next, and that the election will be held in November. Maine, New Hampshire, Connecticut, Rhode Island, Pennsylvania, New Jersey, Maryland, Ohio, Indiana, Michigan, Wisconsin, Iowa, Minnesota, Kansas, and California, have spoken, and, at the advent of the summer solstice, the other States will re-echo the popular sentiments, as so emphatically expressed by their sister Commonwealths. He is no longer the representative of any particular political party, but comes before the loyal voters of the country as an indefatigable, incorruptible, public servant, whose multiform and perplexing duties have been faithfully performed, and who has no other ambition than to so administer the affairs of the nation as will be most conducive to its welfare. Throughout his Presidential career he has never failed to prove himself equal to any emergency that might occur. To use the words of a patriotic Philadelphian, even in the darkest hour of our struggle, when every thing seemed lost, and the feeling of despondency with regard to the future was so great that those who had been confident before lost all hope, he who was at the helm of Government still maintained his self-command and a firm reliance in an overruling Providence, which, in due time, would order all things aright. Coolness, confidence, and courage, are only valuable when they are needed; and he who has passed through ordeals in which the possession of such qualities have been manifested, in no ordinary degree, obtains a hold on the confidence of the world which but few are fortunate enough to secure; men of extraordinary abilities, lacking these qualities, have, on great and trying occasions, too often demonstrated their incapacity for supreme command, like that which belongs to the head of a great government. Considerations such as these will make the people loth to part with one who, in the hour of trial, has proved himself equal to *the emergency.*

As an evidence of the sentiment to which we have referred, we publish the following resolutions, unanimously adopted by the Union League of Philadelphia, on the eleventh of January, 1864:

"*Whereas,* The skill, courage, fidelity and integrity with which, in a period of unparalleled trial, ABRAHAM LINCOLN has conducted the administration of the National Government, have won for him the highest esteem and the most affectionate regard of his grateful countrymen;

"*And whereas,* The confidence which all loyal men repose in his honesty, his wisdom and his patriotism, should be proclaimed on every suitable occasion, in order that his hands may be strengthened for the important work he has yet to perform;

"*And whereas,* The Union League of Philadelphia, composed as it is, of those who, having formerly belonged to various parties, in this juncture recognize no party but their country; and representing, as it does, all the industrial, mechanical, manufacturing, commercial, financial, and professional interests of the city, is especially qualified to give, in this behalf, an unbiased and authentic utterance to the public sentiment; therefore,

"*Resolved,* That to the prudence, sagacity, comprehension and perseverance of Mr. Lincoln, under the guidance of a benign Providence, the nation is more indebted for the grand results of the war, which southern rebels have wickedly waged against liberty and the Union, than to any other single instrumentality; and that he is justly entitled to whatever reward it is in the power of the nation to bestow.

"*Resolved,* That we cordially approve of the policy which Mr. Lincoln has adopted and pursued, as well the principles he has announced as the acts he has performed, and that we shall continue to give an earnest and energetic support to the doctrines and measures by which his administration has thus far been directed and illustrated.

"*Resolved,* That as Mr. Lincoln has had to endure the largest share of the labor required to suppress the rebellion, now rapidly verging to its close, he should also enjoy the largest share of the honors which await those who have contended for the right; and as, in all respects, he has shown pre-eminent ability in fulfilling the requirements of his great office, we recognize with pleasure the unmistakable indications of the popular will in all the loyal States, and heartily join with our fellow-citizens, without any distinction of party, here and elsewhere, in presenting him as the People's candidate for the Presidency at the approaching election.

"*Resolved*, That a Committee of Seventy-six be appointed, whose duty it shall be to promote the object now proposed, by correspondence with other loyal organizations, by stimulating the expression of public opinion, and by whatever additional modes shall, in their judgment, seem best adapted to the end; and that this Committee have power to supply vacancies in their own body and to increase their numbers at their own discretion.

"*Resolved*, That a copy of these proceedings, properly engrossed and attested, be forwarded to President Lincoln; and that they also be published in the loyal newspapers."

GENERAL GRANT MADE A LIEUTENANT-GENERAL.

On the 2d of March, 1864, President Lincoln approved a bill passed by Congress on the 26th of February, reviving the grade of Lieutenant-General, and the same day he nominated for that high office Major-General Grant, the hero of Vicksburg, and on the same day the Senate unanimously confirmed the nomination. On the 9th of March, General Grant, being upon official business at Washington, was invited to the White House, where the President, handing him his commission, addressed him as follows:

" GENERAL GRANT:—The expression of the nation's approbation of what you have already done, and its reliance on you for what remains to do in the existing great struggle, is now presented with this commission, constituting you *Lieutenant-General of the Army of the United States.*

"With this high honor devolves on you an additional responsibility. As the country herein trusts you, so, under God, it will sustain you. I scarcely need add, that with what I here speak for the country, goes my own hearty personal concurrence."

General Grant accepted the commission with characteristic modesty, responding briefly and appropriately to the remarks of the President.

A VIGOROUS PROSECUTION OF THE WAR.

In May, 1864, the President had approved the plans of Lieutenant-General Grant; and the grand combinations of the latter, looking to the breaking up of the Confederate power, and the fall of Richmond, were put in motion Sherman was at work in the South-west, and after taking and destroying Atlanta, he designed marching directly through the heart of Georgia, making Savannah his first objective point; and then, striking northward, he was to compel the evacuation of Columbia, Charleston, and Wilmington, and co-operate with General Grant in the conquest of the rebel capital. Thomas was left in the South-west to check, and if possible, destroy Hood and Johnston; while Grant, aided by the splendid genius and fighting qualities of Meade, Sheridan, and Hancock, were operating in the immediate vicinity of Richmond. The plans were finally all carried out almost to the letter, and General Grant telegraphed to the President, in May, that he "proposed to fight it out on this line if it took all summer." These vast military operations, and the confidence of the great mass of the people in the fidelity of the President, and in the skill of his generals, promoted a great degree of confidence in the speedy ending of the war, with an unconditional restoration of the authority of the Union.

MR. LINCOLN IS RE-NOMINATED FOR THE PRESIDENCY.

On the 7th of June, 1864, the National Union Convention met at Baltimore. The re-nomination of Mr. Lincoln for President of the United States was clearly foreshadowed, and the formal naming of him as the choice of the people for a second term in his high office, was looked for as a matter of course. He was re-nominated by acclamation, and Andrew Johnson of Tennessee, who, like himself, was a self-made man, was nominated for the Vice-Presidency. The platform of principles adopted by the convention was brief and pithy. We transfer some pertinent extracts to our pages.

"*Resolved,* That it is the highest duty of every American citizen to maintain against all their enemies the integrity of the Union and the paramount authority of the Constitution and laws of the United States; and that, laying aside all differences of political opinion, we pledge ourselves as Union men, animated by a common sentiment, and aiming at a common object, to do every thing in our power to aid the Government in quelling by force of arms the rebellion now raging against its authority, and in bringing to the punishment due to their crimes, the rebels and traitors arrayed against it.

"*Resolved,* That we approve the determination of the Government of the United States not to compromise with rebels, nor to offer any terms of peace except such as may be based upon an 'unconditional surrender' of their hostility and a return to their just allegiance to the Constitution and laws of the United States, and that we call upon the Government to maintain this position and to prosecute the war with the utmost possible vigor to the complete suppression of the Rebellion, in full reliance upon the self-sacrifice, the patriotism, the heroic valor, and the undying devotion of the American people to their country and its free institutions.

"*Resolved,* That, as Slavery was the cause, and now constitutes the strength, of this rebellion, and as it must be always and everywhere hostile to the principles of republican government, justice and the national safety demand its utter and complete extirpation from the soil of the republic; and that we uphold and maintain the acts and proclamations by which the Government, in its own defence, has aimed a death-blow at this gigantic evil. We are in favor, furthermore, of such an amendment to the Constitution, to be made by the people in conformity with its provisions, as shall terminate and forever prohibit the existence of Slavery within the limits of the jurisdiction of the United States.

"*Resolved,* That we approve and applaud the practical wisdom, the unselfish patriotism, and unswerving fidelity to the Constitution and the principles of American liberty, with which Abraham Lincoln has discharged, under circumstances of unparalleled difficulty, the great duties and responsibilities of the presidential office; that we approve and indorse, as demanded by the emergency, and essential to the preservation of the nation, and as within the Constitution, the measures and acts which he has adopted to defend the nation against its open and secret foes; that we approve especially the Proclamation of Emancipation, and the employment as Union soldiers of men heretofore held in Slavery; and that we have full confidence in his determination to carry these and all other constitutional measures essential to the salvation of the country into full and complete effect."

On the 29th of August of the same year, the Democratic Convention met at Chicago, and nominated George B. McClellan and George H. Pendleton as its banner bearers. General McClellan being named for the Presidency and Mr. Pendleton for the Vice-presidency. The platform of the party, as laid down by this convention, set forth, among other things, the following:

"*Resolved*, That this Convention does explicitly declare, as the sense of the American people, that after four years of failure to restore the Union by the experiment of war, during which, under the pretence of a military necessity of a war power higher than the Constitution, the Constitution itself has been disregarded in every part, and public liberty and private right alike trodden down, and the material prosperity of the country essentially impaired; justice, humanity, liberty, and the public welfare, demand that immediate efforts be made for a cessation of hostilities, with a view to an ultimate Convention of all the States, or other peaceable means to the end that at the earliest practicable moment peace may be restored on the basis of the Federal Union of the States."

General McClellan, in his letter of acceptance to the committee appointed by the Convention to notify him of his nomination, virtually ignored the portion of the platform given above, and he urged a vigorous prosecution of the war. Much dissatisfaction in the Democratic party grew out of the differences between the sentiments expressed by the platform and those of the principal candidate placed upon it, and for a time it seemed as though the party would be wrecked in advance upon the rock of these differences. Some of the leading peace men of the party refused to support General McClellan, while the War democracy denounced the platform in unmeasured terms.

To use an expression of General McClellan's, the campaign was "short, sharp, and decisive," and the candidates of both parties came in for a liberal share of abuse and ridicule.

PRESIDENT LINCOLN VISITS PHILADELPHIA.

A series of monster fairs was held, in 1864, in the principal cities of the Union, for the purpose of aiding the funds of the United States Sanitary Commission. Philadelphia held her great fair in June, and on the sixteenth of the month, the President and Mrs. Lincoln, paid a visit to the fair buildings, in Logan square. There was a huge crowd present for the purpose of gazing upon the features of their beloved Chief Magistrate. After a collation had been partaken of, Mr. Lincoln made a characteristic address. In speaking of the war, he said:

"War, at the best, is terrible, and this war of ours, in its magnitude and its duration, is one of the most terrible. It has deranged business, totally in many localities, and partially in all localities. It has destroyed property, and ruined homes; it has produced a national debt and taxation unprecedented, at least in this country. It has carried mourning to almost every home, until it can almost be said that the 'heavens are hung in black.'

* * * * * * * * *

"It is a pertinent question, often asked in the mind privately, and from one to the other, 'when is the war to end?' Surely I feel as deep an interest in this question as any other can, but I do not wish to name a day, or month, or a year when it is to end. I do not wish to run any risk of seeing the time come, without our being ready for the end, and for fear of disappointment because the time had come, and not the end. We accepted this war for an object, a worthy object, and the war will end when that object is attained. Under God, I hope it never will until that time. [Great cheering.] Speaking of the present campaign, Gen. Grant is reported to have said, 'I am going through on this line if it takes all summer!' [Cheers.] This war has taken three years; it was begun, or accepted, upon the line of restoring the national authority over the whole national domain—and for the American people, as far as my knowledge enables me to speak, I say, we are going through on this line if it takes three years more. [Cheers.] My friends, I did not know but that I might be called upon to say a few words before I got away from here, but I did not know it was coming just here. [Laughter.] I have never been in the habit of making predictions in regard to the war, but I am almost tempted to make one. If I were to hazard it, it is this: That Grant is this evening, with Gen. Meade and Gen. Hancock, of Pennsylvania, and the brave officers and soldiers with him, in a position from whence he will never be dislodged until Richmond is taken, [loud cheering], and I have but one single proposition to put now, and perhaps I can best put it in the form of an interrogatory. If I shall discover that Gen. Grant, and the noble officers and men under him, can be greatly facilitated in their work by a sudden pouring forward of men and assistance, will you give them to me? [Cries of 'Yes!'] Then, I say, stand ready, for I am waiting for the chance. [Laughter and cheers.] I thank you, gentlemen."

The hint given by the President in his speech, was understood when a call was made the following month for 500,000 more men.

WASHINGTON THREATENED.

Towards the middle of July, 1864, rebel raiders, under command of the traitor Breckinridge, audaciously threatened Washington. They approached as near the capital as Tenallytown, burned the residence of Postmaster Blair, at Silver Springs, destroyed passenger trains on the railroad between Baltimore and the Susquehanna, and burnt a large part of Chambersburg. President Lincoln remained placidly in Washington during this exciting period.

"TO WHOM IT MAY CONCERN."

While these stirring events were in progress near the national capital, representations were made to President Lincoln that certain parties, who professed to represent the rebel government, were at the Clifton House, at Niagara Falls, and anxious to enter into negotiations with a view to the restoration of peace. Clement C. Clay, Beverly Tucker, and George N. Sanders were the active agents of the South in this business, and they succeeded in persuading Mr. Horace Greeley that much good would come of a conference. The project was doubtless a trick to induce Mr. Lincoln to recognize the Southern Confederacy, and to trap him into a betrayal of his plans. But the following manifesto issued by him overturned all those hopes:

"EXECUTIVE MASION, WASHINGTON, *July* 18, 1864.—*To whom it may concern:* Any proposition which embraces the restoration of peace, the integrity of the Union, and the abandonment of slavery, and which comes by and with authority that can control the armies now at war against the United States, will be received and considered by the Executive Government of the United States, and will be met by liberal terms on other substantial and collateral points, and the bearers thereof shall have safe conduct both ways. ABRAHAM LINCOLN."

Mr. Clay and Mr. Holcombe, who were among the chief plenipotentiaries of Jefferson Davis, took high offence at the tone and language of this paper, and they responded to it in a tone of ill temper that evinced their bitter disappointment at the failure of the trap set for the feet of Mr. Lincoln. Their complaints had no other effect than to make their authors ridiculous in the sight of the world.

THE FALL OF ATLANTA.

In the month of September, 1864, intelligence arrived of the fall of Atlanta, and the President appointed a day of Thanksgiving, for the success of an event that none who were not in the secrets of the administration could have imagined the importance of at that time.

MR. LINCOLN IS RE-ELECTED.

The Presidential election took place upon the eighth of November, 1864, and it resulted in the triumph of Mr. Lincoln in every loyal State except Kentucky, New Jersey and Delaware. In some of the States, their soldiers in the field were allowed to vote, and the military vote was almost invariably cast for Lincoln and Johnson. The official returns for the entire vote polled summed up 4,034,789. Of these Mr. Lincoln received 2,223,035, and McClellan received 1,811,754, leaving a majority of 411,281 on the popular vote. Mr. Lincoln was elected by a plurality in 1860. In 1864 his majority was decided and unmistakable.

This result was considered a full endorsement of the

policy of Mr. Lincoln, and the war was more vigorously prosecuted from this time, many of its opponents being at least silenced, if they were not convinced.

MR. LINCOLN MAKES A SPEECH UPON HIS ELECTION.

At a late hour on the night of the election, the President was serenaded by a club of Pennsylvanians, who notified him of the fact of his being the choice of the people for a second term. He responded as follows:

"FRIENDS AND FELLOW-CITIZENS: Even before I had been informed by you that this compliment was paid me by loyal citizens of Pennsylvania friendly to me, I had inferred that you were of that portion of my countrymen who think that the best interests of the nation are to be subserved by the support of the present administration. I do not pretend to say that you, who think so, embrace all the patriotism and loyalty of the country; but I do believe, and I trust without personal interest, that the welfare of the country does require that such support and endorsement be given. I earnestly believe that the consequences of this day's work, if it be as you assume, and as now seems probable, will be to the lasting advantage if not to the very salvation of the country. I cannot, at this hour, say what has been the result of the election, but whatever it may be, I have no desire to modify this opinion: that all who have labored to-day in behalf of the Union organization, have wrought for the best interest of their country and the world, not only for the present but for all future ages. *I am thankful to God for this approval of the people; but while deeply grateful for this mark of their confidence in me, if I know my heart, my gratitude is free from any taint of personal triumph. I do not impugn the motives of any one opposed to me. It is no pleasure to me to triumph over any one, but I give thanks to the Almighty for this evidence of the people's resolution to stand by free government and the rights of humanity*

LAST ANNUAL MESSAGE OF MR. LINCOLN.

On the sixth of December, 1864, Mr. Lincoln sent into Congress his last annual Message. After dwelling at length upon our foreign relations, the state of the country, and the results of the election, which had at once demonstrated the strength of the people and their devotion to the cause of the Union, he said:

"The public purpose to establish and maintain the national authority, is unchanged, and, as we believe, unchangeable. The manner of continuing the effort remains to choose. On careful consideration of all the evidence accessible, it seems to me that no attempt at negotiation with the insurgent leader could result in any good. He would accept nothing short of severance of the Union—precisely what we will not and cannot give. His declarations to this effect are explicit and oft-repeated. He does not attempt to deceive us. He affords us no excuse to deceive ourselves. He cannot voluntarily re-accept the Union. We cannot voluntarily yield it. Between him and us the issue is distinct, single and inflexible. It is an issue which can only be tried by war, and decided by victory. If we yield we are beaten. If the Southern people fail him, he is beaten. Either way, it would be the victory and defeat following war. What is true, however, of him who heads the insurgent cause, is not necessarily true of those who follow. Although he cannot re-accept the Union, they can. * * * * In presenting the abandonment of armed resistance to the National authority, on the part of the insurgents, as the only indispensable condition to ending the war on the part of the government, I retract nothing heretofore said as to slavery. I repeat the declaration made a year ago, that while I remain in my present position I shall not attempt to retract or modify the Emancipation Proclamation, nor shall I return to slavery any person who is free by the terms of that proclamation or by any of the acts of Congress. If the people should, by whatever mode or means, make it an Executive duty to re-enslave such persons, another, and not I, must be their instrument to perform it. In stating a single condition of peace, I mean simply to say that the war will cease on the part of the government whenever it shall have ceased on the part of those who began it."

MORE TROOPS WANTED.

On the 19th of December, 1864, a call was made for 300,000 more men to finish up the great work on hand in the field.

MR. LINCOLN HAS AN INTERVIEW WITH REBEL COMMISSIONERS.

In the early part of February, 1865, application was made to the National Government for permission for Messrs. A. H. Stephens of Georgia, R. M. T. Hunter of Virginia, and J. A. Campbell of Alabama, to pass through the Union lines as *quasi* commissioners from the rebel government to treat for peace. Permission was granted, with the understanding that the parties named were not to be allowed to land. This determination upon the part of the Federal authorities caused much annoyance to the rebel agents, as they made no secret of their desire to visit Washington. Mr. Seward met the distinguished rebels named above, at Fortress Monroe. The Secretary of State telegraphed for the President, and Mr. Lincoln at once repaired to that point, where an interview was had on board the steamer River Queen.

The conference lasted four hours, and was perfectly friendly and good-tempered throughout. Not a word was said on either side indicating any but amicable sentiments. On our side the conversation was mainly conducted by the President; on theirs by Mr. Hunter, Mr. Stephens occasionally taking part. The rebel commissioners said nothing whatever of their personal views or wishes, but spoke solely and exclusively for their government, and, at the outset and throughout the conference, declared their entire lack of authority to make, receive, or consider any proposition whatever looking toward a close of the war, except on the basis of a recognition of the independence of the Confederate States as a preliminary condition. The President presented the subject to them in every conceivable form, suggesting the most liberal and considerate modification of whatever, in the existing legislation and action of the United States Government, might be regarded as specially hostile to the rights and interests, or wounding to the pride of the Southern people—but in no single particular could he induce them to swerve for a moment from their demand for recognition. They did not present this conspicuously as resting on their own convictions or wishes, but as the condition which their government had made absolutely indispensable to any negotiations or discussions whatever concerning peace.

President Lincoln, on the other hand, informed them, at every point, that such recognition was utterly and totally out of the question; that the United States could stop the war and arrest, even temporarily, the movement of its armies, only on the condition precedent, that the authority of the National Government should be recognized and obeyed over the whole territory of the United States. This point conceded, he assured them that upon every other matter of difference they would be treated with the utmost liberality; but without that recognition the war must and would go on.

All the conversation which took place between the respective parties came back to, and turned upon, this radical and irreconcilable difference. Neither side could be swerved a hair's breadth from its position. And, therefore, the attempt at negotiation was an utter failure. Upon separating, it was distinctly understood and explicitly stated that the attitude and action of each Government was to be precisely what it would have been if this interview had never taken place. So this negotiation went for nought, and President Lincoln and Mr. Seward returned to Washington; while the discomfited rebel commissioners made the best of their way back to Richmond.

IS INAUGURATED PRESIDENT OF THE UNITED STATES FOR A SECOND TERM.

On the fourth of March, 1865, Abraham Lincoln was re-inaugurated President of the United States for a second term of four years, the demonstrations on the occasion being of the most imposing description. Arriving at the East portico of the Capitol, the President, President-elect, took a seat provided for him, and the other distinguished persons filling the whole vast platform had places assigned to them. The President, President-elect, then advanced to the front, and Chief Justice Chase administered the oath of office, which the President pronounced in a clear, solemn voice, as follows:—

"I do solemnly swear that I will faithfully execute the office of the President of the United States, and will, to the best of my ability, protect and defend the Constitution of the United States."

The President then delivered his Inaugural Address, as follows:

INAUGURAL ADDRESS.

Fellow-Countrymen—At this second appearing to take the oath of the Presidential office, there is less occasion for an extended address than there was at the first. Then a statement somewhat in detail of a course to be pursued seemed fitting and proper. Now, at the expiration of four years, during which public declarations have been constantly called forth on every point and phase of the great contest which still absorbs the attention and engrosses the energy of the nation, little that is new could be presented. The progress of our arms, upon which all else chiefly depends, is as well known to the public as to myself, and it is, I trust, reasonably satisfactory and encouraging to all.

With high hope for the future, no prediction in regard to it is ventured. On the occasion corresponding to this four years ago, all thoughts were anxiously directed to an impending civil war. All dreaded it. All sought to avert it.

While the Inaugural Address was being delivered from this place, devoted altogether to the saving of the Union without war, insurgent agents were in the city seeking to destroy it without war—seeking to dissolve the Union and divide the effects by negotiation.

Both parties deprecated war, but one of them would make war rather than let the nation survive; and the other would accept war rather than perish—and the war came. One-eighth of the whole population were colored slaves, not distributed generally over the Union, but localized in the Southern part of it.

These slaves constituted a peculiar and beneficial interest. All knew that this interest was somehow the cause of the war. To strengthen, perpetuate and extend this interest was the object for which the insurgents would rend the Union even by war, while the Government claimed no right to do more than to restrict the territorial enlargement of it. Neither party expected for the war the magnitude nor the duration which it has already attained. Neither anticipated that the cause of the conflict might cease with or even before the conflict itself should cease. Each looked for an easier triumph and a result less fundamental and astounding. Both read the same Bible and pray to the same God, and each invokes His aid against the other. It may seem strange that any men should dare to ask a just God's assistance in wringing their bread from the sweat of other men's faces.

But let us judge not that we be not judged. The prayers of both could not be answered; that of neither has been answered fully. The Almighty has His own purposes. "Woe unto the world because of offences, for it must needs be that offences come, but woe to that man by whom the offence cometh." If we shall suppose that American slavery is one of those offences which, in the providence of God, must needs come, but which, having continued through His appointed time, He now wills to remove and that He gives to both North and South this terrible war as the woe due to those by whom the offence came, shall we discern therein any departure from these Divine attributes which the believers in a loving God always ascribe to him? Fondly do we hope, fervently do we pray that this mighty scourge of war may speedily pass away. Yet if God wills that it continue until all the wealth piled by the bondman's two hundred and fifty years of unrequited toil shall be sunk, and until every drop of blood drawn with the lash shall be paid by another drawn with the sword, as was said three thousand years ago, so still it must be said, "the judgments of the Lord are true and righteous altogether."

With malice toward none, with charity for all, with firmness in the right, let us strive on to finish the work we are in, to bind up the Nation's wounds, to care for him who shall have borne the battle and for his widow and his orphan, to do all which may achieve and cherish a just and a lasting peace among ourselves and with all nations.

PRESIDENT LINCOLN GOES TO "THE FRONT."

On the 24th of March, 1865, Mr. Lincoln went to "the front," just as the lines of General Grant were being drawn tighter and tighter around Richmond. He witnessed a part of the assault upon Petersburg, and was at City Point when Richmond fell into the possession of the Federal forces on the 2d of April, 1865. He pushed on to the rebel capital, held a levee in the mansion of the fugitive Jefferson Davis, and left the same evening for City Point, returning to Washington soon after.

GENERAL LEE SURRENDERS.

The fall of Richmond was followed speedily by the surrender of Lee. The terms of capitulation determined upon are embraced in the following note from General Grant to General Lee:

"APPOMATTOX COURT HOUSE, *April 9th.—General Robert E. Lee, Army C. S.*—In accordance with the substance of my letter to you of the 8th inst., I propose to receive the surrender of the army of Northern Virginia on the following terms, to wit: Rolls of all the officers and men to be made in duplicate, one copy to be given to an officer designated by me, the other to be retained by such officer or officers as you may designate, the officers to give their individual paroles not to take up arms against the Government of the United States until properly exchanged, and each company or regimental commander to sign a like parole for the men of their commands. The arms, artillery, and public property to be parked and stacked, and turned over to the officers appointed by me to receive them. This will not embrace the side arms of the officers, nor their private horses or baggage, This done, each officer and man will be allowed to return to their homes, not to be disturbed by United States authority so long as they observe their parole and the laws in force were they may reside.

" *Very Respectfully,* "U. S. GRANT,
" *Lieutenant-General.*"

These easy terms were accepted, and it is known that President Lincoln, in dictating them, was actuated by a kindly spirit of conciliation.

THE PRESIDENT RETURNS TO WASHINGTON.

On the 11th of April, 1865, there was high rejoicing at the National Capital. The public buildings were illuminated at night, in honor of the great victories of the Union arms, and the people were happy at the prospect of a speedy peace. President Lincoln was serenaded at the White House. The President made a responsive speech, in substance as follows:

MR. LINCOLN'S LAST SPEECH.

"We meet this evening not in sorrow, but in gladness of heart. The evacuation of Petersburg and Richmond, and the surrender of the principal insurgent army, give hopes of a righteous and speedy peace, whose joyous expression cannot be restrained. In the midst of this, however, He from whom all blessings flow must not be forgotten. A call for a national thanksgiving is being prepared, and will be duly promulgated. Nor must those whose harder part gives us the cause of rejoicing be overlooked. Their honors must not be parceled out with others. I myself was near the front, and had the high pleasure of transmitting much of the good news to yon. But no part of the honor or execution is mine. To General Grant, his skillful officers and brave men, all belongs. The gallant navy stood ready, but was not in reach to take active part. By these recent successes the re-inauguration of the national authority—reconstruction, which has had a large share of thought from the first—is pressed much more closely upon our attention. It is fraught with great difficulty. Unlike a war between independent nations, there is no authorized organ for us to treat with. No one man has authority to give up the rebellion for any other man. We must simply begin with and mould from disorganized and discordant elements.

* * * * * * * *

"In the annual message of December, 1863, and the accompanying proclamation, I presented a plan of reconstruction, as the phrase goes, which I promised, if adopted by any State, would be acceptable to and sustained by the Executive Government of the nation. I distinctly stated that this was not the only plan which might, possibly, be acceptable; and I also distinctly protested that the Executive claimed no right to say when or whether members should be admitted to seats in Congress from such States. This plan was in advance submitted to the then cabinet, and approved by every member of it. One of them suggested that I should then and in that connection apply the Emancipation Proclamation to the theretofore excepted parts of Virginia and Louisiana, that I should drop the suggestion about apprenticeship for freed people, and that I should omit the protest against my own power in regard to the admission of members of Congress. But even he approved every part and parcel of the plan which has since been employed or touched by the action of Louisiana. The new constitution of Louisiana, declaring emancipation for the whole State, practically applies the proclamation to the part previously excepted. It does not adopt apprenticeship for freed people, and is silent, as it could not well be otherwise, about the admission of members to Congress. So that, as it applied to Louisiana, every member of the Cabinet fully approved the plan. The message went to Congress, and I received many commendations of the plan, written and verbal, and not a single objection to it, from any professed emancipationist, came to my knowledge until after the news reached Washington that the people of Louisiana had begun to move in accordance with it. From about July, 1862, I had corresponded with different persons supposed to be interested in seeking a reconstruction of a State Government for Louisiana. When the message of 1863, with the plan before mentioned, reached New Orleans, General Banks wrote me that he was confident that the people, with his military co-operation, would reconstruct substantially on that plan. I wrote to him and some of them to try it. They tried it, and the result is known. Such has been my only agency in getting up the Louisiana government. As to sustaining it, my promise is out, as before stated. But as bad promises are better broken than kept, I shall treat this as a bad promise and break it whenever I shall be convinced that keeping it is adverse to the public interest; but I have not yet been so convinced.

* * * * * * * *

"We all agree that the seceded States, so called, are out of their proper practical relation with the Union, and that the sole object of the government, civil and military, in regard to those States, is to again get them into their proper practical relation. I believe that it is not only possible, but, in fact, easier, to do this without deciding, or even considering, whether those States have ever been out of the Union, than with it. Finding themselves safely at home, it would be utterly immaterial whether they had been abroad. Let us all join in doing the acts necessary to restore the proper practical relations between those States and the nation, and each forever after innocently indulge his own opinion whether in doing the acts he brought the States from without into the Union, or only gave them proper assistance, they never having been out of it. The amount of constituency, so to speak, on which the Louisiana Government rests, would be more satisfactory to all if it contained 50,000, or 30,000, or even 20,000, instead of 12,000, as it does. It is also unsatisfactory to some that the elective franchise is not given to the colored man. I would myself prefer that it were now conferred on the very intelligent, and on those who serve our cause as soldiers. Still the question is not whether the Louisiana government, as it stands, is quite all that is desirable. The question is, will it be wiser to take it as it is, and help to improve it, or to reject and disperse? Can Louisiana be brought into proper practical relation with the Union sooner by sustaining or by discarding her new State government? Some twelve thousand voters in the heretofore slave State of Louisiana have sworn allegiance to the Union, assumed to be the rightful political power of the State, held elections, organized a State government, adopted a Free State constitution, giving the benefit of public schools equally to black and white, and empowering the legislature to confer the elective franchise upon the colored man. This Legislature has already voted to ratify the constitutional amendment recently passed by Congress, abolishing slavery throughout the nation. These twelve thousand persons are thus fully committed to the Union and to perpetuate freedom in the State; committed to the very things, and nearly all things, the nation wants, and they ask the nation's recognition and its assistance to make good this committal. Now if we reject and spurn them, we do our utmost to disorganize and disperse them. We in fact say to the white man, you are worthless or worse; we will neither help you nor be helped by you. To the blacks we say: This cup of liberty which these, your old masters, held to your lips, we will dash from you, and leave you to the chances of gathering the spilled and scattered contents in some vague and undefined when, where, and how. If this course, discouraging and paralyzing both white and black, has any tendency to bring Louisiana into proper practical relations with the Union, I have so far been unable to perceive it. If, on the contrary, we recognize and sustain the new government of Louisiana, the converse of all this is made true. We encourage the hearts and nerve the arms of 12,000 to adhere to their work, and argue for it, and proselyte for it, and fight for it, and feed it, and grow it, and ripen it to a complete success. The colored man, too, in seeing all united for him, is inspired with vigilance, and energy, and daring to the same end. Grant that he desires the elective franchise, will he not attain it sooner by saving the already advanced steps toward it, than by running backward over them? Concede that the new government of Louisiana is to what it should be as the egg is to the fowl, we shall sooner have the fowl by hatching the egg than by smashing it. [Laughter.]

* * * * * * * *

"Can Louisiana be brought into proper practical relation with the Union sooner by sustaining or by discarding her new State government? What has been said of Louisiana will apply to other States. And yet so great peculiarities pertain to each State, and such important and sudden changes occur in the same State, and withal so new and unprecedented is the whole case, that no exclusive and inflexible plan can safely be prescribed as to details and collaterals. Such exclusive and inflexible plan would surely become a new entanglement. Important principles may and must be inflexible. In the present situation, as the phrase goes, *it may be my duty to make some new announcement to the people of the South.* I am considering, and shall not fail to act when satisfied that action will be proper."

ASSASSINATION OF PRESIDENT LINCOLN.

Henceforward, the Fourteenth day of April, 1865, will stand in the annals of our country equal in importance with the ever memorable Fourth of July, 1776. On the 14th of April, 1861, the national flag was lowered on the ramparts of Fort Sumter to the overwhelming forces of the Rebellion. On the 14th of April, 1865, just four years after the gallant Major Anderson run the Banner down from the flag-staff and bore it away as a holy treasure to the care of the loyal North, the same banner vindicated in a thousand bloody battles, was again flung to the breeze by the same noble hero, over the same spot whence it disappeared in 1861. The 14th of April, 1865, was a day of jubilee throughout the nation. Richmond had been captured. LEE'S army of veterans, the main stay of the Rebellion, was defeated, broken, and prisoners. It's surrender had sealed the fate of treason. JOHNSTON could not hold out before the invincible legions of SHERMAN, and Peace, walking in the footsteps of Victory, was at hand. The nation was exultant. Its great heart throbbed with a joy inexpressible, and throughout the length and breadth of the land preparations for celebrating the Fourteenth day of April had been made. At twelve o'clock, the stars and stripes were floating in every city, town and hamlet, on many a mountain and hill-top, in every valley, and on all the plains, North, East and West, in honor of their restoration to Sumter and their triumph over the black flag of anarchy and slavery.

Monday night, April the 17th, was designed as a night of illumination, and there was not a loyal household in the land that had failed to prepare its flags, its portraits of our heroes, and its candles, lamps or bonfires for the glorious occasion.

But if the day was to be celebrated with such wild demonstrations of delight as our fathers and their children were used to honor the Anniversary of our Independence of Britain, henceforth associated with the laurels of victory are to be found entwined the sombre weeds of woe, the sighing leaves of the yew tree, and the silently waving branches of the willow.

Assassination stalked abroad with the shadows of that eventful night and

ABRAHAM LINCOLN, the respected, revered, and beloved Leader and President, fell beneath the hand of one who had not the courage to look into his manly and honest face and commit the deed, but stealthily and cowardly approached him from behind and fired the fatal shot which deprived the country of its best and purest magistrate since the time of Washington.

During the day, Mr. LINCOLN had been unusually cheerful. His heart which entertained "malice toward none and charity for all" was filled with a happiness which he vainly tried to express in words to those around him. His face told more than his lips could utter, and at the Cabinet Meeting held that day, the members remarked that he was more than ever cheerful, and seemed to feel that the great burden which had been weighing so heavily upon his spirits for the four years previous, was at last lifting from his breast.

The hour had come—the long looked for, the often prayed for hour, when the carnage which treason had initiated was stayed, and smiling Peace again furled her wings over a land restored to harmony. Realizing this, as only the patriotic heart of Mr. LINCOLN could realize so momentous a fact, he was happy in the fullest and broadest sense of the word. Amid the glad thoughts which rushed like waves of joy through his bosom, there was no one which whispered of the terrible fate which awaited him, the horrible shock which with the next morning's dawn was to strike the rejoicing nation, his own dearly loved people, dumb with grief—speechless with a woe that had no voice for utterance.

Late in the afternoon, the Hon. SCHUYLER COLFAX, Speaker of the House of Representatives and a warm personal friend of Mr. LINCOLN, was with the President. Mr. COLFAX had called to pay his last respects to Mr. LINCOLN ere setting out on a tour to the Rocky Mountains. The President, ever mindful of the people, requested him to say to the miners of Nevada and the pioneers of the Far West, that he remembered them with much affection, and he desired that they should be encouraged in their purposes to develope the resources of that hitherto but little known region of our Republic. His sole ambition appeared then, as it always had during the war, and through his whole life, to be that of a benefactor to his country.

During the day, President LINCOLN had been invited to visit Ford's Theatre in the evening, and it was also announced in the papers that Lieutenant-General GRANT would be present. When Speaker COLFAX rose to leave the Presidential Mansion, Mr. LINCOLN asked him if he would not accompany himself and Mrs. LINCOLN to the theatre, but Mr. COLFAX wishing to leave the city in a few hours, declined the urgent invitation, and shaking hands with the President in earnest farewell, and receiving his kind remembrances for the miners of the Far off West, left never again to see his illustrious friend in conscious life.

Mr. LINCOLN, in company with his lady, Miss HARRIS, daughter of Senator HARRIS of New York, and Major RATHBURN of the U. S. A., reached the theatre shortly before nine o'clock, and was received with a perfect tempest of applause, the audience rising, cheering and waving handkerchiefs and hats tumultuously. The President acknowledged the compliment by bowing repeatedly from his box, his face exhibiting a radiant pleasure, indicating the gratitude which filled his heart. It was a proud moment, and yet he was a man who felt no pride except in the discharge and accomplishment of duty.

THE ASSASSINATION.

About ten o'clock in the evening, while the play, "Our American Cousin," was progressing, a stranger, who proved to be John Wilkes Booth, an actor of some note, worked his way into the proscenium box occupied by the presidential party, and leveling a pistol close behind the head of Mr. Lincoln, he fired, and the ball was lodged deep in the brain of the President. The assassin then drew a dirk, and cutting right and left with it, he sprang from the box, flourishing the weapon aloft, and shouted as he reached the stage the motto upon the escutcheon of the State of Virginia, "*Sic Semper Tyrannis!*" The miscreant dashed across the stage, and before the audience or the actors could recover from their amazement and bewilderment, or realize the real position of affairs, the murderer had mounted a fleet horse in waiting in an alley in the rear of the theatre, and galloping off, he escaped for a time.

The screams of Mrs. Lincoln first disclosed to the audience the fact that the President was shot, when all rose, many pressing toward the stage, and hundreds of persons exclaiming, "Hang him! Hang him!" The excitement was of the wildest nature. Many rushed for the President's box, while others cried out, "Stand back! Give him fresh air!" and called for stimulants. It was not known at first where he was wounded, the most of those about him thinking that he was shot through the heart; but after opening his vest, and finding no wound in his breast, it was discovered that he was shot in the head between the left ear and the centre of the back part of the head. In a few moments he was borne to a private house, Mr. PETERSON'S, just opposite the theatre, where the Surgeon-General, and several prominent physicians and surgeons were speedily summoned. Meanwhile the members of the Cabinet, with the exception of Secretary SEWARD, whose life had been attempted by an assassin at about the same hour with the President, assembled in the room where the Chief Magistrate of the nation lay dying.

Secretaries STANTON, WELLES, USHER, MCCULLOCH, Attorney-General SPEED, and Assistant Secretaries MAUNSELL B. FIELD, of the Treasury, and Judge WILLIAM T. OTTO, of the Interior, together with Speaker COLFAX, and several other prominent gentlemen were present. The scene was one of extraordinary solemnity. The history of the world does not furnish a parallel. Quiet, breathing away his life serenely, unconscious of all around, sensible to no pain, lay the great MAN of the Nineteenth Century, passing hence to that immortality which has been accorded by Providence to few of earthly mould.

THE DYING SCENES.

All the long, weary night, the watchers stood by the couch of the dying President. From the moment when the fatal bullet entered his brain he never spoke, never evinced any consciousness, but with closed eyes rested in a repose which appeared to be the quiet of death. Mrs. LINCOLN and Captain ROBERT LINCOLN several times entered the chamber, but their grief was such that they tarried but a brief time, tender friends urging them to remain in the adjoining room.

Day dawned at length, and the tide of life ebbed more rapidly, and at twenty-two minutes past seven o'clock, on the morning of Saturday, April 15th, 1865, the President breathed his last, closing his eyes as if falling to sleep, and his countenance assuming an expression of perfect serenity. There were no indications of pain, and it was not known that he was dead until the gradually decreasing respiration ceased altogether.

The Rev. Dr. Gurley, pastor of the Presbyterian Church, in Washington, which Mr. Lincoln attended regularly with his family, immediately on its being ascertained that life was extinct, knelt at the bedside and offered an impressive prayer, which was responded to by all present.

Dr. Gurley then proceeded to the front parlor, where Mrs. Lincoln, Captain Robert Lincoln, Mr. John Hay, the President's Private Secretary, and others were waiting, where he again offered prayer for the consolation of the family.

The following minutes, taken by Dr. Abbott, show the condition of the President throughout the night:—11 P. M., pulse 44; 11·05 P. M., pulse 45, and growing weaker; 11·10 P. M., pulse 45; 11·15 P. M., pulse 42; 11·20 P. M., pulse 45, respiration 27 to 30; 11·25 P. M., pulse 42; 11·32 P. M., pulse 48 and full; 11·40 P. M., pulse 45; 11·45 P. M., pulse 45, respiration 22; 12·08 A. M., respiration 22; 12·15 A. M., respiration 21, echmose of both eyes; 12·30 A. M., pulse 54; 12·32 A. M., pulse 60; 12·35 A. M., pulse 66; 12·40 A. M., pulse 69; right eye much swollen, and echmose; 12·45 A. M., pulse 70, respiration 27; 12·55 A. M., pulse 80, struggling motion of arms; 1 A. M., pulse 86, respiration 30; 1·30 A. M., pulse 95, appearing easier; 1·45 A. M., pulse 87, very quiet, respiration irregular, Mrs. Lincoln present. 2·10 A. M., Mrs. Lincoln retired with Robert Lincoln to an adjoining room; 2·30 A. M., the President is very quiet, pulse 54, respiration 28; 2·52 A. M., pulse 48, respiration 30; 3 A. M., visited again by Mrs. Lincoln; 3·25 A. M., respiration 24, and regular; 3·25 A. M., prayer by the Rev. Dr. Gurley; 4 A. M., respiration 26 and regular; 4·15 A. M., pulse 60, respiration 25; 5·50 A. M., respiration 28 and regular, sleeping; 6 A. M., pulse failing, respiration 28; 6·30 A. M., still failing and labored breathing; 7 A. M., symptoms of immediate dissolution; 7·22 A. M., death.

Surrounding the death-bed of the President were Secretaries Stanton, Welles, Usher, Attorney-General Speed, Postmaster-General Dennison, M. T. Field, Assistant Secretary of the Treasury; Judge Otto, Assistant Secretary of Interior; General Halleck, General Meigs, Senator Sumner, F. R. Andrews, of New York; General Todd, of Dacotah; John Hay, Private Secretary; Governor Oglesby, of Illinois; General Farnsworth, Mr. and Miss Kenny, Miss Harris, Captain Robert Lincoln, son of the President, and Dr. E. W. Abbott, R. K. Stone, C. D Gatch, Neal Hall, and Leiberman. Secretary McCulloch remained with the President until about 5 A. M., and Chief Justice Chase, after several hours attendance during the night, returned again early in the morning.

A special Cabinet meeting was called immediately after the President's death, by Secretary Stanton, and held in the room where the corpse lay. Secretaries Stanton, Welles, and Usher, Postmaster-General Dennison, and Attorney-General Speed, were present.

THE AUTOPSY.

After his death, a complete examination was made of the wound with the following result: The ball entered the skull midway between the left ear and the centre of the back of the head, and passed nearly to the right eye. The ball and two loose fragments of lead were found in the brain. Singularly enough, both orbital roofs were fractured inwardly, properly from contre-coup. The tenacity of life, was specially noticed by every surgeon in attendance. The brain was taken out, but a considerable portion of it had already escaped from the wound.

The autopsy of the President was made in the presence of Surgeon-General Barnes, Dr. Crane and Dr. Stone, of Washington, and by Drs. Woodward, Notson, and Curtis, of the regular army.

Shortly after the sorrowful event, the President's body

was removed to the Executive Mansion in a hearse, and wrapped in the American flag. It was escorted by a small guard of cavalry, General Augur and other military officers following on foot. A dense crowd accompanied the remains to the White House, where a military guard excluded the crowd, allowing none but persons of the household and personal friends of the deceased to enter the premises.

The corpse was laid out in the room known as the guests' room, in the northwest wing of the White House, dressed in the suit of black clothes worn by him at his last inauguration. A placid smile rested upon the features, and the deceased seemed to be in a calm sleep, while flowers were placed upon the pillow and over the breast above the kindest heart that ever throbbed.

THE MURDERER OF PRESIDENT LINCOLN, AND WHAT BECAME OF HIM.

The murderer of Mr. Lincoln was John Wilkes Booth, an actor, and a native of Harford County, Maryland. During the continuance of the rebellion he was an ardent Secessionist, and he made no concealment of his warm sympathy with armed treason. He had frequently threatened to assassinate the President, and this threat was executed in the tragic and dramatic manner described.

The assassin made his way on horseback into St. Mary's county, where he lay concealed for some days, eluding his pursuers, although the rewards for his capture amounted in the aggregate to over one hundred thousand dollars. It was, however, pretty conclusively ascertained that he was in this locality, and parties of cavalry finally closed in around him, so as to compel him to beat a retreat. On Sunday, April 23d, 1865, Colonel Baker ascertained that Booth, and an accomplice named Harold, had crossed the Potomac river in the neighborhood of Swann Point, and on Monday morning, April 24th, First Lieutenant Edward

Doherty, 16th New York Cavalry, with a detachment of twenty-five cavalrymen of that regiment, and accompanied by some of Colonel Baker's detectives, proceeded by steamer to Belle Plain.

On Tuesday afternoon, April 25th, a man named Jett, by whom Booth and Harold had been ferried across the Rappahannock river at Mathias Point, was arrested. At first, Jett refused to communicate anything; but upon being threatened with instant death if he did not, he agreed to lead the party to the place where Booth and Harold were concealed. They were found on Tuesday night, in a barn, on the premises of Mr. Garrett, about three miles from Port Royal. They had ridden there from the ferry, both mounted on one horse.

The cavalry surrounded the barn and summoned the inmates to surrender. At first Booth insisted that he was alone. He talked with the men for three hours through the crevices of the barn, through which he could see plainly all that were outside, while they could distinguish nothing within. He told Lieutenant Doherty he had a bead drawn upon him, and could shoot him if he chose; but did not fire.

At last, as guerillas were gathering in the vicinity, and Lieutenant Doherty feared his little party might be overpowered and lose the prisoners, he determined to burn them out. The barn was, therefore, set on fire, when Harold gave himself up; but Booth refused to surrender, and prepared to use his weapons. Sergeant Corbett then fired through one of the crevices, and shot Booth in the head. Upon being shot, Booth exclaimed, "It's all up now; I'm gone." He was found to be wounded in the head, very nearly in the same spot where the fatal ball of the assassin entered the head of President Lincoln. A doctor was sent for, and brandy administered, but he died in about two and a half hours after he was shot. He did not deny his crime, but declared that he died for his country. He was armed with two six-barrelled and one seven-barrelled revolvers, and a large knife, probably the same which he flourished on the stage on the occasion of the assassination. He had also three packages of pistol cartridges, some bills of exchange, but only about one hundred and seventy-five dollars in Treasury notes. The bills of exchange were on a Canadian bank, were dated in October, 1864, when Booth was there, and are received as an important link in the chain of evidence showing that the assassination was planned in Canada. The capture occurred about three o'clock on Wednesday morning, April 26th. His left leg was much swollen from an injury received when he leaped from the President's box upon the stage at the theatre, although he had told Dr. Mudd, who had bandaged and set it, that he had been hurt by his horse falling upon it.

His accomplice and companion, David C. Harold, who had been with Booth ever since the crime was consummated, was captured and taken to Washington in company with the body of the dead assassin.

STATEMENTS AND AFFIDAVITS IN RELATION TO THE MURDER.

Mr. Field, Assistant Secretary of the Treasury, describes the scene, and the moment when he received the news of the murder, as follows:

MR. FIELD'S STATEMENT.

"On Friday evening, April 14th, 1865, at about half-past ten o'clock, I was sitting in the reading-room at Willard's Hotel, engaged with a newspaper, when a person hurriedly entered the hotel and passed up the hall, announcing in a loud tone of voice that the President had just heen shot at Ford's Theatre. I started to my feet, and had hardly reached the office when two other persons came in and confirmed the report—which at first I was hardly able to credit. I had parted about fifteen minutes previously with Mr. Mellen, of the Treasury Department, who had retired to his room for the night, and I at once went to him and communicated what had occurred, and we started together for the scene of the tragedy.

"We found the streets already crowded with excited masses of people, and when we reached the theatre there was a very large assemblage in front of it, as well as of the opposite house, belonging to Mr. Peterson, into which the President had been conveyed. The people around the theatre related to us substantially the general facts connected with the assassination which have since been communicated to the public. The impression was prevalent, however, at that time, that the President had been shot in the breast, about the region of the heart, and that the wound might not prove fatal. After a few minutes we crossed the street and endeavored to gain admission into the house where Mr. Lincoln lay. This I effected with some little difficulty.

"The first person whom I met in the hall was Miss Harris, daughter of U. S. Senator Ira Harris, of New York, who had been at the theatre with the Presidential party. She informed me that the President was dying, but desired me not to communicate the fact to Mrs. Lincoln, who was in the front parlor. Several other persons who were there confirmed the statement as to Mr. Lincoln's condition. I then entered the front parlor, where I found Mrs. Lincoln in a state of indescribable agitation. She repeated over and over again, 'Why didn't he kill me? Why didn't he kill me?'

"I asked if there was any service I could render her, and she requested me to go for Dr. Stone, or some other eminent physician. Both Dr. Stone and Surgeon-General Barnes had been already sent for, but neither had yet arrived. On my way out I met Major T. T. Eckert, of the War Department, who told me that he was himself going for Dr. Stone. I then went for Dr. Hall, one of the most distinguished surgeons in the District. I found him at home, and he at once accompanied me. When we again reached the neighborhood of the house access had become very difficult, guards having been stationed on every side.

"After much effort I was enabled to obtain admission for Dr. Hall, but was not at that time permitted to enter myself; accordingly, I returned to Willard's. The whole population of the city was by this time out, and all kinds of conflicting stories were being circulated. At three or four o'clock I again started for Mr. Peterson's house. This time I was admitted without difficulty. I proceeded at once to the room in which the President was dying. It was a small chamber, in an extension or back building, on the level with the first or parlor floor. The President was lying on his back, diagonally across a low double bedstead, his head supported by two pillows on the outer side of the bed.

"The persons in the room were the Secretaries McCulloch, Stanton, Welles, and Harlan, Postmaster-General Dennison, the Attorney-General, the Assistant Secretary of the Interior,

Senator Sumner of Massachusetts, General Halleck, General Augur, General Meigs, General J. F. Farnsworth of Illinois, General Todd of Dacotah, the President's Assistant Private Secretary, Major Hay, the medical gentlemen, and perhaps two or three others. Dr. Stone was sitting on the foot of the bed. An army surgeon was sitting opposite the President's head, occasionally feeling his pulse, and applying his fingers to the arteries of the neck and the heart.

"Mr. Lincoln seemed to be divested of all clothing except the bed coverings. His eyes were closed, and the lids and surrounding parts so injected with blood as to present the appearance of having been bruised. He was evidently totally unconscious, and was breathing regularly but heavily, and with an occasional sigh escaping with the breath. There was scarcely a dry eye in the room, and the scene was the most solemn and impressive one I ever witnessed. After a while, Captain Robert Lincoln, of General Grant's staff, and eldest son of the President, entered the chamber, and stood at the headboard, leaning over his father.

"For a time his grief completely overpowered him, but he soon recovered himself and behaved in the most manly manner until the closing of the scene. As the morning wore on, the condition of the President remained unchanged until about seven o'clock. In the meantime, it came on to rain heavily, and the scene from the windows was in dreary sympathy with that which was going on within. Just before this, Mrs. Lincoln had been supported into the chamber, and had thrown herself moaning upon her husband's body. She was permitted to remain but a few minutes, when she was carried out in an almost insensible condition.

"At about seven o'clock, the President's breathing changed in a manner to indicate that death was rapidly approaching. It became low and fitful, with frequent interruptions. Several times I thought that all was over, until the feeble respiration was resumed. At last, at just twenty-two minutes past seven o'clock, without a struggle, without a convulsive movement, without a tremor, he ceased breathing—and was no more.

"Thus died this great, pure, kind-hearted man, who never willingly injured a human being—the greatest martyr to liberty the world has ever seen.

"Shortly after his death, finding that his eyes were not entirely closed, I placed my hands upon them. One of the attendant surgeons first put nickel cents upon them, and then substituted silver half dollars. It was twenty minutes or half an hour before the body commenced to grow cold. The lower jaw began to fall slightly, and the lower teeth were exposed. One of the medical gentlemen bound up the jaw with a pocket handkerchief. Mr. Stanton threw down the window-shades, and I left the Chamber of Death. Immediately after the decease, the Rev. Dr. Gurley had offered up a fervent and affecting prayer in the room, interrupted only by the sobs of those present.

"When I left the room he was again praying in the front parlor. Poor Mrs. Lincoln's moans were distressing to listen to. After the prayer was over I entered the parlor, and found Mrs. Lincoln supported in the arms of her son Robert. She was soon taken to her carriage. As she reached the front door she glanced at the theatre opposite, and exclaimed several times, 'Oh, that dreadful house!' 'That dreadful house!' Immediately thereafter guards were stationed at the door of the room in which the President's body lay. In a few minutes I left myself. It is hoped that some historical painter will be found capable of portraying that momentous death-scene."

MAJOR RATHBONE'S STATEMENT.

In connection with the murder of Mr. Lincoln, we give the statements of Major RATHBONE and Miss HARRIS, who were in the President's box at the time. Being the only persons, except Mrs. LINCOLN, who were present when Booth executed his foul purpose, their statements are of great interest, delineating as they do the scenes which immediately transpired. Major RATHBONE appeared before the investigating Magistrate, and testified as follows:

"That on the 14th April, 1865, at about twenty minutes past eight o'clock in the evening, he, with Miss Clara H. Harris, left his residence, at the corner of Fifteenth and H streets, and joined the President and Mrs. Lincoln, and went with them in their carriage to Ford's Theatre, in Tenth street. The box assigned to the President is in the second tier, on the right-hand side of the audience, and was occupied by the President and Mrs. Lincoln, Miss Harris, and the deponent—and by no other person. The box is entered by passing from the front of the building, in the rear of the dress-circle, to a small entry or passage-way about eight feet in length and four feet in width.

"This passage-way is entered by a door which opens on the inner side. The door is so placed as to make an acute angle between it and the wall behind it on the inner side. At the inner end of this passage-way is another door standing squarely across, and opening into the box. On the left-hand side of the passage-way, and very near the inner end, is a third door, which also opens into the box. This latter door was closed. The party entered the box through the door at the end of the passage-way. The box is so constructed that it may be divided into two by a movable partition, one of the doors described opening into each. The front of the box is about ten or twelve feet in length, and in the centre of the railing is a small pillar overhung with a curtain. The depth of the box from front to rear is about nine feet. The elevation of the box above the stage, including the railing, is about ten or twelve feet.

"When the party entered the box, a cushioned arm-chair was standing at the end of the box furthest from the stage and nearest the audience. This was also the nearest point to the door by which the box is entered. The President seated himself in this chair—and except that he once left the chair for the purpose of putting on his overcoat, remained so seated until he was shot. Mrs. Lincoln was seated in a chair between the President and the pillar in the centre above described. At the opposite end of the box—that nearest the end of the stage—were two chairs. In one of these, standing in the corner, Miss Harris was seated. At her left hand, and along the wall running from that end of the box to the rear, stood a small sofa. At the end of this sofa, next to Miss Harris, this deponent was seated. The distance between this deponent and the President, as they were sitting, was about seven or eight feet; and the distance between this deponent and the door was about the same.

"The distance between the President, as he sat, and the door, was about four or five feet. The door, according to the recollection of this deponent, was not closed during the evening. When the second scene of the third act was being performed, and while this deponent was intently observing the proceedings upon the stage, with his back towards the door, he heard the discharge of a pistol behind him, and looking around, saw, through the smoke, a man between the door and the President. At the same time deponent heard him shout some word, which deponent thinks was 'Freedom!' This deponent instantly sprang towards him and seized him; he wrested himself from the grasp and made a violent thrust at the breast of deponent with a large knife. Deponent parried the blow by striking it up, and received a wound several inches deep in his left arm, between the elbow and the shoulder. The orifice of the wound is about an inch and a half in length, and extends upwards towards the shoulder several inches. The man rushed to the front of the box, and deponent endeavored to seize him again, but only caught his clothes as he was leaping over the railing of the box. The clothes, as deponent believes, were torn in this attempt to seize him.

"As he went over upon the stage, deponent cried out with a loud voice:—'Stop that man!' Deponent then turned to the President; his position was not changed; his head was slightly bent forward, and his eyes were closed. Deponent saw that he was unconscious, and supposing him mortally wounded, rushed to the door for the purpose of calling medical aid. On reaching the outer door of the passage-way as above described, deponent found it barred by a heavy piece of plank, one end of which was secured in the wall, and the other resting against the door. It had been so securely fastened that it required considerable force to remove it. This wedge or bar was about four feet from the floor. Persons upon the outside were beating against the door for the purpose of entering. Deponent removed the bar, and the door was opened.

"Several persons who represented themselves to be surgeons were allowed to enter. Deponent saw there Colonel Crawford, and requested him to prevent other persons from entering the box. Deponent then returned to the box, and found the surgeons examining the President's person. They had not yet discovered the wound. As soon as it was discovered it was determined to remove him from the theatre. He was carried out, and this deponent then proceeded to assist Mrs. Lincoln, who was intensely excited, to leave the theatre. On reaching the head of the stairs, deponent requested Major Potter to aid him in assisting Mrs. Lincoln across the street to the house to which the President was being conveyed. The wound which deponent had received had been bleeding very profusely, and on reaching the house, feeling very faint from the loss of blood, he seated himself in the hall, and soon after fainted away, and was laid upon the floor. Upon the return of consciousness, deponent was taken in a carriage to his residence.

"In the review of the transaction, it is the confident belief of this deponent that the time which elapsed between the discharge of the pistol and the time when the assassin leaped from the box, did not exceed thirty seconds. Neither Mrs. Lincoln nor Miss Harris had left their seats. "H. R. RATHBONE.

"*Subscribed and sworn before me this 17th day of April,* 1865.

"A. B. OLIN, *Justice Supreme Court, D. C.*"

AFFIDAVIT OF MISS HARRIS.

"*District of Columbia, City of Washington,* ss.:—CLARA H. HARRIS, being duly sworn, says that she has read the foregoing affidavit of Major Rathbone, and knows the contents thereof; that she was present at Ford's Theatre with the President, and Mrs. Lincoln, and Major Rathbone on the evening of the 14th of April instant; that at the time she heard the discharge of the pistol she was attentively engaged in observing what was transpiring upon the stage, and looking round she saw Major Rathbone spring from his seat and advance to the opposite side of the box; that she saw him engaged as if in a struggle with another man, but the smoke with which he was enveloped prevented this deponent from seeing distinctly the other man; that the first time she saw him distinctly was when he leaped from the box upon the stage; that she then heard Major Rathbone cry out, 'Stop that man!' and this deponent then immediately repeated the cry, 'Stop that man! Won't somebody stop that man?' A moment after some one from the stage asked, 'What is it?'

or 'What is the matter?' and deponent replied, 'The President is shot.' Very soon after, two persons, one wearing the uniform of a naval surgeon and the other that of a soldier of the Veteran Reserve Corps, came upon the stage, and the deponent assisted them in climbing up to the box.

"And this deponent further says that the facts stated in the foregoing affidavit, so far as the same came to the knowledge or notice of this deponent, are accurately stated therein.

"CLARA H. HARRIS.

"*Subscribed and sworn before me this* 17*th day of April,* 1865.

"A. B. OLIN, *Justice of Supreme Court, D. C.*"

SURGEON GENERAL BARNES' STATEMENT.

On the night of the assassination, Surgeon General Barnes was met in front of Willard's Hotel by an officer pale and breathless, who informed him that the President had been shot. Supposing that the deed was done at the White House, General Barnes hurried thitherward. Stopping at the Surgeon General's office to give orders for assistance, he found a summons to the bedside of Secretary Seward, who had been attacked by an assassin. Believing that the two stories were from this, Barnes hurried to the chamber of Mr. Seward. He found him lying upon the bed with one cheek cut open and part of the flesh lying upon the pillow. The room presented a horrible scene. Blood was everywhere. The attendants were helpless. A deed of horror had been enacted; but there was no one to explain its details. Dr. Barnes immediately gave his attention to Mr. Seward; but soon afterward Dr. Norris arrived, and, turning over the Secretary to his care, the Surgeon General proceeded to look after the Assistant Secretary, Frederick Seward, who was lying insensible upon a sofa in the adjoining room. In the meantime other surgical attendants had come, among whom was Dr. Notson, and while ministering to the wounded at Secretary Seward's, the Surgeon-General was summoned to the dying murdered President.

DESCRIPTION OF FORD'S THEATRE.

Ford's Theatre is situated on Tenth street, just above E street, in Washington. It is a large edifice, constructed of brick, and of plain appearance. Its internal arrangements are somewhat novel, differing from those in our large cities. There are eight private boxes instead of six, as is the case in the Philadelphia theatres. The four lower boxes, two on each side of the stage, are scarcely more than loopholes, and are very excellent points from which those who wish to see and remain unseen may take inspection. The apertures which appear above the stage are about three feet square. Consequently the boxes immediately above them are elevated but a short distance above the stage, a distance which any one could easily leap, even were his nerves not freshly braced from the commission of a murder.

The four upper boxes are *the* boxes of the theatre, and are very elegant and spacious. They give a tone of elegance to the auditorium, and are sumptuously appointed. It is in them that the most magnificent displays of toilette are made upon nights of opera, and that at once command the whole house, and are central points of inspection from it. Each accommodates quite a party, and the *locale* is so arranged that the greater portion of the occupants, except those in the back of the box, are in full view of the audience.

The box which the President occupied, and which was known as "THE PRESIDENT'S BOX," consisted of the two upper boxes on the right hand side of the house as you face the stage, thrown into one. Mr. Lincoln was always accompanied by a party, which, although limited to personal friends and foreign officials, to whom courtesy required the extension of an invitation, was always sufficiently large to render more than one box necessary for comfort.

The proprietor of the theatre had, therefore, at the commencement of the season, made arrangements by which these two boxes could at any time be thrown into one. They were fitted up with great elegance and taste. The curtains were of fine lace and buff satin, the paper dark and figured, the carpet Turkey, the seats velvet, and the exterior ornamentations were lit up with a chaste chandelier suspended from the outside. A winding staircase leads up to the lobbies which conduct to the box, and unless the arrangements are more stringent than they used to be, no decently dressed person would find much difficulty, probably, in entering one of these boxes after they had once been opened for the ingress of the party using them.

The parquet consists of cane-seat chairs, rising in very gradual elevation, so that even the most distant observers obtain a fair view of the stage, and the entire parquette on an opera night, viewed from the stage or private boxes, resembles an exquisitely variegated parterre. The first tier or balcony is very commodious, and opens into a retiring-saloon, elegantly illuminated and appointed. A second tier, corresponding to the family circle, completed the portion of the house dedicated to the accommodation of the audience. The house would hold probably between two and three thousand people.

There are two alleys at Ford's Theatre. One leads from the stage, along the east side of the theatre, between the theatre and a refreshment saloon, and so out to Tenth street. The alley is neatly paved, and is boarded and papered on both sides. The entry to it from the stage is through a glass door, and the exit from it on to Tenth street through a wooden one.

The other passage-way leads from the back of the theatre to a small alley which communicates with Ninth and other streets, and conducts to a livery-stable locality.

It was in this alley that the horse of the murderer was kept waiting.

The Tenth street door would have been too public, and escape, even temporary, a matter of impossibility. But the escape by the alley leading from the back of the stage was comparatively safe.

There are two doors there, one used for the egress and ingress of the actors, and the other devoted to the accommodation of scenery and machinery. It was through the smaller one that the assassin made his exit.

THE FUNERAL.

In Cabinet Council it was determined that Wednesday, the 19th of April, 1865, should be devoted to the obsequies at the Capital, and acting Secretary of State, MR. HUNTER, issued the following dispatch to the people of the United States:

"TO THE PEOPLE OF THE UNITED STATES:—The undersigned is directed to announce that the funeral ceremonies of the late lamented Chief Magistrate will take place at the Executive Mansion, in this city, at 12 o'clock noon, on Wednesday, the 19th inst. The various religious denominations throughout the country are invited to meet in their respective places of worship at that hour, for the purpose of solemnizing this occasion with appropriate ceremonies.

(Signed) "WM. HUNTER,
"*Acting Secretary of State.*
"*Department of State, Washington, April 17th,* 1865."

Tuesday, April 18th, was set apart for the citizens of Washington to visit the remains lying in state at the White House, and fully twenty thousand persons, irrespective of rank or color, looked upon the face of the dead President, and passed out with eyes weeping and hearts overburdened with grief.

THE OBSEQUIES.

Wednesday, April 19th, dawned with a clear sky and a genial sun. Washington was in the deepest mourning.

All the stores were closed as they had been since the assassination. Sadness was depicted on every countenance, and soon the streets were thronged with military, societies, and citizens, wending their way to Pennsylvania Avenue and the White House. All the public buildings were draped in black, and every house in the city hung out the sombre crape.

At ten o'clock those invited to attend the funeral ceremonies in the White House began to assemble, while all the avenues leading to it were crowded with the military forming for procession, and the sidewalks were blockaded with an anxious and orderly multitude of spectators.

THE SCENES AT THE WHITE HOUSE.

By 10.30 it was almost impossible to wend one's way to the White House. None were admitted except by cards, which were inscribed as follows:

GREEN ROOM.
ADMIT THE BEARER TO THE
EXECUTIVE MANSION,
ON WEDNESDAY
THE 19TH OF APRIL, 1865.

In the centre of the East Room was the catafalque. Around the coffin was a large wreath of white camelias, orange blossoms, and evergreens. At the feet was a beautiful anchor, of choicest flowers, sent by Hon. Mrs. Sperry, of Connecticut; at the head was a cross of white camelias, and the delicate white exotics which, with a basket of flowers, was the present of Mrs. James H. Orne, of Philadelphia. A number of wreaths were scattered around in profusion.

Upon the centre, east side of the catafalque, was the

PRESIDENT AND CABINET.

Upon their right was the

DIPLOMATIC CORPS.

THE ASSISTANT SECRETARIES.

GOVERNORS OF STATES AND TERRITORIES.

THE JUDICIARY.

THE ARMY AND NAVY.

THE NEW YORK DELEGATION.

PALL BEARERS.

Upon the left of the President were the

SUPREME COURT.

THE SENATE.

MEMBERS OF THE HOUSE OF REPRESENTATIVES.

ILLINOIS AND KENTUCKY DELEGATION.

THE CLERGY.

CITY AUTHORITIES.

Upon the west side were the Press; upon the south side, and at the foot of the catafalque, were the family of Mr. Lincoln.

The guard of honor, consisting of Major-General Hunter and Brigadier-General Dyer, marched in silence to and fro. The lilies, the orange blossoms, and the choicest of flowers that decked the corpse filled the room with the sweetest fragrance. The windows, shrouded with crape, kept out the light, and made the gloom, that all felt, seem like being in a living tomb!

The echoes of the funeral dirges in the distance seemed like the terrible murmur of the avenging God's wrath at the impiety of the awful crime that brought all here as mourners. As the various delegations came in they quietly took the places assigned them. Not a word was spoken loudly. Whispers faint, as though the loved one was sleeping after his weary troubles and all feared to wake him, were the only noises that marred the death-like stillness of the room, which had been the scene of two similar services. First, over the body of William Henry

Harrison, then over the gallant General Zachary Taylor, now over Mr. Lincoln, beloved more than any man since the days of Washington.

The exceeding great grief of Mrs. Lincoln was such that she was unable to be present at the services, and the chairs for herself and her sons were vacant.

The mourners present were:

Hon. J. G. Nicolay, the President's Confidential Secretary, and his colleague, Major John Hay.

Mr. N. W. Edwards and Mr. C. M. Smith, brothers-in-law of Mrs. Lincoln.

Dr. L. Beecher Todd, of Lexington, Kentucky, and General J. B. S. Todd, of Dacotah, cousins of Mrs. Lincoln.

Upon the left of President Johnson, was Ex-Senator P. King, of New York; and upon his right, Hannibal Hamlin, Ex-Vice-President.

Behind Mr. King, was Mr. Stanton, Secretary of War.

Behind the President, was Secretary McCulloch.

Behind Mr. Hamlin, were Chief Justice Chase, and Secretaries Welles, Dennison, Speed, and Usher.

At twelve o'clock the room was filled, the President and Cabinet having entered last.

Rev. Dr. Gurley then announced the order of exercises, which were opened by Rev. Dr. Hall reading the funeral service of the Episcopal Church, commencing "I am the resurrection and the life, saith the Lord."

THE WHOLE AUDIENCE JOIN IN THE PRAYERS.

This was followed by a fervent prayer by Bishop Simpson, of the Methodist Episcopal Church, which was not only appropriate but effective in all respects. He closed with the Lord's Prayer, in which the whole audience joined as if by one voice. All those present were melted to tears under its effect.

BISHOP SIMPSON'S PRAYER.

"In the course of his prayer the Bishop said that in the hands of God were the issues of life and death. Our sins had called for his wrath to descend upon us as individuals and as a community. For the sake of our blessed Redeemer, forgiveness was asked for all our trangressions, and that all our iniquities may be washed away. While we bow under this sad bereavement which has caused a wide spread gloom, not only in this circle but over the entire land, an invocation was made that all might submit to God's holy will. Thanks were returned for the gift of such a man as our Heavenly Father had just taken from us, and for the many virtues which distinguished all his transactions; for the integrity, honesty and transparency of character bestowed upon him, and for having given him counsellors to guide our nation through periods of unprecedented sorrow. He was permitted to live to behold the breaking of the clouds which overhung our national sky, and the disintegration of the rebellion. Going up the mount he beheld the land of promise, with its beauty and happiness, and the glorious destiny reserved for us as a nation. Thanks were also returned that his arm was strengthened and wisdom and firmness given to his heart to pen a declaration of emancipation by which were broken the chains of millions of the human race. God be thanked that the assassin who struck down the Chief Magistrate had not the hand to again bind the suffering and oppressed. The name of the beloved dead would ever be identified with all that is great and glorious with humanity on earth. God grant that all who stand here entrusted with the administration of public affairs may have the power, strength and wisdom to complete the work of His servant so gloriously begun, and may the successor of the deceased President not bear the sword in vain. God grant that strength may be given to him and to our military to perfect victory, and to complete the contest now nearly closed. May the spirit of rebellion soon pass away. May the last vestige of slavery, which caused the rebellion, be driven from our land. God grant that the sun may shine on a free people from the Atlantic to the Pacific, and from the lakes to the Gulf. May He not only safely lead us through the struggle, but give us peace with all nations of the earth. Give us hearts to deal justly with them, and give them hearts to deal justly with us, so that universal peace may reign on earth. We raise our hearts to Thee, to plead that Thy blessing may descend on the family of the deceased. God bless the weeping widow as in her broken-heartedness she bows under a sad stroke more than she can bear. Encircle her in Thy own arms. God, be gracious with the children left behind him. Endow his sons with wisdom from on high; endow them with great usefulness. May they appreciate the patriotic example and virtues of their father, and walk in his footsteps. We pray Thee to make the assassination of personal profit to our hearts, while by the remains of the deceased, whom we had called a friend, do Thou grant us peace and repentance of our sins. So that at the end of life we may be gathered where assassins are not found, where sorrow and sickness never come; but all gather in peace and love around the Father's throne in glory. We pray Thee that our Republic may be made the stronger for this blow. While here we pledge ourselves to set our faces as a flint against every form of opposition which may rise up for its destruction; so that we, the children, may enjoy the blessed advantages of a government delivered from our fathers."

THE FUNERAL ORATION.

After the prayer, the Rev. Dr. Gurley, of the Presbyterian Church, which the President and family attended, delivered an eloquent and impressive funeral oration, as follows:

"As we stand here to-day mourners around this coffin and around the lifeless remains of our beloved Chief Magistrate, we recognize and we adore the sovereignty of God. His throne is in the heavens, and His kingdom ruleth over all. He hath done and hath permitted to be done whatsoever He pleased. Clouds and darkness are round about Him; righteousness and judgment are the habitation of His throne. His way is in the sea and His path in the great waters, and His footsteps are not known. Canst thon by searching find out God? Canst thou find out the Almighty unto perfection? It is as high as heaven. What canst thou do? Deeper than hell. What canst thou know? The measure thereof is longer than the earth and broader than the sea. If He cut off and shut up, or gather together; then who can hinder Him? For He knoweth vain men; He seeth wickedness. Also, will He not then consider it. We bow before His infinite majesty. We bow—we weep—we worship.

"'There reason fails with all her powers
There faith prevails, and love adores.'

"It was a cruel, cruel hand, that dark hand of the assassin, which smote our honored, wise and noble President, and filled the land with sorrow. But above and beyond that hand there is another, which we must see and acknowledge. It is the chastening hand of a wise and faithful Father. He gives us the bitter cup; and the cup that our Father hath given us shall we not drink it? God of the just, Thou gavest us the cup. We yield to Thy behest, and drink it up. Whom the Lord loveth He chasteneth. Oh, how these blessed words have cheered and strengthened and sustained us through all these long and weary years of civil strife, while our friends and brothers on so many ensanguined fields were falling and dying for the cause of liberty and Union. Let them cheer and strengthen and sustain us to-day. True, this new sorrow and chastening has come in such an hour and in such a way as we thought not, and it bears the impress of a rod that is very heavy, and of mystery that is very deep. That such a life should be sacrificed at such a time, by such a foul and diabolical agency; that the man at the head of the nation, whom the people had learned to trust with a confiding and a loving confidence, and upon whom more than upon any other were centered, under God, our best hopes for the true and speedy pacification of the country, the restoration of the Union, and the return of harmony and love; that he should be taken from us, and taken just as the prospect of peace was brightly opening upon our torn and bleeding country, and just as he was beginning to be animated and gladdened with the hope of ere long enjoying with the people the blessed fruit and reward of his and their toil and care and patience, and self-sacrificing devotion to the interests of liberty and the Union—oh! it is a mysterious and a most afflicting dispensation. But it is our Father in heaven, the God of our fathers, who permits us to be so suddenly and sorely smitten, and we know that His judgments are right, and that in faithfulness He has afflicted us in the midst of our rejoicings. We needed this stroke, this dealing, this discipline, and therefore He has sent it. Let us remember our affliction has not come forth of the dust, and our trouble has not sprung out of the ground. Through and beyond all second causes let us look and see the sovereign permissive agency of the first great cause. It is His prerogative to bring light out of darkness and good out of evil. Surely the wrath of man shall praise Him, and the remainder of wrath He will restrain. In the light of a clear day we may yet see that the wrath which planned and perpetrated the death of the President was overruled by Him, whose judgments are unsearchable and His ways past finding out, for the highest welfare of all those interests which are so dear to the Christian, patriot and philanthropist, and for which a loyal people have made such an unexampled sacrifice of treasure and of blood. Let us not be faithless, but believing.

"'Blind unbelief is prone to err,
And scan his work in vain;
God is his own interpreter,
And he will make it plain.'

"We will wait for His interpretation, and we will wait in faith, nothing doubting. He who has led us so well, and defended and prospered us so wonderfully during the last four years of toil, and struggle, and sorrow, will not forsake us now. He may chasten, but He will not destroy. He may purify us more and more in the furnace of trial, but He will not consume us: no, no. He has chosen us, as He did His people of old in the furnace, of affliction, and He has said of us as He said of them, 'This people have I formed for myself: they shall show forth my praise.' Let our principal anxiety now be that this new sorrow may be a sanctified sorrow; that it may lead us to deeper repentance, to a more humbling sense of our dependence upon God, and to the more unreserved consecration of ourselves and all that we have to the cause of truth and justice, of law and order, of liberty and good government, of pure and undefiled religion. Then, though weeping may endure for a night, joy will come in the morning. Blessed be God, despite of the great, and sudden, and temporary darkness, the morning has begun to dawn—the morning of a bright and glorious day, such as our country has never seen. That day will come and not tarry, and the death of a hundred presidents and their cabinets can never, never prevent it. While we are hopeful, however, let us also be humble. The occasion calls us to prayerful and tearful humiliation. It demands of us that we lie low, very low, before Him who has stricken us for our sins. Oh that all our rulers and all our people may bow in the dust to-day beneath the chastening hand of God, and may their voices go up to Him as one voice, and their hearts go up to Him as one heart, pleading with Him for mercy and for grace to sanctify our great and sore bereavement, and for wisdom to guide us in this our time of need. Such a united cry and pleading will not be in vain. It will enter into the ear and heart of Him who sits upon the throne and He will say to us as to his ancient Israel, 'In a little wrath I hid my face from thee for a moment; but with everlasting kindness will I have mercy upon thee, saith the Lord, thy redeemer.' I have said that the people confided in the late lamented President with a full and a loving confidence. Probably no man since the days of Washington was ever so deeply and firmly imbedded and enshrined in the very hearts of the people as Abraham Lincoln. Nor was it a mistaken confidence and love. He deserved it—deserved it well—deserved it all. He merited it by his character, by his acts and by the whole tenor and tone and spirit of his life. He was simple and sincere, plain and honest, trustful and just, benevolent and kind. His perceptions were quick and clear, his judgments were calm and accurate, and his purposes were good and pure, beyond a question. Always and everywhere he aimed and endeavored to be right and to do right. His integrity was thorough, all pervading, all controlling, and incorruptible. It was the same in every place and relation. In the consideration and the control of matters, great or small, the same firm and steady principle of power and beauty, that shed a clear and crowning lustre upon all his other excellences of mind and heart, and recommended him to his fellow-citizens as the man who, in a time of unexampled peril, when the very life of the nation was at stake, should be chosen to occupy—in the country and for the country—its highest post of power and responsibility. How wisely and well, how purely and faithfully, how firmly and steadily, how justly and successfully, he did occupy that post and meet its grave demands, in circnmstances of surprising trial and difficulty, is known to you all, is known to the country and the world. He comprehended from the first the perils to which treason had exposed the freest and best government on the earth, the vast interests of liberty and humanity that were to be saved or lost forever, in the urgent impending conflict. He rose to the dignity and momentousness of the occasion, saw his duty as Chief Magistrate of a great and imperilled people, and he determined to do his duty and his whole duty, seeking the guidance and leaning upon the arm of Him of whom it is written, 'He giveth power to the faint, and to them that have no might He increases their strength.' Yes, he leaned upon His arm; he recognized and received the truth that 'the kingdom is the Lord's, and He is the Governor among the nations.' He remembered that 'God is in history,' and he felt that no where had His hand and His mercy been so marvellously conspicuous as in the history of this nation. He hoped and prayed that 'that same hand would continue to guide us, and that same mercy continue to abound to us in the time of our greatest need.' I speak what I know, and testify what I have often heard him say, when I affirm that that guidance and mercy were the prop on which he humbly and habitually leaned; that they were the best hope he had for himself and for his country. Hence when he was leaving his home in Illinois and coming to this city to take his seat in the Executive chair of a disturbed and troubled nation; he said to the old and tried friends who gathered joyfully around him and bade him farewell, 'I leave you with this request—pray for me.' They did pray for him. And millions of others prayed for him. Nor did they pray in vain. Their prayers were heard, and the answer appears in all his subsequent history. It shines forth with a heavenly radiance in the whole course and tenor of his administration, from its commencement to its close. God raised him up for a great and glorious mission, furnished him for his work and aided him in its accomplishment. Nor was it merely by strength of mind and honesty of heart and purity and pertinacity of purpose that he furnished him in addition to these things; he gave him a calm and abiding confidence in the overruling providence of God, and in the ultimate triumph of truth and righteousness through the power and blessing of God. This confidence strengthened him in all his hours of anxiety and toil, and inspired him with calm and cheering hope, when others were inclining to despondency and gloom. Never shall I forget the emphasis and the deep emotion with which he said in this very room to a company of clergymen and others, who called to pay him their respects in the darkest days of our civil conflict. 'Gentlemen, my hope of success in this great and terrible struggle, rests on that immutable foundation, the justice and goodness of God.' And when events are very threatening, and prospects very dark, 'I still hope that in some way which man cannot see, all will be well in the end; because our cause is just and God is on our side.' Such was his sublime and holy faith, and it was an anchor to his soul, both sure and steadfast; it made him firm and strong; and emboldened him in the pathway of duty, however rugged and perilous it might be. It made him valiant for the right, for the cause of God and humanity, and it held him in steady, patient, and unswerving adherence to a policy of administration which, he thought, and which we all now think, both God and humanity required him to adopt. We admired and loved him on many accounts, for strong and various reasons. We admired his childlike simplicity, freedom from guile and deceit; his staunch and sterling integrity; his kind and forgiving temper; his industry and patience; his persistent, self-sacrificing devotion to all the duties of his eminent position, from the least to the greatest: his readiness to hear and consider the cause of the poor and humble, the suffering and the oppressed; his charity towards those who questioned the correctness of his opinions and the wisdom of his policy; his wonderful skill in reconciliating the differences among the friends of the Union, leading them away from obstructions, and inducing them to work together and harmoniously for the common weal; his true and enlarged philanthropy that knew no distinction of color or race, but regarded all men as brethren and endowed alike by their Creator with certain inalienable rights, amongst which are life, liberty, and the pursuit of happiness; his inflexible purpose that what freedom had gained in our terrible strife should never be lost, and that the end of the war should be the end of slavery, and, as a consequence, of rebellion; his readiness to spend and be spent for the attainment of such a triumph—a triumph, the blessed fruits of which should be as wide-spreading as the earth and as enduring as the sun. All these things commanded and fixed our admiration and the admiration of the world, and stamped upon his character and life the unmistakable impress of greatness. But, more sublime than any or all of these, more holy and influential, more beautiful and strong and sustaining was his abiding confidence in God, and in the final triumph of truth and righteousness, through Him and for His sake. This was his noblest virtue, his grandest principle, the secret alike of his strength, his patience, and his success; and this, it seems to me, after being near him steadily and with him often for more than four years, is the principle by which more than by any other, he being dead, yet speaketh.

"Yes, by his steady enduring confidence in God, and in the

complete ultimate success of the cause of God, which is the cause of humanity, more than in any other way does he now speak to us, and to the nation he loved and served so well. By this he speaks to his successor in office, and charges him to have faith in God. By this he speaks to the members of his Cabinet, the men with whom he counselled so often and was associated with so long, and he charges them to have faith in God. By this he speaks to all who occupy positions of influence and authority in these sad and troublesome times, and he charges them all to have faith in God. By this he speaks to this great people as they set in sackcloth to-day and weep for him with a bitter wailing, and refuse to be comforted; and he charges them to have faith in God; and by this he will speak through the ages, and to all rulers and peoples in every land, and his message to them will be:—'Cling to liberty and right; battle for them; bleed for them; die for them, if need be, and have confidence in God.' Oh! that the voice of this testimony may sink down into our hearts to-day and every day, and into the heart of the nation, and exert its appropriate influence upon our feelings, our faith our patience and our devotion to the cause, now dearer to us than ever before, because consecrated by the blood of the most conspicuous defender, its wisest and most fondly trusted friend. He is dead, but the God in whom he trusted lives, and He can guide and strengthen his successor as He guided and strengthened him. He is dead, but the memory of his virtues, of his wise and patriotic counsels and labors, of his calm and steady faith in God lives, is precious, and will be a power for good in the country quite down to the end of time. He is dead; but the cause he so ardently loved, so ably, patiently, faithfully represented and defended, not for himself only, not for us only, but for all people, in all their coming generations, till time shall be no more—that cause survives his fall, and will survive it. The light of its brightening prospects flashes cheeringly to-day around the gloom occasioned by his duties, and the language of God's united providences is telling us that, though the friends of liberty die, liberty itself is immortal; there is no assassin strong enough, and no weapon deadly enough to quench its inextinguishable life or arrest its onward march to the conquest and empire of the world. This is our confidence and this is our consolation as we weep and mourn to-day. Though our beloved President is slain, our beloved country is saved, and so we sing of mercy as well as of judgment. Tears of gratitude mingle with those of sorrow, while there is also the dawning of a brighter, happier day upon our stricken and weary land. God be praised that our fallen chief lived long enough to see the day dawn and the day star of joy and peace arise upon the nation. He saw it and he was glad. Alas! alas! he only saw the dawn. When the sun has risen full orbed, and a glorious and a happy reunited people are rejoicing in its light, it will shine upon his grave. But that grave will be a precious and a consecrated spot. The friends of liberty and of the Union will repair to it in years and ages to come to pronounce the memory of its occupant blessed, and gathering from his very ashes and from the rehearsal of his deeds and virtues fresh incentives to patriotism. They will then renew their vows of fidelity to their country and their God. And now I know not that I can more appropriately conclude this discourse, which is but a sincere and simple utterance of the heart; than by addressing to our departed President, with some slight modification, the language which Tacitus, in his life of Agricola, addressed to his venerated and departed father-in-law:—'With you we may now congratulate. You are blessed, not only because your life was a career of glory, but because you were released when, your country safe, it was happiness to die. We have lost a parent, and, in our distress, it is now an addition to our heartfelt sorrows that we had it not in our power to commune with you on the bed of languishing and receive your last embrace. Your dying words would have been ever dear to us. Your commands we should have treasured up and graved them on our hearts. This sad comfort we have lost, and the wound for that reason pierces deeper. From the world of spirits behold your disconsolate family and people. Exalt our minds from fond regret and unvailing grief to the contemplation of your virtues. These we must not lament. It were impiety to sully them with a tear. To cherish their memory, to embalm them with our praises, and so far as we can to emulate your bright example, will be the truest mark of your respect, the best tribute we can offer. Your wife will thus preserve the memory of the best of husbands, and thus your children will prove their final piety. By dwelling constantly on your words and actions they will have an illustrious character before their eyes; and not content with the base image of your mortal frame, they will have what is more valuable—the form and features of your mind. Busts and statues, like their originals, are frail and perishable. The soul is formed of finer elements, and its inward form is not to be expressed by the hand of an artist with unconscious matter. Our manners and our morals may in some degree trace the resemblance. All of you that gained our love and raised our admiration still subsist, and will ever subsist, preserved in the minds of men, the register of ages and the records of fame. Others, matured on the stages of life, and who were the worthies of a former day, will sink for want of a faithful historian into the common lot of oblivion, inglorious and unremembered; but you, our lamented friend and head, delineated with truth and fairly consigned to posterity, will survive yourself and triumph over the injuries of time.'"

At the conclusion of the sermon, the Rev. Dr. GRAY, of the Baptist church, closed the solemnities by prayer. The coffin was then closed, and carried out by twelve sergeants of the Veteran Reserve Corps.

ORDER OF THE PROCESSION.

The following order of procession was strictly carried out by the officers in command :—

Funeral Escort in Column of March.
One Regiment of Cavalry.
Two Batteries of Artillery.
Battalion of Marines.
Two Regiments of Infantry.
Commander of Escort and Staff.
Dismounted Officers of Marine Corps
Navy and Army in the order named.
Mounted Officers of Marine Corps.
Navy and Army in the order named.
All Military Officers to be in uniform, with Side Arms.

CIVIC PROCESSION.

Marshal.
Clergy in Attendance.
The Surgeon-General of the United States and Physicians to the deceased.

PALL BEARERS.	HEARSE.	PALL BEARERS.

On the part of the Senate.	*On the part of the House.*
Mr. Foster, Connecticut,	Mr. Dawes, Massachusetts.
Mr. Morgan, New York,	Mr. Coffroth, Pennsylvania,
Mr. Johnson, Maryland,	Mr. Smith, Kentucky,
Mr. Yates, Illinois,	Mr. Colfax, Indiana,
Mr. Wade, Ohio,	Mr. Worthington, Nevada,
Mr. Conness, California.	Mr. Washburne, Illinois.
Army.	*Navy.*
Lieut. Gen. U. S. Grant,	Vice-Admiral D. G. Farragut,
Maj. General H. W. Halleck.	Rear-Admiral W.B. Shubrick.
Br't Brig. Gen. W.A. Nichols.	Col. Jacob Zellin, M. C.
Civilians.	*Civilians.*
C. H. Browning,	Thomas Corwin,
George Ashmun.	Simon Cameron.

THE FAMILY.

Relatives.
The Delegations of the States of Illinois and Kentucky as Mourners.

THE PRESIDENT.
The Cabinet Ministers.
The Diplomatic Corps.
Ex-Presidents.
The Chief Justice,
And Associate Justices of Supreme Court.
The Senate of the United States,
Preceded by its Officers.
The House of Representatives of the United States, preceded by its Officers.
Legislatures of the several States and Territories.
The Federal Judiciary, and the Judiciary of the several States and Territories.
The Assistant Secretaries of State, Treasury, War, Navy, and Interior, and the Assistant Postmaster-General and Assistant Attorney-General.
Officers of Smithsonian Institution.
The Members and Officers of the Sanitary and Christian Commissions.
Corporate Authorities of Washington and Georgetown, and other cities.
Delegations of the several States.
The Reverend Clergy of the various Denominations.
The Clerks and Employees of the several Departments and Bureaus,
Preceded by the Heads of such Bureaus and their respective Chief Clerks.
Such Societies as may wish to join the Procession.
Citizens and Strangers.

The head of the column reached the Capitol at 3 P. M., passing up Pennsylvania Avenue upon the north side of the Capitol. When the infantry reached the Senate door, they filed into the yard on the east front, and opened column, forming a hollow square in the yard in front of the Rotunda. The artillery and cavalry then passed on towards the old Capitol. When they had passed, the commander of escort and staff and the army and navy officers passed into the east front yard, the equestrians passing on.

The coffin was then borne into the Rotunda of the Capitol, and a Guard of Honor assigned to duty for the several hours of the afternoon and evening.

Never before had Washington beheld so solemn a

pageant as that which moved up Pennsylvania Avenue on the 19th of April, 1865; a day now trebly memorable in our annals as the day when the first blood of the Revolution was shed at Lexington, the first blood spilled by the Rebellion at Baltimore in 1861, and the day when the body of our martyred President, ABRAHAM LINCOLN, was borne through the streets of our National Capital on its way to its resting-place in the West.

The body remained lying in state in the Capitol over Thursday, thousands of persons visiting the corpse.

DEPARTURE FROM WASHINGTON.

On Friday morning, April 21st, at seven o'clock, the coffin was taken to the depot, and deposited in the funeral car. Hon. Edwin M. Stanton, Hon. Gideon Welles, Hon. Hugh McCulloch, Hon. Jno. P. Usher, Lieut. General U. S. Grant, and Gen. M. C. Meigs left the escort at the depot, and at 8 A. M. the train left. At least ten thousand persons were out to see the departure. A special train was provided for the occasion, and the route to Springfield, Illinois, was designated by an order from the War Department, and the railroads over which the remains passed, were declared military roads, subject to the order of the War Department, and the railroads, locomotives, cars and engines engaged on said transportation, were subject to the military control of Brigadier-General McCallum. No person was allowed to be transported on the cars constituting the funeral train, save those who were specially authorized by the orders of the War Department. The funeral train consisted of nine cars, including baggage and hearse car, which proceeded over the entire route from Washington to Springfield. The time schedule for the transportation was as follows:—

Leave Washington, Friday, April 21, 8 A. M.
Arrive at Baltimore, Friday, April 21, 10 A. M.
Leave Baltimore, Friday, April 21, 3 P. M.
Arrive at Harrisburg, Friday, April 21, 8·20 P. M.
Leave Harrisburg, Saturday, April 22, 12 M.

Arrive at Philadelphia, Saturday, April 22, 4·30 P. M.
Leave Philadelphia, Monday, April 24, 4 A. M.
Arrive at New York, Monday, April 24, 10 A. M.
Leave New York, Tuesday, April 25, 4 P. M.
Arrive at Albany, Tuesday, April 25, 11 P. M.
Leave Albany, Wednesday, April 26, 4 P. M.
Arrive at Buffalo, Thursday, April 27, 7 A. M.
Leave Buffalo, Thursday, April 27, 10·10 A. M.
Arrive at Cleveland, Friday, April 28, 7 A. M.
Leave Cleveland, Friday, April 28, midnight.
Arrive at Columbus, Saturday, April 29, 7·30 A. M.
Leave Columbus, Saturday, April 29, 8 P. M.
Arrive at Indianapolis, Sunday, April 30, 7 A. M.
Leave Indianapolis, Sunday, April 30, midnight.
Arrive at Chicago, Monday, May 1, 11 A. M.
Leave Chicago, Tuesday, May 2, 9·30 P. M.
Arrive at Springfield, Monday, May 3, 8 A. M.

At various points on the route where the remains were to be taken from the hearse-car by State or municipal authorities, to receive public honors, according to the aforesaid programme, the authorities were to make such arrangements as might be fitting and appropriate to the occasion, under the direction of the military commander of the division, department, or district; but the remains continued always under the special charge of the officers and escort assigned by the War Department.

The route from Columbus to Indianapolis was via the Columbus and Indianapolis Central Railway, and from Indianapolis to Chicago, via Lafayette and Michigan city. In order to guard against accident, the train did not move faster than twenty miles an hour.

Accompanying the remains were a distinguished party of friends and mourners: Judge David Davis, Judge United States Supreme Court; N. W. Edwards; General J. B S. Todd; Charles Alexander Smith. Guard of Honor—namely: General E. D. Townsend; Brigadier-General Charles Thomas; Brigadier-General A. D. Eaton; Brevet-Major-General J. G. Barnard; Brigadier-General G. D. Ramsay; Brigadier-General A. P. Howe; Brigadier-General D. C. McCallum; Major-General David

Hunter; Brigadier-General J. C. Caldwell; Rear-Admiral C. H. Davis, United States Navy; Captain William R. Taylor, United States Navy; Major T. Y. Field, United States Marine Corps. (The foregoing constituted a guard of honor.) Dr. Charles B. Brown, embalmer; Frank T. Sands, undertaker; and on the part of the Senate and House of Representatives: Maine, Mr. Pike; New Hampshire, Mr. Rollins; Vermont, Mr. Baxter; Massachusetts, Mr. Hooper; Connecticut, Mr. Dixon; Rhode Island, Mr. Anthony; New York, Mr. Harris; Pennsylvania, Mr. Cowan; Ohio, Mr. Schenck; Kentucky, Mr. Smith, Indiana, Mr. Julian; Minnesota, Mr. Ramsay; Michigan, Mr. T. W. Ferry; Iowa, Mr. Harlan; Illinois, Mr. Yates, Mr. Washburne, Mr. Farnsworth, and Mr. Arnold; California, Mr. Shannon; Oregon, Mr. Williams; Kansas, Mr. Clarke; Western Virginia, Mr. Whaley; Nevada, Mr. Nye; Nebraska, Mr. Hitchcock; Colorado, Mr. Bradford; Idaho, Mr. Wallace; New Jersey, Mr. Newell; Maryland, Mr. Phelps; George T. Brown, Sergeant-at-arms of the Senate; and N. G. Ordway, Sergeant-at-arms House of Representatives.

The delegates from Illinois were: Governor Richard J. Oglesby; General Isham N. Haynie, Adjutant-General State of Illinois; Colonel James H. Bowen, A. D. C.; Colonel M. H. Hanna, A. D. C.; Colonel D. B. James, A. D. C.; Maj. S. Waite, A. D. C.; Col. D. L. Phillips, United States Marshal Southern District of Illinois, A. D. C.; Hon. Jesse K. Dubois; Hon. J. T. Stuart; Col. John Williams; Dr. S. H. Melvin; Hon. S. M. Cullum; General John A. McClernand; Hon. Lyman Trumbull; Hon. J. S. V. Reddenburg; Hon. Thomas J. Dennis; Lieutenant-Governor William Bross; Hon. Francis E. Sherman, Mayor of Chicago; Hon. Thomas A. Haine; Hon. John Wentworth; Hon. S. S. Hays; Colonel R. M. Hough; Hon. S. W. Fuller; Capt. J. B. Turner; Hon. I. Lawson; Hon. C. L. Woodman; Hon. G. W. Gage;

G. H. Roberts, Esq; Hon. J. Commisky; Hon. T. L. Talcott; Governor Morton, of Indiana; Gov. Brough, of Ohio; Gov. Stone, of Iowa, together with their aids and reporters for the press.

ALONG THE ROUTE.

As the train moved on to Baltimore, thousands of Marylanders assembled by the way-side to catch a glimpse of the car which contained the corpse of the deceased President.

ARRIVAL AT BALTIMORE.

When the Monumental city was reached, an immense throng crowded the streets, anxious to do homage to all that remained of their noble chief. The arrival was heralded by a salvo of artillery, and the large funeral procession which, at a short notice, had been prepared to escort the deceased and retinue through the city, formed in column, and the line of march was taken up. Succeeding the military was the civic procession, headed by Governor Bradford. All the associations of Baltimore turned out in full numbers, and the rear was brought up by an immense throng of colored people, all wearing badges of mourning.

The cortege moved to the Post-office Building, where the remains were placed in state, and an opportunity was given the citizens to see the corpse. At 3 o'clock P. M. the coffin was removed to the depot, and the train departed for Harrisburg, amid the firing of minute guns and the sorrows of a people who felt that the Republic had indeed lost its best friend.

Governor Curtin and staff met the train on the borders of Pennsylvania, and accompanied it to Harrisburg. At York, Pa., six ladies, dressed in deep black, were kindly permitted by General McCallum to enter the funeral car and place upon the coffin a beautiful wreath of white roses, camelias, and other rare flowers. Silently they performed their last tribute to the illustrious patriot, and when they retired from the car there were no dry eyes among the military chieftains who stood guard over the bier.

ARRIVAL AT HARRISBURG.

Although the train arrived at the Capital of Pennsylvania during a fearful storm of thunder, lightning, and rain, the people were gathered on the streets and lined the way to the Capitol building, where the body was conveyed and placed in state until the next day, April 22d, at 12 o'clock, when it was taken to the depot, and, amid the tears and lamentations of the whole city and surrounding country, placed on the cars for Philadelphia. Along the entire route, thousands of people assembled to see the train pass by, all business in the towns and on the farms having been suspended.

ARRIVAL AT PHILADELPHIA.

At half-past four the same afternoon, the train reached the Baltimore depot at Broad and Washington. Hours before, tens of thousands of men, women and children had crowded all the streets leading to this great avenue.

The Procession was formed, and moved over the designated route to Independence Hall, the coffin being carried through the square from the Walnut street entrance, the grounds being illuminated with calcium lights, red, white and blue colors, and the members of the Union League standing on each side of the main avenue, dressed in deep black, and white gloves, with a splendid band performing funeral dirges. The coffin was taken into Independence Hall and placed on an oblong platform in the centre of the hall, covered with black cloth, and lay directly north and south, the head towards the south, and directly opposite "Old Independence Bell." The lid of the coffin was removed far enough to expose to view the face and breast of the deceased. An American flag, the one used to cover the coffin during the funeral procession, was thrown back at the foot of the coffin, and a number of wreaths of exotics laid upon it. A magnificent floral device, composed of a large wreath of brilliant-colored flowers, and containing a beautiful American shield in the centre, also composed of choice flowers, occupied a prominent position on the lid of the coffin.

At the head of the coffin was suspended a highly wrought cross, composed of japonicas, with a centre consisting of jet black exotics. The device contained the following inscription:

> "To the memory of our beloved President, from a few ladies of the United States Sanitary Commission."

On the "Old Independence Bell," and near the head of the coffin, rested a large and beautifully made floral anchor, composed of the choicest exotics. This beautiful offering came from the ladies of St. Clement's church. Four stands, two at the head and two at the foot of the coffin, were draped in black cloth, and contained rich candelabras with lighted wax candles. Directly to the rear of these were placed three additional stands, also containing candelabras with burning tapers; and again, another row of four stands, containing candelabras also, brought up the rear, making in all eighteen candelabras and one hundred and eight burning wax tapers. Between this flood of light, shelving were erected, on which were placed rare vases filled with japonicas, heliotropes, and other rare flowers. These vases were about twenty-five in number. A most delicious perfume stole through every part of the hall, which, added to the soft yet brilliant light of the wax tapers, the elegant uniforms of the officers on duty, etc., constituted a scene of oriental magnificence but seldom witnessed.

The Hall at large was completelv shrouded with black

cloth, arranged in a very graceful and appropriate manner. The old chandelier that hangs from the centre of the room, and which was directly over the coffin of the deceased, was entirely covered, and from it radiated in every direction festoons of black cloth, forming a sort of canopy over the entire room. The walls of the room presented the appearance of having been papered with black. The celebrated historical pictures that ornament the hall were, with few exceptions, hid from view. The statue of Washington, at the east end of the room, stood out, however, in bold relief against the black background. The only pictures visible were the full-length portraits of William Penn, Lafayette, Washington, and Chevalier Gerard, and the smaller ones of Martha Washington, Stephen Decatur, and one or two others. Wreaths of immortelle were hung on the black drapery that covered the walls, and were placed about midway between the floor and ceiling.

One of the wreaths that lay near the head of the coffin contained a card bearing the following inscription:

> "Before any great national event I have always had the same dream. I had it the other night. It is of *a ship sailing rapidly.*"

These words were used by Mr. Lincoln in a conversation not long since.

And thus Abraham Lincoln, the martyr of the nineteenth century, was laid in solemn repose beneath the roof which once covered the grand old heroes and statesmen of the Revolution. Cold and lifeless he lay in the same chamber where our fathers subscribed their names to the immortal Magna Charta of our liberties, the Declaration of American Independence. On the 22d of February, 1861, he was in that Hall, and under the inspiration of its sacred memories, while raising the national flag above its hallowed roof, he uttered these significant words:

"It was something in the Declaration of Independence, giving "liberty not only to the people of this country, but hope to the "world for all future time. It was that which gave promise "that in due time the weights should be lifted from the shoul-"ders of all men, and that all should have an equal chance. * * * "Now, my friends, can the country be saved upon that basis? "If it can, I will consider myself one of the happiest men in the "world if I can help to save it. *But if this country cannot be "saved without giving up that principle, I was about to say, I "would rather be assassinated upon this spot than to surren-"der it.*"

It was proper that ABRAHAM LINCOLN, the champion of freedom, the martyr to those principles, should rest over the holy Sabbath in the sanctuary of the republic. It was fitting that his remains should repose during the sacred hours beneath the eyes of the statesmen and patriots who look down from the walls of that consecrated temple, a temple dedicated nearly a century since by our fathers as a shrine to human freedom, a shrine to which all time would come with reverence and affection. It was meet that the Sacrifice of the nineteenth century should be laid in awful glory at the feet of his statue whose memory we were taught to love and honor in our infancy—GEORGE WASHINGTON.

At ten o clock in the evening, a limited number of visitors, embracing the City Councils, members of the Courts, and citizens, to the number of two or three thousand, were admitted, Mayor Henry occupying a position at the head of the coffin, while the following officers of the army formed the guard of honor.

GUARD OF HONOR.

Major-General David Hunter.
Brigadier-General E. D. Townsend.
Brigadier-General Charles Thomas.
Brigadier-General A. B. Eaton.
Brigader-General J. G. Barnard.

Brigadier-General J. G. Ramsey.
Brigadier-General A. P. Howe.
Brigadier-General D. C. McCallum.
Brigadier-General J. C. Caldwell.
Rear-Admiral C. H. Davis, U. S. Navy.
Captain W. R. Taylor, U. S. Navy.
Major T. Y. Field, U. S. Marine Corps.

Six o'clock, Sabbath morning, the 23d of April, 1865, was fixed as the hour when the remains were to be exposed to public view. Long before the hour arrived, thousands of people were on the streets and formed into lines, patiently and silently awaiting the time when the doors should be opened. The entrances were through two windows on Chestnut street, and the exits through the windows facing them on Independence Square, temporary steps having been placed in position for that purpose. By this arrangement two lines of spectators were admitted at a time, passing on either side of the coffin. So great was the anxiety of our citizens to view the body of their late beloved Chief Magistrate, that hundreds of them remained around Independence Hall all night, waiting anxiously for the doors, or rather the windows, to be thrown open.

At the hour of six o'clock a double line of applicants were formed, extending as far west as Eighth street, and east to Third street. By eleven o'clock the lines extended from the Hall west as far as the Schuylkill, and east as far as the Delaware. The residents of West Philadelphia flocked across the Market street bridge by hundreds, while the Camden ferry-boats apparently brought across the Delaware about one-half of the population of New Jersey. So it was throughout the day and night, until one o'clock on the morning of the 24th, when the lid of the coffin was closed down and thousands of persons found themselves disappointed in getting a glimpse of him whom they held so dear in memory. At least one hundred and twenty thousand people passed through the Hall during the twenty-four hours.

At three o'clock on Monday morning, April 24th, the mournful cortege left Philadelphia for New York. As the draped cars passed through New Jersey, the people of that State evinced the same grief, and paid the same honors to the funeral train as had hitherto been done by the people of Maryland and Pennsylvania.

Gov. PARKER, of New Jersey, and staff, met the escort at the State line, and accompanied it to New York. At Trenton, Rahway, Elizabeth, Newark, and Jersey City, as well as at all the intermediate points, bells were tolled, minute guns were fired, and immense assemblages of citizens were gathered.

ARRIVAL AT NEW YORK.

On arriving at New York, the remains were carried in solemn procession to the City Hall, where they were placed in state. The interior of the City Hall was elaborately draped and festooned with mourning emblems, presenting a sombre and solemn appearance. The room in which the remains of the President were deposited was thoroughly draped in black. The centre of the ceiling was dotted with silver stars relieved by black; the drapery was finished with heavy silver fringe, and the curtains of black velvet were fringed with silver and gracefully looped The coffin rested on a raised dais, on an inclined plane, the inclination being such that the face of the departed patriot was in view of visitors while passing for two or three minutes.

The coffin was laid on the dais in the presence of Generals Dix, Burnside, Van Vliet, Peck, Ullman, Sandford, and Townsend; Admiral Spaulding; Commodores Meade and Rice; the members of the Press, and a number of eminent civilians. The embalmers then re-arranged the body, which had been somewhat disturbed by the journey, after which the lid was removed, affording a view of the face and upper portion of the breast.

The people were admitted early the same afternoon, and from that time until twelve M., the next day, Tuesday, the 25th, a continuous stream passed through the hall. At one o'clock the remains were placed upon the hearse, and an immense procession escorted them to the Hudson River Railroad Depot, whence they departed for Albany.

ALBANY, SYRACUSE, AND BUFFALO.

At every point between the two cities, great concourses of people assembled, and when the train arrived at the State Capital of New York, a procession accompanied the remains to the Capitol building, where they were placed in State. At four P. M., on the 26th, they were again borne to the funeral car, and the train departed on its solemn journey to the Great West. Syracuse, Buffalo, and each town and village on the line paid their last tribute to the dead statesman.

CLEVELAND AND COLUMBUS.

The same sad duties were rendered by the people of Ohio, the body being transferred from the train at Cleveland, and also at Columbus, where it was placed in the Capitol for several hours, giving thousands of the citizens an opportunity to view all that remained of ABRAHAM LINCOLN.

ARRIVAL AT INDIANAPOLIS.

In Indiana, the State in which Mr. Lincoln had spent some ten years of his early life, the most intense exhibitions of grief and respect were evinced. GOV. MORTON, a warm personal friend of the deceased President, joined the train at the State line, his suite consisting of his staff and all the chief officers of the State, military and civil. On Sunday morning, April 30th, the train reached Indianapolis, and though a heavy rain prevailed, the entire population of the city and the adjacent country were gathered to receive the remains. The coffin was borne beneath a magnificent arch, into the Capitol, and placed under the great dome, the splendid structure being festooned with black. The preparations here were of the most expensive and elaborate nature, and were said to be by far the most elegant and appropriate witnessed on the entire route. All through the Sabbath the people passed in an almost endless line by the coffin, the scene proving one of most extraordinary solemnity. All the children of the Sunday-schools were admitted, and the City Councils of Cincinnati and Louisville, together with Gov. BRAMLETTE of Kentucky, were present.

ARRIVAL AT CHICAGO.

At midnight of Sunday, April 30th, the remains were escorted to the cars at Indianapolis, and the train left for Chicago, where it arrived at eleven A. M., May 1st, 1865.

Minute guns and the tolling of bells announced the arrival of the remains, and the multitude stood in profound silence, with uncovered heads, as the coffin was slowly borne to the funeral car, under a grand arch across Park place. The arch was fifty-one feet in span, sixteen feet deep and forty feet high, its centre draped with the national flags and mourning emblems, and containing several inscriptions, including one as follows: "We Mourn the Man with Heaven-born Principles." The remains were conveyed to the rotunda of the Court-house. Among the mottoes was "Illinois clasps to her bosom her slain but glorified son." The number of people in the city at the time the processsion moved was not less than a quarter of a million.

ARRIVAL AT SPRINGFIELD.

At eight o'clock in the evening of May 1st, the coffin was again closed, and borne to the cars on its journey to

Springfield, the earthly resting-place of its sacred treasure. The next morning, May 2d, the funeral train reached the city, and the corpse was conveyed to the State Capitol and revealed to the view of the dead President's late fellow-citizens. The grief expressed here surpassed that of all other communities. To thousands of the people MR. LINCOLN had been personally known, and their affection and sorrow for his untimely death was of a deeper nature than that of any of his countrymen. Bells were tolled, funeral guns fired, and a universal woe overspread the city. Many thousand people visited the Capitol during the day and night.

THE FUNERAL AT SPRINGFIELD.

The funeral took place on the fourth of May, and at noon twenty-one guns were fired, and afterward single guns at intervals of ten minutes. About noon, the remains were brought from the State House and placed in a hearse, which was surrounded by a magnificent crown of flowers. Meanwhile a chorus of hundreds of voices, accompanied by a brass band, sang the following hymn from the portico of the Capitol.

"Children of the heavenly King,
Let us journey as we sing."

The funeral procession was under the imediate direction of Major-General Hooker, Marshal-in-chief, Brigadier-General Cook and staff, and Brevet Brigadier-General Oakes and staff. The military and the firemen made a fine appearance. The guard of honor consisted of General Barnard; Rear-Admiral Davis; and Generals McCallum, Ramsay, Caldwell, Thomas, Howe, Townsend, and Eakin; and Captain Field, of the Marine Corps. The relations and family friends of the deceased were in carriages. Among them were Judge Davis, of the Supreme Court, the officiating clergyman, Bishop Simpson, Dr. Gurley, and others. In the procession were the Governors of several States, members of Congress, the State and municipal authorities, and delegations from adjoining States. The long line of civilians was closed by the Free Masons, Odd Fellows, and citizens at large, including colored persons. The hearse was immediately followed by the horse formerly belonging to Mr. Lincoln. Its body was covered with black cloth, trimmed with silver fringe. Never before was there so large a military and civic display in Springfield. There were immense crowds of people in the immediate vicinity of the Capitol to see the procession as it passed, and the people for several miles occupied the side-ways.

The procession arrived at Oak Ridge Cemetery at one o'clock. On the left of the vault in which the remains of the President were deposited immediately on their arrival, was a platform on which singers and an instrumental band were in place, and these united in the chanting and singing of appropriate music, including a burial hymn by the deceased President's pastor, the Rev. Dr. Gurley. On the right was the speaker's stand, appropriately draped with mourning.

The vault is erected at the foot of a knoll in a beautiful part of the grounds, which contains forest trees of all varieties. It has a doric gable resting on pilasters, the main wall being rustic. The vault is fifteen feet high and about the same in width, with semi-circular wings of bricks projecting from the hill-sides. The material is limestone, procured at Joliet, Illinois. Directly inside of the ponderous doors is an iron grating. The interior walls are covered with black velvet, dotted with evergreens. In the centre of the velvet is a foundation of brick, capped with a marble slab, on which the coffin rests. The front of the vault is trimmed with evergreens. The dead march in "Saul" was sung, accompanied by the band, as the remains were deposited. Thousands of persons were assembled at the cemetery before the arrival of the procession, occupying the succession of green hills, and the scene was one of the most intense solemnity. The landscape was beautiful in the light of an unclouded sun.

The religious exercises were commenced by the singing of a dirge. Then followed the reading of appropriate portions of the Scriptures and a prayer. After a hymn sung by the choir, the Rev. Mr. Hubbard read the last inaugural of President Lincoln. Another dirge was sung by the choir, when Bishop Simpson delivered the funeral oration. It was in the highest degree solemn, eloquent, and patriotic, and portions of it were applauded. Then followed another dirge and hymn, when benediction was pronounced by the Rev. Dr. Gurley. The procession was then re-formed, and returned to the city.

REMINISCENCES.

We have followed the remains of President Lincoln from Washington, the scene of his assassination, to Springfield, his former home and now to be his final resting-place. He had been absent from that city ever since he left it in February, 1861, for the National Capital, to be inaugurated as President of the United States. We have seen him lying in state in the Executive Mansion, where the obsequies were attended by numerous mourners, some of them clothed with the highest public honors and responsibilities which our republican institutions can bestow, and by the diplomatic representatives of foreign Governments. We have followed the remains from Washington, through Baltimore, Harrisburg, Philadelphia, New York, Albany, Buffalo, Cleveland, Columbus, Indianapolis, and Chicago to Springfield, a distance in circuit of fifteen hundred or eighteen hundred miles. On the route millions of people have appeared to manifest by every means of which they were capable, their deep sense of the public loss, and their appreciation of the many virtues which adorned the life of Abraham Lincoln. All classes, without distinction of politics, spontaneously united in the posthumous honors. All hearts seemed to beat as one at the bereavement; and now funeral processions are ended, our mournful duty of escorting the mortal remains of Abraham Lincoln hither is performed. We have seen them deposited in the tomb. The bereaved friends, with subdued and grief-stricken hearts, have taken their adieu and turn their faces homeward, ever to remember the affecting and impressive scenes which they have witnessed. The injunction, so often repeated on the way, "Bear him gently to his rest," has been obeyed, and the great heart of the nation throbs heavily at the portals of the tomb.

BISHOP SIMPSON'S FUNERAL ORATION.

"FELLOW-CITIZENS OF ILLINOIS AND OF MANY PARTS OF OUR ENTIRE UNION:—Near the capital of this large and growing State of Illinois, in the midst of this beautiful grove, and at the open mouth of the vault which has just received the remains of our fallen chieftain, we gather to pay a tribute of respect and drop the tears of sorrow around the ashes of the mighty dead. A little more than four years ago, from his plain and quiet home in yonder city, he started, receiving the parting words of the concourse of friends who gathered around him, and in the midst of the dropping of the gentle shower he told of the pains of parting from the place where his children had been born and his home had been made so pleasant by early recollections. And as he left he made an earnest request in the hearing of some who are present, that as he was about to enter upon responsibilities which he believed to be greater than any which had fallen upon any man since the days of Washington, the people would offer up their prayers that God would aid and sustain him in the work they had given him to do. His company left your quiet city. But as it went snares were in waiting for the Chief Magistrate. Scarcely did he escape the dangers of the way or the hands of the assassin as he neared Washington, and I believe he escaped only through the vigilance of the officers and the prayers of the people; so that the blow was suspended for more than four years, which was at last permitted, through the providence of God, to fall. How different the occasion which witnessed his departure and that which witnessed his return! Doubtless you expected to take him by the hand, to feel the warm grasp which you felt in other days, and to see the tall form walking among you which you had delighted to honor in years past. But he was never permitted to return until he came with lips mute and silent, his frame encoffined, and a weeping nation following as his mourners. Such a scene as his return to you was never witnessed among the events of history. There have been great processions of mourners. There was one for the patriarch Jacob, which came up from Egypt, and the Egyptians wondered at the evidence of reverence and filial affection which came from the hearts of the Israelites. There was mourning when Moses fell upon the heights of Pisgah and was hid from human view. There have been mournings in the kingdoms of the earth when kings and warriors have fallen; but never was there in the history of man such mourning as that which has accompanied the funeral procession and has gathered around the mortal remains of him who was our loved one, and who now sleeps among us. If we glance at the procession which followed him we see how the nation stood aghast. Tears filled the eyes of many sunburned faces. Strong men, as they clasped the hands of their friends, were unable to find vent for their grief in words. Women and little children caught up the tidings as they ran through the land and were melted into tears. The nation stood still. Men left their plows in the fields and asked what the end would be. The hum of manufactures ceased and the sound of the hammer was not heard. Busy merchants closed their doors, and in the exchange gold passed no more from hand to hand. Three weeks have passed. The nation has scarcely breathed easily yet. A mournful silence is abroad upon the land. Nor is this mourning confined to any class or to any district of the country. Men of all political parties and of all religious creeds seem united in paying this mournful tribute. The Archbishop of the Roman Catholic Church in New York and a Protestant minister walked side by side in the sad procession, and a Jewish Rabbi performed a part of the solemn service. There are gathered around his tomb representatives of the army and navy, senators, judges, governors and officers of all the branches of the government and members of all the civic associations, with men and women from the humblest as well as the highest occupations. Here and there, too, are tears, as sincere and warm as any that drop, which come from the eyes of those whose kindred and whose race have been freed from their chains by him whom they mourn as their deliverer. Far more have gazed on the face of the departed than ever looked upon the face of any other departed man. More eyes have looked upon the procession for sixteen hundred miles or more by night and by day, by sunlight, dawn, twilight and by torchlight, than ever before watched the progress of a procession. We ask why this wonderful mourning, this great procession? I answer: First, a part of the interest has arisen from the times in which we live, and in which he that has fallen was a principal actor. It is a principle of our nature that feelings once excluded from the object by which they are excited, turn readily to some other object which may for the time being take possession of the mind. Another principle is, that the deepest affections of our hearts gather around some human form in which are incarnated the loving thoughts and ideas of the passing age. If we look, then, at the times, we see an age of excitement. For four years the popular heart has been stirred to its utmost depths. War had come upon us, dividing families, separating nearest and dearest friends—a war, the extent and magnitude of which no one could estimate—a war in which the blood of brethren was shed by a brother's hand. A call for soldiers was made by this voice, now hushed, and all over this land—from hill to mountain, from plain to valley—they sprung up, hundreds of thousands of bold hearts, ready to go forth and save our National Union. This feeling of excitement was transferred next into a feeling of deep grief, because of the dangers in which our country was placed. Many said, Is it possible to save our nation? Some in our own country, and nearly all the leading men in other countries, declared it to be impossible to maintain the Union; and many an honest heart was deeply pained with apprehensions of common ruin; and many, in grief, and almost in despair, anxiously inquired, 'What shall the end of these things be?' In addition, the wives had given their husbands, and mothers their sons. In the pride and joy of their hearts, they saw them put on their uniform—they saw them take their martial step—and they tried to hide their deep feelings of sadness. Many dear ones slept on the battle-field—never, never, to return again—and there was mourning in every mansion and in every cabin in our broad land. Then came a feeling to deepen sadness, as the story came of prisoners tortured to death, or starved, through the mandates of those who are called the representatives of the Chivalry, or who claim to be the honorable ones of the earth; and as we read the stories of frames attenuated, and reduced to mere skeletons, our grief turned partly to horror, and partly into a cry for vengeance. Then, the feeling was changed to one of joy. There came signs of the end of the rebellion. We followed the career of our glorious Generals. We saw our army, under the command of the brave officer who is guiding this procession, climb up the heights of Lookout Mountain, and drive the rebels from their strongholds. Another brave General swept through Georgia, South and North Carolina, and drove the combined armies of the rebels before him—while the honored Lieutenant-General held Lee and his hosts in a death-grasp. Then the tidings came that Richmond was evacuated, and that Lee had surrendered! The bells rang merrily all over the land. The booming of cannon was heard. Illuminations and torch-light processions manifested the general joy, and families were looking for the speedy return of their loved ones from the field of battle. Just in the midst of the wildest joy—in one hour, nay, in one moment—the tidings rang throughout the land that Abraham Lincoln, the best of Presidents, had perished by the hands of an assassin! And then, all that feeling which had been gathered for four years—in forms of excitement, grief, horror, and joy—turned into one wail of woe: a sadness inexpressible, anguish unutterable. But it is not the time merely which caused this mourning—the mode of his death must be taken into account. Had he died on a bed of illness, with kind friends around him; had the sweat of death been wiped from his brow, by gentle hands, while he was yet conscious; could he have had the power to speak words of affection to his stricken widow; words of counsel to us all, like those which we heard in his parting for Washington—in his inaugural, which shall now be immortal—how it would have softened or assuaged something of the grief. There might at least have been preparation for the event. But no moment of warning was given to him or to us. He was stricken down when his hopes for the end of the rebellion were bright, and the prospects of a joyous life were before him. There was a Cabinet meeting that day, said to have been the most cheerful and happy of any held since the beginning of the rebellion. After this meeting, he talked with his friends, and spoke of the four years of tempest, of the storm being over, and of the four years of pleasure and joy now awaiting him, as the weight of care and anguish would be taken from his mind, and he could have happy days with his family again. In the midst of these anticipations, he left his house, never to return alive. Though the evening was Good Friday—the saddest day in the whole calendar for the Christian Church—henceforth in this country to be made still sadder, if possible, by the memory of our nation's loss. And so filled with grief was every Christian's heart, that even all the joyous thoughts of Easter Sunday failed to remove the crushing sorrow under which the true worshipper bowed in the house of God. But the great cause of this mourning is to be found in the man himself. Mr. Lincoln was no ordinary man; and I believe the conviction has been growing on the nation's mind, as it certainly has been on my own, especially in the last years of his administration, that, by the hand of God, he was especially singled out to guide our government in these troublous times. And it seems to me that the hand of God may be traced in many of the events connected with his history.

"*First*, then, I recognize that in his physical education which he received, and which prepared him for enduring Herculean labors in the toils of his boyhood and the labors of his manhood, God was giving him an iron form. Next to this, was his identification with the heart of the great people—understanding their feelings, because he was one of them, and connected with them in their movements and life. His education was simple. A few months spent in the school-house, gave him the elements of education. He read few books, but mastered all he read. 'Bunyan's Progress' and the 'Life of Washington' were his favorites. In these we recognize the works which gave the bias to his character, and which partly moulded his style. His early life, with its varied struggles, joined him indissolubly to the weeping masses, and no elevation in society diminished his respect for the sons of toil. He knew what it was to fell the tall trees of the forest, and to stem the current of the swift Mississippi. His home was in the growing West, the heart of the Republic; and, invigorated by the wind which swept over its groves, he learned the lesson of self-reliance which sustained him in seasons of adversity. His genius was soon recognized, as true genius always will be. He was placed in the Legislature of a State. Already acquainted with the principles of law, he devoted his thoughts to matters of public interest, and began to be looked on as the coming statesman. As early as 1849 he presented resolutions in the Legislature asking for emancipation in the District of Columbia, although, with rare exceptions, the whole popular mind of his State was opposed to the measures. From that hour he was a steady and uniform friend of humanity, and was preparing for the conflict of later years. If you ask on what mental characteristics his greatness rested, I answer, on a quick and ready perception of facts, and a memory unusually tenacious and retentive, and on a logical turn of mind which followed sterlingly and unwaveringly every link in the chain of thought on any subject which he was called on to investigate. I think there have been minds more decided in their character, more comprehensive in their scope, but I doubt if there has been a man who could follow, step by step, with logical power, the points which he desired to illustrate. He gained the power by the close study of geometry, and by a determination to persevere in truth. It is said of him, that in childhood, when he had any difficulty, in listening to a conversation, to understand what people meant, if he retired to rest he could not sleep till he tried to understand the precise points intended, and, when understood, to convey it in a clearer manner to those who had listened with him. Who that has read his messages fails to perceive the directness and the simplicity of his style; and this very trait, which was scoffed at and derided by his opposers, is now recognized as one of the strong points of that mighty mind which has so powerfully influenced the destiny of the nation, and which shall for ages to come influence the destiny of humanity. It is not, however, chiefly by his mental faculties that he gained such a control over mankind. His moral power gave him prominence. The convictions of men that Abraham Lincoln was an honest man, led them to yield to his guidance. As has been said of Cobden, whom he greatly respected, he made all men feel and own the sense of himself, and recognize in him, individually, a self-relying power. They saw in him a man whom they believed would do that which was right, regardless of all consequences. It was this moral feeling which gave him the greatest hold on the people, and made his utterances almost oracular. When the nation was angered by the perfidy of foreign nations in allowing privateers to be fitted out, he uttered the significant expression—'One war at a time'—and it stilled the national heart. When his own friends were divided as to what steps should be taken as to slavery, that simple utterance—'I will save the Union if I can with slavery; but, if not, slavery must perish: for the Union must be preserved'—became the rallying word. Men felt that the struggle was for the Union, and all other questions must be subsidiary. But after all the acts of a man, shall his fall be perpetuated? What are his acts? Much praise is due to the men who aided him. He called able counsellors around him, and able Generals into the field—men who have borne the sword as bravely as any human arm has borne it. He had the aid of prayerful and thoughtful men everywhere. But under his own guiding hands the movements of our land have been conducted.

"Turn towards the different departments. We had an unorganized militia—a mere skeleton army; yet under his care that army has been enlarged into a force which for skill, intelligence, efficiency and bravery surpasses any which the world has ever seen. Before its veterans the renowned veterans of Napoleon shall pale—and the mothers and sisters on these hillsides and all over the land shall take to their arms again braver men than ever fought in European wars. The reason is obvious. Money, or a desire for fame collected their armies, or they were rallied to sustain favorite theories or dynasties; but the armies he called into being fought for liberty, for the Union, and for the right of self-government; and many of them felt that the battles they won were for humanity everywhere, and for all time; for I believe that God has not suffered this terrible rebellion to come upon our land merely as a chastisement to us or a lesson to our age. There are moments which involve in themselves eternities. There are instants which seem to contain germs which shall develop and bloom forever. Such a moment comes in the tide of time to our land when a question must be settled. The contest was not for the republic merely, not for the Union simply, but to decide whether the people, as a people, in their entire majesty, were destined to be the government, or whether they were to be subjects of tyrants, or autocrats, or to class-rule of any kind. This is the great question for which we have been fighting, and its decision is at hand, and the result of the contest will affect the ages to come. If successful, republics will spread, in spite of monarchism, all over this earth. (*Exclamations of Amen*," " *Thank God!*") I turn from the Army to the Navy. What was it when the war commenced? Now we have our ships of war at home and abroad—to guard privateers in foreign sympathizing ports as well as to take care of every part of our own coast. They have taken forts that military men said could not be taken, and a brave admiral, for the first time in the world's history, lashes himself to the mast, there to remain as long as he had a particle of skill or strength to watch over his ship while it engaged in the perilous contest of taking the strong forts of the enemy. I turn to the Treasury Department. Where shall the money come from? Wise men predicted ruin, but our National credit has been maintained, and our currency is safer to-day than it ever was before. Not only is this so, but through our National bonds, if properly used, we shall have a permanent basis for our currency; and they are also an investment so desirable for capitalists of other nations, that under the laws of trade, I believe, the centre of exchange will be transferred from England to the United States. But the great act of the mighty chieftian, on which his fame shall rest long after his frame shall moulder away, is that of giving freedom to a race. We have all been taught to revere the sacred character of Moses, of his power, and the prominence he gave to the moral law. How it lasts, and how his name towers among the names in Heaven, and how he delivered three millions of his kindred out of bondage; and yet we may assert that Abraham Lincoln, by his Proclamation, liberated more enslaved people than ever Moses set free, and these not of his kindred or of his race. Such a power, or such an opportunity, God has seldom given to man. When other events shall have been forgotten, when this world shall have become a network of republics, when every throne shall have been swept from the face of the earth, when literature shall enlighten all minds, when the claims of humanity shall be recognized every where, this act shall still be conspicuous on the pages of history, and we are thankful that God gave to Abraham Lincoln the decision, wisdom and grace to issue that Proclamation which stands high above all other papers which have been penned by uninspired men. Abraham Lincoln was a good man. He was known as an honest, temperate, forgiving man, a just man, a man of noble heart in every way. As to his religious experience, I cannot speak definitely, because I was not privileged to know much of his private sentiments. My acquaintance with him did not give me the opportunity to hear him speak on this topic. I know, however, he read the Bible frequently; loved it for its great truths and for its profound teachings, and he tried to be guided by its precepts. He believed in Christ, the Saviour of sinners, and I think he was sincerely trying to bring his life into the principles of revealed religion. Certainly, if ever there was a man who illustrated some of the principles of pure religion, that man was our departed President. Look over all his speeches; listen to his utterances. He never spoke unkindly of any man; even the rebels received no words of anger from him; and the last day illustrated, in a remarkable manner, his forgiving disposition. A despatch was received that afternoon, that Thompson and Tucker were trying to make their escape through Maine, and it was proposed to arrest them. Mr. Lincoln, however, preferred rather to let them quietly escape, and this morning we read the Proclamation offering twenty-five thousand dollars each for the arrest of these men, as aiders and abettors of his assassination. So that in his expiring acts he was saying: 'Father forgive them; they know not what they do!' As a rule I doubt if any President has ever shown such trust in God, or in public documents so frequently referred to Divine aid. Often did he remark to friends and to delegations that his hope for our success rested in his conviction that God would bless our efforts because we were trying to do right. To the address of a large religious body he replied, 'Thanks be unto God, who, in our national trials, giveth us the churches.' To a minister who said he hoped the Lord was on our side, he replied that it gave him no concern whether the Lord was on our side or not, for, he added, 'I know that the Lord is always on the side of the right,' and with a deep feeling, added, 'But God is my witness that it is my constant anxiety and prayer, that both myself and this nation should be on the Lord's side.' In his domestic life he was exceedingly kind and affectionate. He was a devoted husband and father.

"During his Presidential term he lost his second son, Willie. To an officer of the army he said not long since, 'Do you ever find yourself talking with the dead?' and added, 'Since Willie's death I catch myself every day involuntarily talking with him, as if he were with me.' On his widow, who is unable to be here, I need only invoke the blessing of Almighty God that she may be comforted and sustained. For his son, who has witnessed the exercises of this hour, all that I can desire is that the mantle of his father may fall upon him. (*Exclamations of 'Amen.'*) Let us pause a moment in the lesson of the hour before we part. This man, though he fell by the hand of the assassin, still he fell under the permissive hand of God. He had some wise purpose in allowing him so to fall. What more could he have desired of life for himself? Were not his honors full? There was no office to which he could aspire. The popular heart clung around him as around no other man. The nations of the world have learned to honor him. If rumors of a desired alliance with England be true, Napoleon trembled when he heard of the fall of Richmond, and asked what nation would join him to protect him against our government. Besides the goodness of such a man his fame was full. his work was done, and he sealed his glory by becoming the nation's great martyr for liberty. He appears to have had a strange presentiment early in political life, that some day he would be President. You see it, indeed, in 1839. Of the slave power he said: 'Broken by it? I, too, may be asked to bow to it. I never will. The probability that we may fail in the struggle ought not to deter us from the support of a cause which I deem to be just. It shall not deter me. If I ever feel the soul within me elevate and expand to those dimensions not wholly unworthy of its Almighty architect, it is when I contemplate the cause of my country, deserted by all the world besides, and I standing up boldly and alone and hurling defiance at her vicarious oppressors. Here, without contemplating consequences, before high Heaven and in the face of the world, I swear eternal fidelity to the just cause, as I deem it, of the land, of my life, my liberty and my love.' And yet secretly he said to more than one, 'I never shall live out the four years of my term. When the rebellion is crushed my work is done.' So it was. He lived to see the last battle fought and to dictate a despatch from the home of Jefferson Davis. Lived till the power of the rebellion was broken; and then, having done the work for which God had sent him, angels, I trust, were sent to shield him from one moment of pain or suffering, and to bear him from this world to that high and glorious realm where the patriot and the good shall live forever. His example teaches young men that every position of eminence is open before the diligent and the worthy, to the active men of the country. His example urges the country to trust in God and do right. Standing as we do to-day by his coffin and his sepulchre, let us resolve to carry forward the policy which he so nobly and wholly began. Let us do right to all men. Let us vow in the sight of Heaven to eradicate every vestige of human slavery, to give every human being his true position before God and man, to crush every form of rebellion, and to stand by the flag which God has given us. How joyfully we ought to be that it floated over parts of every State before Mr. Lincoln's career was ended. How singular is the fact that the assassin's foot was caught in the folds of the flag, and to this we are indebted for his capture. The flag and the traitor must ever be enemies. The traitors will probably suffer by the change of rulers, for one of sterner mould, who himself has deeply suffered from the rebellion, now wields the sword of justice. Our country, too, is stronger for the trial through which it has passed. A republic was declared by monarchies too weak to endure a civil war, yet we have crushed the most gigantic rebellion in history, and have grown in strength and population every year of the struggle. We have passed through the ordeal of a popular election while swords and bayonets were in the field, and have come out unchanged; and now, in an hour of excitement, with a large minority who pre-

16

ferred another man for President, and the bullet of the assassin having laid our President prostrate, has there been a mutiny? has any rival proposed his claim? In an army of nearly a million of men, no officer or soldier has uttered one word of dissent, and in an hour or two after Mr. Lincoln's death, another leader, with constitutional powers, occupied his chair, and the government moved forward without one single jar. The world will learn that republics are the strongest governments on earth. And now, my friends, in the words of the departed, 'with malice towards none, free from all feeling of personal vengeance, yet believing the sword must not be drawn or borne in vain, let us go forward in our painful duty.' Let every man who was a Senator or Representative in Congress, and who aided in beginning this rebellion, and thus led to the slaughter of our sons and daughters, be brought to a speedy and to certain punishment. Let every officer educated at public expense, and who, having been advanced to position, has perjured himself and has turned his sword against the vitals of his country, be doomed to this. I believe in the will of the American people. Men may attempt to compromise, and to restore these traitors and murderers to society again; but the American people will arise in their majesty and sweep all such compromises and compromisers away, and shall declare that there shall be no peace to rebels; but to the deluded masses we shall extend the arms of forgiveness. We will take them to our hearts and walk with them side by side as we go forward to work out a glorious destiny. The time will come when, in the beautiful language of him whose lips are forever closed, 'The mystic cords of memory, which stretch from every battle field and from every patriot's grave, shall yield a sweeter music when touched by the angels of our better nature.' To the ambitious there is the fearful lesson of the four candidates for Presidential honors in 1860. Two of them, Douglas and Lincoln, once competitors, but now sleeping patriots, rest from their labors; Bell perished in poverty and misery, as a traitor might perish, and Breckenridge is a frightened fugitive, with the brand of traitor on his brow. That will be vouched by the angels of our better nature. (Cries of "good, good.")

ABRAHAM LINCOLN IS MOURNED BY TWENTY-FIVE MILLIONS OF PEOPLE.

Thus was laid to his silent rest the most illustrious citizen of the Nineteenth century. No other mortal ever went to his tomb amid such expressions of grief. Twenty-five millions of people mourned him as children mourn the loss of a father. The emancipated blacks felt that they had parted with their earthly saviour, the man who, under GOD, had been raised up to redeem them from oppression. And now, as we write, the wail of old England, the sorrows of all Europe, the sighs of every breast which contains a heart throbbing with the love of liberty, come borne to us by every burdened breeze from over the Atlantic. The world sympathizes with America in her grief, and the world accords to our cherished dead the meed of praise, the proud height of fame to which Mr. Lincoln's pure life, honest heart, and unsullied private and public character entitled him before the eyes of man and angels.

In his career we have seen how the flat-boatman and rail-splitter of the West climbed step by step until he reached the highest round of political preferment, as well as the loftiest place in the affections of his countrymen. We have seen how honesty of purpose won its way while beset by the wiles of political chicanery and deceit. We have seen how sterling principle lived down fierce opposition until the false and the wrong were forced to yield to the true and the just. We have seen a grand illustration of the practical democratic republicanism of our American system, in elevating a man from the humblest ranks of the people to the loftiest place on earth. And, finally, we have seen how the malignant hate of foiled traitors sped the Parthian arrow to the murdering of the most illustrious citizen of the Republic.

> "An eagle, tower'ing in his pride of place,
> Was by a mousing owl hawked at and killed."

But the principles enunciated and struggled for by Abraham Lincoln are as imperishable as truth itself, and having performed his great mission upon earth, he has gone to meet his reward in another sphere, leaving to his fellow citizens, and to posterity, the enjoyment of the great reforms of which he was the instrument in the hands of Providence, and to American youth the influence of his grand example.

THE FIRST PLOT TO ASSASSINATE PRESIDENT LINCOLN.

The murder of Mr. Lincoln, more than four years after his induction into the office of President of the United States, is not the fulfilment of a recent intention, nor is the guilt of it confined to the actual murderer and his present active accomplices. Soon after the first election of Mr. Lincoln, a plot was matured for his assassination, which was vaguely rumored at the time of its intended execution, but which was never exposed in any formal manner, and hence never obtained general credence. As we are in possession of its outlines, and the means by which it was defeated, the mention of the circumstances may now be received with a degree of interest which they could not heretofore have excited. It is proper to say that we state them substantially as they were reported some time ago, by a gentleman who was chiefly instrumental in defeating the conspiracy. In the month of January, 1861, a gentleman, holding a position in this city, which made him a proper agent to act on the information, was waited upon by a lady, who stated to him her suspicions or knowledge—whence derived we are not able to say—of a plot to assassinate Mr. Lincoln when on his way from his home, in Illinois to Washington, to be inaugurated as President. The active parties, or some of them, in the business, were understood to be in Baltimore. At all events, the gentleman considered that the intelligence had sufficient foundation to make it his duty to satisfy himself whether it might be correct. He accordingly employed a detective officer, a man who had in his profession become notable for his sagacity and success, to go to Baltimore and adopt his own course to detect the parties to and plan of the conspiracy. The officer went to Baltimore, and opened an office as some sort of broker or agent, under an assumed name. Being supplied with needful funds, he made occasions to become acquainted with certain classes of secessionists, and by degrees was on free and easy terms with them. He took each man in his humor, dined and supped with some, gambled with others, "treated" and seconded dissipations in more ways than need be expressly stated, until he had secured enough of their confidence to be familiar with the particulars of their schemes. Meanwhile it had been ascertained that on the line of the Baltimore Railroad there were men engaged in military drilling. Several other detectives were employed by the chief to discover the purpose of those organizations; and, disguised as laborers or farm hands, they got themselves mustered in. One of the military companies proved to be loyal in its purpose; another, under pretence of being prepared to guard one or more of the bridges north of Baltimore, was designed for quite an opposite purpose. It will be remembered that some time before Mr. Lincoln set out from his home for Washington, his intended route thither was published. A part of the programme was that he should visit Harrisburg and Philadelphia. We believe that Mr. Lincoln was not advised especially of any personal danger until he was about to go to Harrisburg, and then, at the instance of the gentleman referred to, he was urged to proceed without delay to Washington. He replied, however, that he had promised the people of Harrisburg to answer their invitation, and he would do so if it cost him his life. He accordingly visited Harrisburg on the 22d of February, 1861. It was intended he should rest there that evening. But under the management of "the gentleman," another arrangement was effected. The night train from Philadelphia to Baltimore and Washington left at half past ten o'clock in the evening. It was determined that Mr. Lincoln should go secretly by that train on the evening of the 23d; and to enable him to do so, a special train was provided to bring him secretly from Harrisburg to Philadelphia. After dark, in the former city, when it was presumed he had retired to his hotel, he accordingly took the special train, and came to Philadelphia. Meanwhile, in anticipation of his coming, "the gentleman" had insured the detention of the Philadelphia and Baltimore train, under the pretence that a parcel of important documents for one of the departments in Washington must be dispatched by it, but which might not be ready until after the regular time of the starting of that train. By a similar representation, the connecting train from Baltimore to Washington was also detained. Owing to the late hour at which the special train left Harrisburg with Mr. Lincoln, it did not, as was anticipated, reach this city until after the usual Philadelphia and Baltimore time. Mr. Lincoln was accompanied by the officer who had been employed in Baltimore. A formidable bundle of old railroad reports had been made up in the office of the Philadelphia and Baltimore Company, which the officer, duly instructed, had charge of. On the arrival of the Harrisburg train, Mr. Lincoln took a carriage in waiting, and with his escort was driven to the depot at Broad and Prime streets. The officer made some ostentatious bustle, arriving with his parcel for which the train was detained, and passing through the depot entered the cars, Mr. Lincoln in his company. As Mr. Lincoln passed through the gate, the man attending it remarked: "Old fellow, it's well for you the train was detained to-night, or you wouldn't have gone in it." No one aboard the train but the agent of the company and the officer knew of Mr. Lincoln's being in it. He was conducted to a sleeping car, and thus was kept out of the way of observation. To guard against any possible communication by telegraph at this time, the circuit was broken, to be united when it would be safe to do so. The plan of the conspirators was to break or burn one of the bridges north of Baltimore, at the time of Mr. Lincoln's anticipated approach, on the following day; and in the confusion incident to the stoppage of the train, to assassinate him in the cars. Hence the extra precaution above mentioned, regarding the telegraph. In due time the train with Mr. Lincoln reached Washington, and he being safe there, the officer, as previously instructed, sent a dispatch to "the gentleman" that "the parcel of documents had been delivered." The public, and, above all, the conspirators, awoke on the morning of the 24th to be astonished with the intelligence that Mr. Lincoln had arrived in Washington. It may be well to mention here that the story of his disguise in a "Scotch cap" and cloak, was untrue. He wore his ordinary traveling cap, and was in no sense of the word disguised.

We give this narrative, assured that in no essential particular can it vary from the circumstantial account of "the gentlemen," to whose precautions may be properly attributed the frustation of the first plot to assassinate Abraham Lincoln. In confirmation of the view that this plot was within the knowledge of certain eminent secessionists in Washington, it may be stated that a gentleman, who was a member of the "Peace Convention," then in session, heard one of the Southern members exclaim, when Mr. Lincoln's arrival in Washington was mentioned, "My God! how did he get here?" The surprise was too significant to be mistaken, when afterwards remembered and associated with other circumstances.

TRIBUTES TO THE MEMORY OF PRESIDENT LINCOLN.

The history of Mr. LINCOLN's life would be incomplete, did we not introduce several of the eloquent tributes paid to his memory by some of the most distinguished of our public men and pulpit orators. The noble sentences uttered by SCHUYLER COLFAX, of Indiana, at Bryan Hall, Chicago, will be read with intense interest and satisfaction by the American people. No one knew the lamented dead better than he. There was a unity of heart between the two, and Mr. LINCOLN rarely took any step affecting the interests of the nation without making known his intentions to and consulting with Mr. COLFAX, in whose judgment he placed the utmost confidence. A strong affection existed between them, each admiring and respecting the other, for the honesty, firmness, and integrity of character which have made the names of ABRAHAM LINCOLN and SCHUYLER COLFAX household words throughout the land.

GGORGE BANCROFT, the historian, also laid his tribute of respect upon the tomb of the martyr, in a eulogy remarkable for its eloquence and sententiousness; while HENRY WARD BEECHER, the orator of the American pulpit, delivered in the Plymouth Church, Brooklyn, a sermon on the death of the President which has not been surpassed by any funeral oration called forth by the event which threw the country into mourning.

General HIRAM WALBRIDGE, of New York, one of the most prominent men in the North—a man who was politically opposed to the election of Mr. LINCOLN, but a man of undoubted patriotism—at an immense meeting held in memory of the deceased President, delivered an address worthy of the distinguished speaker and of the hallowed character of which he spoke.

The Orations are subjoined, and will be found complete.

ABRAHAM LINCOLN—HIS RELIGIOUS CHARACTER AND NOBILITY OF HEART—ADDRESS OF THE HON. SCHUYLER COLFAX, AT BRYAN HALL, CHICAGO, SUNDAY, APRIL 30, 1865.

Every seat in Bryan Hall, and every inch of standing room, was occupied by the audience, who came, notwithstanding the inclemency of the weather, to hear SCHUYLER COLFAX, the Speaker of the National House of Representatives, speak of the virtues and character of the dead President.

The Chair was occupied by JOHN V. FARWELL, Esq., the President of the Northwestern Pranch of the Christian Commission. The services were opened with Prayer by Professor F. W. FISK, D. D., of the Chicago Theological Seminary; after which Mr. FARWELL introduced the eloquent speaker, in a few befitting and appropriate remarks. Mr. COLFAX was loudly applauded. After requesting the audience to omit all manifestations of applause, Mr. COLFAX said :

HON. SCHUYLER COLFAX'S ADDRESS.

"Over two centuries and a half have passed away since the Ruler of any great nation of the world has fallen by the murderous attack of an assassin ; and, for the first time in our history, there is blood on the Presidential Chair of the Republic. Death is almost always saddening. The passing away of some dear friend from our earthly sight forever, fills the heart with sorrow. When it strikes down one who fills honorably a position of influence and power, as in the case of our two Presidents who died of disease in the White House, the sincerest grief is felt throughout the land. But when this affliction is aggravated by death coming through the hand of a murderer, it is not strange that the wave of woe sweeps gloomily over a nation, which sits down to mourn in sackcloth, and feels in every individual heart as if there was one dead at their own hearthstones. It seems, too, as if this wicked deed was intensified, in all its horror, by every attendant circumstance. The fatal shot was fired on the very day when the nation's flag was again unfurled in triumph over that fort in Charleston harbor, which, in four years' time, had been the cradle and the grave of the Rebellion. It was at an hour when the death of the President could not be of the slightest avail to the treasonable conspiracy against the Republic, which its military leaders acknowledged, at last, was powerless and overthrown. And it was aimed, alas, with too sure a hand, at the life of that one man in the Government whose heart was tenderest towards the would-be assassins of the nation's life.

"You may search history, ancient and modern, and when the task is ended, all will concede that Abraham Lincoln was the most merciful ruler who ever put down a powerful rebellion. He had so won the hearts of the people, and so entwined himself in their regard and affection, that he was the only man living who could have stood in the breach between the leaders of this iniquity and the wrath of the country they had plunged into bloody war. Feeling, as so many did, that his kindly heart almost forgot justice in its throbbings for mercy, yet, knowing his unfaltering devotion to his country his inflexible adherence to principle, his unyielding determination for the restoration of our national unity, there was a trust in him almost filial in its loving confidence, that whatever he should finally resolve on would prove in the end to be for the best. Had he been an unforgiving ruler; had his daily practice been to sit in his high place and there administer with unrelenting severity the penalties of offended law; had he proclaimed his resolution to consign all the plotters against his country to the gallows they had earned, we might have understood why the Rebel assassins conspired against his life. But no assassination in history—not even that of Henry IV. of France, for which Ravaillac was torn in pieces by horses—nor William of Orange—approximates in utterly unpalliated infamy to this.

"In the midst of the national rejoicings over the assured triumph of the national cause—with illuminations and bonfires blazing in every town, and the merry peal of the festive bell in every village, our cities blossoming with flags, our hearts beating high with joy, the two great armies of Grant and Lee fraternizing together after their long warfare, and exulting together over the return of peace—we were brought from the utmost heights of felicity to the deepest valleys of lamentation. No wonder that Rebel Generals acknowledged that it sent down their cause through all the coming centuries to shameless dishonor. For, disguise it as some may seek to do, behind the form of the assassin as his finger pulled the fatal trigger, looms up the dark and fiendish Spirit of the Rebellion, which, baffled in its work of assassinating the nation's life, avenged itself on the life of him who represented the nation's contest and the nation's victory. As surely as the infamous offer of twenty-five thousand crowns, by Philip of Spain, to whomsoever would rid the world of the pious William of Orange, the purest and best-loved ruler of his times—who, by a striking coincidence, was called Father William, as we called our beloved President

Father Abraham—as surely as this public offer, with its false denunciations of William's offences, inspirited the murderous Balthazar to shoot him through the body, so surely are the Chiefs of this gigantic rebellion of our times responsible for the fatal bullet that carried death to our Chief Magistrate and filled the land with unavailing sorrow.

"Unrebuked by them, history repeated itself in the following infamous proffer, published in the Selma (Alabama) *Dispatch* of last December, and copied approvingly into other Rebel organs:

"'ONE MILLION DOLLARS WANTED, TO HAVE PEACE BY THE FIRST OF MARCH.—If the citizens of the Southern Confederacy will furnish me with the cash, or good securities, for the sum of One Million Dollars, I will cause the lives of Abraham Lincoln, William H. Seward, and Andrew Johnson, to be taken by the 1st of March next. This will give us peace, and satisfy the world that cruel tyrants cannot live in a land of liberty. If this is not accomplished, nothing will be claimed beyond the sum of fifty thousand dollars, in advance, which is supposed to be necessary to reach and slaughter the three villains.

"'I will give, myself, one thousand dollars towards this patriotic purpose.

"'Every one wishing to contribute will address Box X, Cahawba, Ala.

"'*December* 1, 1864.'

"And, to fix upon them the brand, ineffaceably and forever, as the miscreant leaped upon the stage, his shout of Virginia's motto, '*Sic semper tyrannis*,' with his own addition, 'The South is avenged,' proclaims to the civilized world, which will be filled with horror at the deed, as well as to posterity, which will ever loathe the crime and the cause for whose interest it was committed, the authorship of this unparalleled atrocity. It seems, however, but a natural sequel to the infamous plot to murder him as he passed through Baltimore when first elected; to the brutalities on our dead soldiers at Bull Run, burying them face downwards, and carving up their bones into trinkets; to the piracies on the high seas, and attempts to burn women and children to death in crowded hotels and theatres; to Fort Pillow massacres, and to the systematic and inexpiable starvation of thousands of Union prisoners in their horrid pens.

"I can scarcely trust myself to attempt the portraiture of our Martyred Chief, whose death is mourned as never man's was mourned before; and who, in all the ages that may be left to America, while time may last, will be enshrined in solemn memory with the Father of the Republic which he saved. How much I loved him personally I cannot express to you. Honored always by his confidence, treated ever by him with affectionate regard; sitting often with him familiarly at his table; his last visitor on that terrible night; receiving his last message, full of interest to the toiling miners of the distant West; walking by his side from his parlor to the door, as he took his last steps in that Executive Mansion he had honored; receiving the last grasp of that generous and loving hand, and his last good-bye; declining his last kind invitation to join him in those hours of relaxation which incessant care and anxiety seemed to render so desirable, my mind has since been tortured by regrets that I had not accompanied him. If the knife which the assassin had intended for Grant had not been wasted, as it possibly would not have been, on one of so much less importance in our national affairs, perchance a sudden backward look at that eventful instant might have saved that life, so incalculably precious to wife, and children, and country—or, failing in that, might have hindered or prevented the escape of his murderer. The willingness of any man to endanger his life for another's, is so much doubted, that I scarcely dare to say how willingly I would have risked my own to preserve his, of such priceless value to us all. But if you can realize that it is sweet to die for one's country—as so many scores of thousands, from every State, and county, and hamlet, have proven in the years that are passed, you can imagine the consolation there would be to any one, even in his expiring hours, to feel that he had saved the land from the funereal gloom which, but a few days ago, settled down upon it, from ocean to ocean, and from capitol to cabin, at the loss of one for whom even a hecatomb of victims could not atone.

"Of this noble-hearted man, so full of genial impulses, so self-forgetful, so utterly unselfish, so pure, and gentle, and good, who lived for us, and at last died for us, I feel how inadequate I am to portray his manifold excellencies, his intellectual worth, his generous character, his fervid patriotism. Pope celebrated the memory of Robert Harley, the Lord of Oxford, a privy counsellor of Queen Anne, who himself n arrowly escaped assassination, in lines that seem prophetic of Mr. Lincoln's virtues:

> "'A soul supreme in each hard instance tried;
> Above all pain, all anger, and all pride,
> The rage of power, the blast of public breath,
> The lust of lucre, and the dread of death.'

"No one could ever convince the President that he was in danger of violent death. Judging others by himself, he could not realize that any one could seek his blood. Or he may have believed, as Napoleon wrote to Jerome, that no public man could effectually shield himself from the danger of assassination. Easier of access to the public at large than had been any of his predecessors; admitting his bitterest enemies to his reception-room alone; restive under the cavalry escort, which Secretary Stanton insisted should accompany him last summer in his daily journeys between the White House and his summer residence, at the Soldier's Home, several miles from Washington, at a time, too, as since ascertained in the details of this long-organized plot, discovered since his death, when it was intended to gag and handcuff him, and carry him to the Rebel capital as a hostage for their recognition; sometimes escaping from their escort by anticipating their usual hour of attendance; walking about the grounds unattended; he could not be persuaded that he run any risk whatever.

"Being at City Point after the evacuation of Richmond, he determined to go thither: not from idle curiosity, but to see if he could not do something to stop the effusion of blood and hasten the peace for which he longed. The ever-watchful Secretary of War hearing of it, implored him by telegraph not to go, and warned him that some lurking assassin might take his life. But, armed with his good intentions—alas, how feeble a shield they proved against the death-blow afterwards—he went, walked fearlessly and carelessly through the streets, met and conferred with a Rebel leader who had remained there, and when he returned to City Point telegraphed to his faithful friend and constitutional adviser, who till then had feared, as we all did at that time, for his life—'I received your despatch last night, went to Richmond this morning, and have just returned. ABRAHAM LINCOLN.' When I told him, on that last night, how uneasy all had been at his going, he replied, pleasantly, and with a smile (I quote his exact words): 'Why, if any one else had been President and gone to Richmond, I would have been alarmed too; but I was not scared about myself a bit.' If any of you have ever been at Washington, you will remember the footpath, lined and embowered with trees, leading from the back door of the War Department to the White House.

"One night, and but recently too, when, in his anxiety for news from the army, he had been with the Secretary in the telegraph office of the Department, he was about starting home at a late hour by this short route, Mr. Stanton stopped him, and said, 'You ought not to go that way—it is dangerous for you even in the daytime, but worse at night.' Mr. Lincoln replied, 'I don't believe there's *any* danger there, day or night.' Mr. Stanton responded, solemnly, 'Well, Mr. President, you shall not be killed returning that dark way from my Department while I am in it; you *must* let me take you round by the avenue in my carriage.' And Mr. Lincoln, joking the Secretary on his imperious military orders, and his needless alarm on his account, as he called it, entered his carriage and was driven by the well-lighted avenue to the White House.

"And thus he walked through unseen dangers without 'the dread of death;' his warm heart so full of good-will, even to his enemies, that he could not imagine there was any one base enough to slay him; and the death-dealing bullet was sped to its mark in a theatre, where, but little over an hour before, he had been welcomed, as he entered, by a crowded audience rising, and with cheers and waving of handkerchiefs, honoring him with an ovation of which any one might well be proud. Some regret that he was there at all. But, to all human appearance, he was safer there, by far, than in his own reception-room, where unknown visitors so often entered alone. He found there a temporary respite, occasionally, from the crowds who thronged his anterooms, relaxation from the cares and perplexities which so constantly oppressed him, keeping his mind under the severest tension, like the bent bow, till it almost lost its spring, and, on this fatal night—to be so black an one hereafter in our calendar—going with reluctance, and, as he expressed it to Mr. Ashmun and myself, only because General Grant, who had been advertised with himself to be present, had been compelled to leave the city, and he did not wish to disappoint those who would expect to see him there.

"Of the many thousands of persons I have met in public or private life, I cannot call to mind a single one who exceeded him in calmness of temper, in kindness of disposition, and in overflowing generosity of impulse. I doubt if his most intimate associate ever heard him utter bitter or vindictive language. He seemed wholly free from malignity or revenge; from ill-will or injustice. Attacked ever so sharply, you all remember that he never answered railing with railing. Criticised ever so unjustly, he would reply with no word of reproof, but patiently and uncomplainingly, if he answered at all, strive to prove that he stood on the rock of right. When, from the halls of Congress or elsewhere, his most earnest opponents visited the White House with business, they would be met as frankly, listened to as intently, and treated as justly as his most intimate friends. It could be said of him as Pyrrhus said of Fabricius when the latter, though in hostile array, exposed to his enemy the treachery of his physician, who proffered to poison him—'It is easier to turn the sun from his career than Fabricius from his honesty.' Men of all parties will remember, when the exciting contest of last fall ended in his triumphant re-election, his first word thereafter, from the portico of the White House, was that he could not and would not exult over his countrymen who had differed with his policy.

"And thus he ruled—and thus he lived—and thus he died. The wretch who stood behind him and sent his bullet crashing through that brain, which had been devising plans of reconciliation with the country's deadliest foes, as he leaped upon the stage and exulted over the death of him whom he denounced as a tyrant, uttered as foul a falsehood as the lying witnesses who caused the conviction and the crucifixion of the Son of Man, on the same Good Friday, nearly two thousand years ago. I would not compare the human with the Divine, except in that immeasurable contrast of the finite with the Infinite. But his whole life proves to me that if he could have had a single moment of consciousness and of speech, his great heart would have prompted him to pray for those who had plotted for his blood, 'Father, forgive them, for they know not what they do!'

"He bore the nations perils, and trials and sorrows, ever on his mind. You knew him, in a large degree, by the illustrative stories of which his memory and his tongue were so prolific, using them to point a moral, or to soften discontent at his decisions. But this was the mere badinage which relieved him for the moment from the heavy weight of public duties and responsibilities under which he often wearied. Those whom he admitted to his confidence, and with whom he conversed of his feelings, knew that his inner life was checkered with the deepest anxiety and most discomforting solicitude. Elated by victories for the cause which was ever in his thoughts, reverses to our arms cast a pall of depression over him. One morning, over two years ago, calling upon him on business, I found him looking more than usually pale and careworn, and inquired the reason. He replied, with the bad news he had received at a late hour the previous night, which had not yet been communicated to the press—adding, that he had not closed his eyes or breakfasted; and, with an expression I shall never forget, he exclaimed, 'How willingly would I exchange places to-day with the soldier who sleeps on the ground in the Army of the Potomac!'

"He was as free from deceit as from guile. He had one peculiarity which often misled those with whom he conversed. When his judgment, which acted slowly, but which was almost as immovable as the eternal hills when settled, was grasping some subject of importance, the arguments against his own desires seemed uppermost in his mind, and in conversing upon it he would present these arguments to see if they could be rebutted. He thus often surprised both friend and foe in his final decisions; always willing to listen to all sides till the latest possible moment; yet, when he put down his foot, he never took a backward step. Once, speaking of an eminent statesman, he said: 'When a question confronts him, he always and naturally argues it from the stand-point of which is the better policy; but with me,' he added, 'my only desire is to see what is right.' And this is the key to his life. His parents left Kentucky for Indiana in his childhood, on account of slavery in the former State; and he thus inherited a dislike for that institution. As he said recently to Governor Bramlette, of his native State, 'if slavery is not wrong, nothing is wrong.' Moving to Illinois, he found the prejudices here against anti-slavery men, when he entered on public and professional life, more intense than in any other free State in the Union. But he never dissembled, never concealed his opinions.

"Entering, in 1858, on that contest with his great political rival, but personal friend, Judge Douglas, which attracted the attention of the whole Union, he startled many of his friends by the declaration of his convictions that the Union could not permanently endure half slave and half free, that ultimately it would be either the one or the other, or be a divided house that could not stand; that he did not expect the Union to be dissolved, or the house to fall, but that it would cease to be divided, and that the hope of the Republic was in staying the spread of slavery that the public mind might rest in the hope of its ultimate extinction. And, though he coupled this with declarations against Congressional interference with it in existing States, it was not popular, and kept him in the whole canvass upon the defensive. But to every argument against it his calm reply was, in substance, 'such is my clear conviction, and I cannot unsay it.'

"His frankness in expressing unpopular opinions was manifested also, when in Southern Illinois, before an audience almost unanimously hostile to the sentiments, he declared, in the same close and doubtful contest, that, when the Declaration of Independence proclaimed that all men were created free and equal, it did not mean white men alone, but negroes as well; and that their rights to life, liberty, and the pursuit of happiness, were as inalienable as the noblest of the land. He claimed no power over State laws in other States which conflicted with these rights, or curtailed them; but with unfaltering devotion to his conscientious conviction, and regardless of its effects upon his political prospects, he never wavered in his adherence to this truth. And yet, when elected President of the United States, he executed the Fugitive Slave Law, because his oath of office as the Executive, in his opinion, required it. When urged to strike at slavery under the war power, he replied in a widely published letter, 'My paramount object is to save the Union, and I would save it in the shortest way. If I could save the Union without freeing any slaves, I would do it. If I could save it by freeing all the slaves, I would do it; and if I could do it by freeing some and leaving others alone, I would also do that. But I intend no modification of my oft-expressed personal wish that all men everywhere could be free.' And, when at last the hour arrived when, in his honest opinion, the alternative between the death of slavery and the death of the Union confronted him, then, and not till then, he struck at the cause of all our woes with the battle axe of the Union.

"Signing that immortal proclamation, which made him the Liberator of America, on the afternoon of January 1st, 1863, after hours of New Year's hand shaking, he said to me and other friends that night—'The signature looks a little tremulous, for my hand was tired, but my resolution was firm. I told them in September, if they did not return to their allegiance and cease murdering our soldiers, I would strike at this pillar of their strength. And now the promise shall be kept; and not one word of it will I ever recall.' And the promise was kept, and every word of it has stood. Thank God, when slavery and treason benumbed that hand in death, they could not destroy that noble instrument to which that hand had given a life that shall never die. A great writer said that when Wilberforce stood at the bar of God, he held in his hand the broken shackles which on earth had bound hundreds of thousands of his fellow-men. But, when baffled treason hurried Abraham Lincoln into the presence of his Maker, he bore with him the manacles of four millions whom he had made free; fetters that no power on God's foot-stool is strong enough to place again on their enfranchised limbs.

"No man, in our era, clothed with such vast power, has ever used it so mercifully. No ruler holding the keys of life and death, ever pardoned so many and so easily. When friends said to him they wished he had more of Jackson's sternness, he would say, 'I am just as God made me, and cannot change.' It may not be generally known that his door-keepers had standing orders from him that no matter how great might be the throng, if either Senators or Representatives had to wait, or to be turned away without an audience, he must see before the day closed, every messenger who came to him with a petition for the saving of life. One night in February I left all other business to ask him to respite the son of a constituent, who was sentenced to be shot, at Davenport, for desertion. He heard the story with his usual patience, though he was wearied out with incessant calls, and anxious for rest, and then replied:—'Some of our generals complain that I impair discipline and subordination in the army by my pardons and respites, but it makes me rested, after a hard day's work, if I can find some good excuse for saving a man's life, and I go to bed happy as I think how joyous the signing of my name will make him and his family and his friends.' And with a happy smile beaming over that care-furrowed face, he signed that name that saved that life.

"But Abraham Lincoln was not only a good and a just and a generous and a humane man. I could not be just to that well-rounded character of his, without adding that he was also a praying man. He has often said that his reliance in the gloomiest hours, was on his God, to whom he appealed in prayer, although he had never become a professor of religion. To a clergyman who asked him if he loved his Saviour, he replied, and he was too truthful for us to doubt the declaration:

"'When I was first inaugurated I did not love Him; when God took my son I was greatly impressed, but still I did not love Him; but when I stood upon the battle-field of Gettysburg, I gave my heart to Christ, and I can now say I do love the Saviour.'

"The Bible was always in his reception room. I have doubted the report that he read an hour in it every day, for he often came

17

direct from his bed to his reception room, so anxious was he to accommodate members who had important business, and it would sometimes be two or three hours before he would playfully say to some friend whose turn had come, 'Won't you stay here till I get some breakfast?' But he must have read the Bible considerably, for he often quoted it. One day that I happened to come in he said, 'Mr. — has just been here attacking one of my Cabinet, but I stopped him with this text,' and he read from the Proverbs a text, I had never heard quoted before, as follows: 'Accuse not a servant to his master.'

"You cannot fail to have noticed the solemn and sometimes almost mournful strain that pervades many of his addresses. When he left Springfield in 1861 to assume the Presidency, his farewell words were as follows:

"'My Friends:—No one not in my position can appreciate the sadness I feel at this parting. To this people I owe all that I am. Here I have lived more than a quarter of a century; here my children were born, and here one of them lies buried. I know not how soon I shall see you again. A duty devolves upon me which is, perhaps, greater than that which has devolved upon any other man since the days of Washington. He never would have succeeded except for the aid of Divine Providence, upon which he at all times relied. I feel that I cannot succeed without the same Divine aid which sustained him, and on the same Almighty Being I place my reliance for support; and I hope you, my friends, will all pray that I may receive that Divine assistance, without which I cannot succeed, but with which success is certain. Again, I bid you all an affectionate farewell.'

"Before that murderous blow closed his eyes in death, that 'success' for which he had struggled was assured; that 'duty' devolved upon him had been performed. But the friends to whom with the, 'sadness he felt at parting,' he bade this 'affectionate farewell,' can only look at the lifeless corpse, now slowly borne to their midst.

"When in the same month, he raised the national flag over Independence Hall at Philadelphia, he said to the assembled tens of thousands: 'It was something in the Declaration of Independence giving liberty, not only to the people of this country, but hope to the world for all coming time. It was that which gave promise that in due time the weights should be lifted from the shoulders of all men, and that all should have an equal chance. * * * * Now, my friends, can this country be saved upon that basis? If it can, I will consider myself one of the happiest men in the world, if I can help to save it. But if this country cannot be saved without giving up that principle, I was about to say that I would rather be assassinated upon the spot than to surrender it. I have said nothing but what I am willing to live by, and if it be the pleasure of Almighty God, to die by.'

"He seemed, as he thus spoke, to have the dark shadow of his violent death before him. But even in its presence he declared that he would rather be assassinated than to surrender a principle; and that while he was willing to live by it, yet, if it was God's pleasure, he was equally willing to die by it. He was assassinated; but his name and principles will live while history exists and the Republic endures.

"So, too, in the conclusion of his first inaugural, he appealed in the language of entreaty and peace to those who had raised their mailed hands against the life of their father-land:

"'You can have no conflict without being yourselves the aggressors. You have no oath registered in Heaven to destroy the Government, while I have the most solemn one to preserve, protect and defend it. The mystic cord of memory, stretching from every battle-field and patriot grave to every living heart and hearthstone all over this broad land, will yet swell the chorus of the Union, when again touched, as surely they will be, by the better angels of our nature.'

"In the funeral exercises in the East Room, on the 19th of April, the very anniversary of the day when the blood of murdered Massachusetts soldiers stained the stones of the city of Baltimore, Dr. Gurley quoted the President's solemn reply to a company of clergymen who called on him in one of the darkest hours of the war, when, standing where his lifeless remains then rested, he replied to them in tones of deep emotion:

"'Gentlemen, my hope of success in this great and terrible struggle rests on that immutable foundation, the justness and goodness of God. And when events are very threatening and prospects very dark, I still hope in some way which man cannot see, all will be well in the end, because our cause is just, and God is on our side.'

"You cannot have forgotten this impressive invocation with which he closed his Proclamation of Emancipation:

"'And, upon this last, sincerely believed to be an act of justice, warranted by the Constitution on military necessity, I invoke the considerate judgment of mankind, and the gracious favor of Almighty God.'

"The solemn words of his last inaugural sound in my ears to-day as I heard them fall from his lips on the steps of the Capitol. There was no exultation over his own success, though he was the first Northern President who had ever been re-elected. There was no bitterness against the men who had filled our land with new made graves, and who were striving to stab the nation to its death. There was no confident and enthusiastic prediction of the country's triumph. But with almost the solemn utterances of one of the Hebrew Prophets; as if he felt he was standing, as he was, on the verge of his open grave, and addressing his last official words to his countrymen, with his lips touched by the finger of Inspiration, he said:

"'The Almighty has his own purposes. 'Woe unto the world because of offences, for it must needs be that offences come; but woe to that man by whom the offence cometh.' If we shall suppose that American slavery is one of those offences, which, in the providence of God must needs come, but which having continued through His appointed time, He now wills to remove, and that He gives to both North and South this terrible war as the woe due to those by whom the offence came, shall we discern therein any departure from those Divine attributes which the believers in a living God always ascribe to Him? Fondly do we hope, fervently do we pray, that the mighty scourge of war may soon pass away. Yet, if God will that it continue until all the wealth piled by the bondman's two hundred and fifty years of unrequited toil shall be sunk, and until every drop of blood drawn with the lash shall be paid with another drawn with the sword, as was said three thousand years ago, so still it must be said, 'The judgments of the Lord are true and righteous altogether.'

"'With malice towards none, with charity for all, with firmness in the right as God gives us to see the right, let us strive on to finish the work we are in, to bind up the nations wounds, to care for him who shall have borne the battle and for his widow and orphans, to do all which may achieve and cherish a just and lasting peace among ourselves and with all nations.'

"What a portraiture of his own character he unconsciously draws in this closing paragraph. 'With malice towards none, with charity for all, with firmness in the right as God gives us to see the right?' *And yet, they slew him.*

"Bear with me further while I quote the letter, when, in the midst of the exciting canvass of last fall, in which he was so deeply interested, during the very week that he was being denounced in this city as scarcely any man had ever been denounced before, he shut out the thoughts of these cruelly unjust aspersions to write in this deeply impressive strain to a Philadelphia lady, then resident in England:—

"'EXECUTIVE MANSION, *Washington, September* 6, 1864.

"'ELIZA GURNEY:—*My Esteemed Friend:*—I have never forgotten, probably never shall forget, the very impressive occasion, when yourself and friends visited me on a Sabbath forenoon, two years ago, nor has your kind letter, written nearly a year later, ever been forgotten.

"'In all it has been your purpose to strengthen my reliance on God, I am much indebted to the good Christian people of the country for their constant prayers and consolations, and to no one of them more than yourself. The purposes of the Almighty are perfect and must prevail, though we erring mortals may fail to perceive them in advance.

"'We hoped for a happy termination of this terrible war long before this, but God knows best, and has ruled otherwise. We shall acknowledge His wisdom and our own errors therein.

Meanwhile we must work earnestly in the best light He gives us, trusting that so working still conduces to the great end He ordains. Surely He intends some great good to follow this mighty convulsion, which no mortal could stay. Your people—the Friends—have had and are having very great trials on principles and faith. *Opposed to both war and oppression, they can only practically oppose oppression by war.* In this hard dilemma some have chosen one horn and some the other. For those appealing to me on conscientious grounds, I have done, and shall do the best I can in my own conscience, and my oath to the law. That you believe this I doubt not, and believing it, I shall still receive, for our country and myself, your earnest prayers to our Father in Heaven.

"'Your sincere friend,

"'A. LINCOLN.'

"Nor should I forget to mention here that the last act of Congress ever signed by him, was one requiring that the motto, in which he sincerely believed, 'In God we trust,' should hereafter be inscribed upon all our national coin. But April came at last, with all its glorious resurrection of spring, that spring which he was not to see ripening into summer. The last sands in the hour-glass of his life were falling. His last moment drew nigh, for his banded assassins, foiled in an attempt to poison him last year (a plot only discovered since detectives have been tracking the mysteries of his death,) had resolved this time on striking a surer blow. Victory after victory crowned our national armies. A hundred captured rebel banners filled the War Department. Scores of thousands of Rebel soldiers had surrendered, and all over the Republic the joyous acclaim of millions hailed the promised land of Peace.

"But our beloved leader was to enter another land of rest. Thank Heaven, though wicked men may kill the body, they can not kill the immortal soul. And, if the spirits of the good men who have left us are permitted to look back on the land they loved in life, it is not presumptuous to believe that Washington and Lincoln, from the shining courts above, look down to-day with paternal interest on the nation, which, under Providence, the one had founded and the other saved, and which will entwine their names together in hallowed recollection forever.

"But, in his last hours, all the affectionate traits of character which I have so inadequately delineated shone out in more than wonted brilliancy. How his kindly heart must have throbbed with joy, as on the very day before his death he gladdened so many tens of thousands of anxious minds by ordering the abandonment of the impending but now not needed draft. With what generous magnanimity he authorized our heroic Lieutenant-General to proffer terms unparalleled in their liberality, to the Army of Virginia, so long the bulwark of Rebellion. And the very last official act of his life was, when learning by telegraph that very Friday afternoon, that two of the leaders and concoctors of the Rebellion were expected to arrive disguised, in a few hours, at one of our ports, to escape to Europe, he instructed our officers not to arrest them, but let them flee the country. He did not wish their blood, but their associates thirsted for his, and in a few short hours after this message of mercy to save their friends from death sped on the wings of lightning, with wicked hands they slew him. No last words of affection to weeping wife and children did they allow him. No moment's space for prayer to God. But in order that consciousness might end with the instant, the pistol was held close to the skull, that the bullet might be buried in his brain.

"Thus lived and thus died our murdered President. But, as the ruffian shot down the pilot at our helm, just as the Ship of State, after all its stormy seas, was sailing prosperously into port; another, whose life, like that of Seward and Stanton, had been marked for that very night of horrors, but who had been saved, sprang to the rudder, and the noble ship holds on her course, without a flutter in her canvass, or a strain upon her keel. Andrew Johnson, to whom the public confidence was so quickly and worthily transferred, is cast in a sterner mould than him whose place he fills. He has warred on traitors in his mountain home as they have warred on him; and he insists, with this crowning infamy filling up their cup of wickedness, that treason should be made odious, and that mercy to the leaders who engendered it is cruelty to the nation.

"The text of Holy Writ, which he believes in for them, is in the twenty-sixth verse of the seventh chapter of Ezra. 'Let judgment be executed speedily upon him, whether it be unto death, or to banishment, or to confiscation of goods, or to imprisonment;' and to this do not all loyal hearts respond Amen.

"And thus, though the President is slain, the Nation lives. The statesman who has so successfully conducted our foreign correspondence as to save us from threatened and endangering complications and difficulties abroad, and who, with the President, leaned over to mercy's side, so brutally bowie-knifed as he lay helpless upon his bed of anguish, is happily to be spared us, and the conspiracy which intended a bloody harvest of six patriots' lives, reaped with its murderous sickle but one.

"But that one, how dear to all our hearts, how priceless in its worth, how transparent and spotless its purity of character. In the fiery trial to which the nation has been subjected we have given of the bravest and best of the land. The South is billowed with the graves where sleep the patriot martyrs of Constitutional liberty till the resurrection morn. The vacant chair at the table of thousands upon thousands tells of those who, inspired by the sublimest spirit of self-sacrifice, have died that the Republic might survive. Golden and living treasures have been heaped upon our country's altar. But, after all these costly sacrifices had been offered, and the end seemed almost at hand, a costlier sacrifice had to be made; and from the highest place in all the land the victim came. Slaughtered at the moment of victory the blow was too late to rob him of the grand place he has won for himself in history.

"'We know him now. All narrow jealousies
Are silent. And we see him as he moved,
How modest, kindly, all compassionate, wise,
With what sublime repression of himself,
And in what limits and how tenderly.
Whose glory was redressing human wrongs;
Not making his high place the lawless perch
Of winged ambitions, nor a vantage ground
Of pleasure. But through all this tract of years,
Wearing the white flower of a blameless life.'

"Murdered, coffined, buried, and will live with those few immortal names who were not born to die; live as the Father of the Faithful in the time that tried men's souls; live in the grateful hearts of the dark-browed race he lifted from under the heel of the oppressor to the dignity of freedom and of manhood; live in every bereaved circle which has given father, husband, son or friend to die, as he did, for his country; live with the glorious company of martyrs to liberty, justice and humanity, that trio of Heaven-born principles; live in the love of all beneath the circuit of the sun who loathe tyranny, slavery and wrong. And leaving behind him a record that shows how honesty and principle lifted him, self-made as he was, from the humblest ranks of the people to the noblest station on the globe, and a name that shall brighten under the eye of posterity as the ages roll by.

"'From the top of Fame's ladder he stepped to the sky.'"

Notwithstanding the request of the speaker that the audience would not applaud, it was impossible to restrain them, and Mr. Colfax was repeatedly interrupted.

HON. GEORGE BANCROFT'S ORATION.

"Our grief and horror at the crime which has clothed the continent in mourning, find no adequate expression in words and no relief in tears. The President of the United States of America has fallen by the hands of an assassin. Neither the office with which he was invested by the approved choice of a mighty people, nor the most simple-hearted kindliness of nature could save him from the fiendish passions of relentless fanaticism. The wailings of the millions attend his remains as they are borne in solemn procession over our great rivers, along the seaside, beyond the mountains, across the prairie, to their final resting-place in the valley of the Mississippi. The echoes of his funeral knell vibrate through the world, and the friends of freedom of every tongue and in every land are his mourners.

"Too few days have passed away since ABRAHAM LINCOLN stood in the flush of vigorous manhood, to permit any attempt at an analysis of his character or an exposition of his career. We find it hard to believe that his large eyes, which in their softness and beauty expressed nothing but benevolence and gentleness, are closed in death; we almost look for the pleasant smile that brought out more vividly the earnest cast of his features, which were serious even to sadness. A few years ago he was a village attorney, engaged in the support of a rising family, unknown to fame, scarcely named beyond his neighborhood; his Administration made him the most conspicuous man in his country, and drew on him first the astonished gaze, and then the respect and admiration of the world.

"Those who come after us will decide how much of the wonderful results of his public career is due to his own good common sense, his shrewd sagacity, readiness of wit, quick interpretation of the public mind, his rare combination of fixedness and pliancy, his steady tendency of purpose; how much to the American people, who, as he walked with them side by side, inspired him with their own wisdom and energy; and how much to the overruling laws of the moral world, by which the selfishness of evil is made to defeat itself. But after every allowance, it will remain that members of the government which preceded his administration opened the gates to treason, and he closed them; that when he went to Washington the ground on which he trod shook under his feet, and he left the republic on a solid foundation; that traitors had seized public forts and arsenals, and he recovered them for the United States, to whom they belonged; that the capital, which he found the abode of slaves, now the home only of the free; that the boundless public domain which was grasped at, and, in a great measure, held for the diffusion of slavery, is now irrevocably devoted to freedom; that then men talked a jargon of a balance of power in a republic between Slave States and Free States, and now the foolish words are blown away forever by the breath of Maryland, Missouri and Tennessee; that a terrible cloud of political heresy rose from the abyss, threatening to hide the light of the sun, and under its darkness a rebellion was rising into indefinable proportions; now the atmosphere is purer than ever before, and the insurrection is vanishing away; the country is cast into another mould, and the gigantic system of wrong, which had been the work of more than two centuries, is dashed down, we hope forever. And as to himself personally: he was then scoffed at by the proud as unfit for his station, and now, against the usage of later years, and in spite of numerous competitors, he was the unbiassed and the undoubted choice of the American people for a second term of service. Through all the mad business of treason he retained the sweetness of a most placable disposition; and the slaughter of myriads of the best on the battle-field, and the more terrible destruction of our men in captivity by the slow torture of exposure and starvation, had never been able to provoke him into harboring one vengeful feeling or one purpose of cruelty.

"How shall the nation most completely show its sorrow at Mr. LINCOLN'S death? How shall it best honor his memory? There can be but one answer. He was struck down when he was highest in its service, and, in strict conformity with duty, was engaged in carrying out principles affecting its life, its good name, and its relations to the cause of freedom and the progress of mankind. Grief must take the character of action, and breathe itself forth in the assertion of the policy to which he fell a sacrifice. The standard which he held in his hand must be uplifted again, higher and more firmly than before, and must be carried on to triumph. Above every thing else, his proclamation of the 1st day of January, 1863, declaring throughout the parts of the country in rebellion the freedom of all persons who had been held as slaves, must be affirmed and maintained.

"Events, as they rolled onward, have removed every doubt of the legality and binding force of that proclamation. The country and the rebel government have each laid claim to the public service of the slave, and yet but one of the two can have a rightful claim to such service. That rightful claim belongs to the United States, because every one born on their soil, with the few exceptions of the children of travelers and transient residents, owes them a primary allegiance. Every one so born has been counted among those represented in Congress; every slave has ever been represented in Congress—imperfectly and wrongly it may be—but still has been counted and represented. The slave born on our soil always owed allegiance to the General Government. It may in time past have been a qualified allegiance, manifested through his master, as the allegiance of a ward through its guardian or of an infant through its parent. But when the master became false to his allegiance the slave stood face to face with his country, and his allegiance, which may before have been a qualified one, became direct and immediate. His chains fell off, and he stood at once in the presence of the nation, bound, like the rest of us, to its public defence. Mr. LINCOLN'S proclamation did but take notice of the already existing right of the bondman to freedom. The treason of the master made it a public crime for the slave to continue his obedience; the treason of a State set free the collected bondmen of that State.

"This doctrine is supported by the analogy of precedents. In the times of feudalism the treason of the lord of the manor deprived him of his serfs; the spurious feudalism that existed among us differs in many respects from the feudalism of the middle ages, but so far the precedent runs parallel with the present case—for treason the master then, for treason the master now, loses his slaves.

"In the middle ages the sovereign appointed another lord over the serfs and the land which they cultivated: in our day the sovereign makes them masters of their own persons, lords over themselves.

"It has been said that we are at war, and that emancipation is not a belligerent right. The objection disappears before analysis. In a war between independent powers the invading foreigner invites to his standard all who will give him aid, whether bond or free, and he rewards them according to his ability and his pleasure with gifts or freedom; but when at a peace he withdraws from the invaded country he must take his aiders and comforters with him; or if he leaves them behind, where he has no court to enforce his decrees, he can give them no security, unless it be by the stipulations of a treaty. In a civil war it is altogether different. There, when rebellion is crushed, the old government is restored, and its courts resume their jurisdiction. So it is with us; the United States have courts of their own, that must punish the guilt of treason and vindicate the freedom of persons whom the fact of rebellion has set free.

"Nor may it be said, that because slavery existed in most of the States when the Union was formed, it cannot rightfully be interfered with now. A change has taken place, such as MADISON foresaw, and for which he pointed out the remedy. The constitutions of States had been transformed before the plotters of treason carried them away into rebellion. When the Federal Constitution was formed, general emancipation was thought to be near: and everywhere the respective legislatures had authority, in the exercise of their ordinary functions, to do away with slavery; since that time the attempt has been made in what are called Slave States to make the condition of slavery perpetual; and events have proved with clearness of demonstration, that a constitution which seeks to continue a caste of hereditary bondmen through endless generations is inconsistent with the existence of republican institutions. So, then, the new President and the people of the United States must insist that the proclamation of freemen shall stand as a reality. And moreover, the people must never cease to insist that the constitution shall be so amended as utterly to prohibit slavery on any part of our soil for evermore.

"Alas! that a State in our vicinity should withhold its assent to this last beneficent measure; its refusal was an encouragement to our enemies equal to the gain of a pitched battle, and delays the only hopeful method of pacification. The removal of the cause of the rebellion is not only demanded by justice; it is the policy of mercy, making room for a wider clemency; it is the part of order against a chaos of controversy; its success brings with it true reconcilement, a lasting peace, a continuous growth of confidence through an assimilation of the social condition. Here is the fitting expression of the mourning of to-day. And let no lover of his country say that this warning is uncalled for. The cry is delusive that slavery is dead. Even now it is nerving itself for a fresh struggle for continuance.

"No sentiment of despair may mix with our sorrow. We owe it to the memory of the dead, we owe it to the cause of popular liberty throughout the world, that the sudden crime which has taken the life of the President of the United States shall not produce the least impediment in the smooth course of public affairs. This great city, in the midst of unexampled emblems of deeply-seated grief, has sustained itself with composure and magnanimity. It has nobly done its part in guarding against the derangement of business or the slightest shock to public credit. The enemies of the republic put it to the severest trial, but the voice of faction has not been heard—doubt and despondency have been unknown. In serene majesty the country rises in the beauty and strength and hope of youth, and proves to the world the quiet energy and the durability of institutions growing out of the reason and affection of the people.

"Heaven has willed it that the United States shall live. The nations of the earth cannot spare them. All the worn-out aristocracies of Europe saw in the spurious feudalism of slaveholding their strongest outpost, and banded themselves together with the deadly enemies of our national life. If the Old World will discuss the respective advantages of oligarchy or equality; of the union of church and state, or the rightful freedom of religion; of land accessible to the many or of land monopolized by an ever-decreasing number of the few, the United States must live to control the decision by their quiet and unobtrusive example. It has often and truly been observed that the trust and affection of the masses gather naturally round an individual; if the inquiry is made whether the man so trusted and beloved shall elicit from the reason of the people enduring institutions of their own, or shall sequester political power for a superintending dynasty, the United States must live to solve the problem. If a question is raised on the respective merits of TIMOLEON or JULIUS CÆSAR, of WASHINGTON or NAPOLEON, the United States must be there to call to mind that there were twelve Cæsars, most of them the opprobrium of the human race, and to contrast with them the line of American presidents.

"The duty of the hour is incomplete, our mourning is insincere if, while we express unwavering trust in the great principles that underlie our government, we do not also give our support to the man to whom the people have entrusted its administration.

"ANDREW JOHNSON is now, by the constitution, the President of the United States, and he stands before the world as the most conspicuous representative of the industrial classes. Left an orphan at four years old, poverty and toil were his steps to honor. His youth was not passed in the halls of colleges; nevertheless he has received a thorough political education in statesmanship in the school of the people and by long experience of public life. A village functionary; member successively of each branch of the Tennessee legislature, hearing with a thrill of joy the words: 'The Union, it must be preserved;' a representative in Congress for successive years; Governor of the great State of Tennessee, approved as its Governor by re-election; he was at the opening of the Rebellion a Senator from that State in Congress. Then at the Capitol, when Senators, unrebuked by the government, sent word by telegram to seize forts and arsenals, he alone from that Southern region told them what the government did not dare to tell them, that they were traitors, and deserved the punishment of treason. Undismayed by a perpetual purpose of public enemies to take his life, bearing up against the still greater trial of the persecution of his wife and children, in due time he went back to his State, determined to restore it to the Union, or die with the American flag for his winding sheet. And now, at the call of the United States, he has returned to Washington as a conqueror, with Tennessee as a Free State for his trophy. It remains for him to consummate the vindication of the Union.

"To that Union Abraham Lincoln has fallen a martyr. His death, which was meant to sever it beyond repair, binds it more closely and more firmly than ever. The blow aimed at him, was aimed not at the native of Kentucky, not at the citizen of Illinois, but at the man who, as President, in the executive branch of the government, stood as the representative of every man in the United States. The object of the crime was the life of the whole people; and it wounds the affections of the whole people. From Maine to the southwest boundary on the Pacific, it makes us one. The country may have needed an imperishable grief to touch its inmost feeling. The grave that receives the remains of Lincoln, receives the martyr to the Union; the monument which will rise over his body will bear witness to the Union; his enduring memory will assist during countless ages to bind the States together, and to incite to the love of our one undivided, individual country. Peace to the ashes of our departed friend, the friend of his country and his race. Happy was his life, for he was the restorer of the republic; he was happy in his death, for the manner of his end will plead forever for the union of the States and the freedom of man."

HENRY WARD BEECHER'S TRIBUTE.

On Sunday, April 23d, 1865, the Plymouth street Church, Brooklyn, was filled to overflowing long before the hour of service, it having been announced that Mr. Beecher would deliver an appropriate sermon on the event which had cast the nation into mourning. Thousands were turned away, and hundreds hung about the outer door in the vain hope of hearing. The church was very neatly and effectively draped in black and white, and upon the pastor's desk was placed a basket of beautiful flowers. At half-past ten Mr. Beecher went to his platform, the whole of which was occupied by men and women, while small boys fringed the front.

After the reading of the 90th Psalm, and conducting the ordinary services of invocation and praise, Mr. Beecher delivered the following

SERMON,

Taking for his text the first five verses of the last chapter of Deuteronomy:

1. And Moses went up from the plains of Moab, unto the Mountains of Nebo, to the top of Pisgah, that is over against Jericho; and the Lord showed him the land of Gilead, unto Dan.
2. And all Naphtali, and the land of Ephraim and Manasseh, and all the land of Judah, unto the utmost sea.
3. And the South, and the plain of the valley of Jericho, and the city of palm trees, unto Zoar.
4. And the Lord said unto him, This is the land which I sware unto Abraham, unto Isaac, and unto Jacob, saying I will give it unto thy seed; I have caused thee to see it with thine eyes, but thou shalt not go over thither.
5. So Moses, the servant of the Lord, died there in the land of Moab, according to the word of the Lord.

"There is no historic figure more noble than that of the Jewish lawgiver. After many thousand years, the figure of Moses is not diminished, but stands up against the background of early days, distinct and individual as if he lived but yesterday. There is scarcely another event in history more touching than his death. He had borne the great burdens of state for forty years, shaped the Jews to a nation, filled out their civil and religious polity, administered their laws, and guided their steps, or dwelt with them in all their sojourning in the wilderness, had mourned in their punishment, kept step with their marches and led them in wars, until the end of their labors drew nigh, the last stages were reached, and Jordan only lay between them and the promised land.

"The Promised Land! Oh, what yearnings had heaved his breast for that Divinely promised place! He had dreamed of it by night and mused by day; it was holy, and endeared as God's favored spot; it was to be the cradle of an illustrious history.

All his long, laborious and now weary life, he had aimed at this as the consummation of every desire, the reward of every toil and pain. Then came the word of the Lord to him, 'Thou must not go over. Get thee up into the mountain, look upon it and die.' From that silent summit the hoary leader gazed to the North, to the South, to the West, with hungry eyes. The dim outlines rose up, the hazy recesses spoke of quiet valleys. With eager longing, with sad resignation, he looked upon the promised land, that was now the forbidden land. It was a moment's anguish. He forgot all his personal wants and drank in the vision of his people's home. His work was done. There lay God's promise fulfilled. There was the seat of coming Jerusalem, there the city of Jehovah's King, the sphere of judges and prophets, the mount of sorrow and salvation, the country whence were to fly blessings to all mankind. Joy chased sadness from every feature, and the prophet lay him down and died.

"Again, a great leader of the people has passed through toil, sorrow, battle and war, and came near to the promised land of peace, into which he might not pass over. Who shall recount our martyr's sufferings for the people? Since the November of 1860, his horizon has been black with storms. By day and by night he trod its way of danger and darkness. On his shoulders rested a Government, dearer to him than his own life. At its life millions were striking at home; upon us foreign eyes were lowered, and it stood like a lone island in a sea full of storms, and every tide and wave seemed eager to devour it. Upon thousands of hearts great sorrows and anxieties have rested, but upon not one such and in such measure, as upon that simple, truthful, noble soul, our faithful and sainted Lincoln. Never rising to the enthusiasm of more impassioned natures in hours of hope, and never sinking with the mercurial in the hours of defeat to the depths of despondency, he held on with immovable patience and fortitude, putting caution against hope that it might not be premature, and hope against caution that it might not yield to dread and danger. He wrestled ceaselessly through four black and dreadful purgatorial years, when God was cleansing the sins of this people as by fire.

"At last the watchman beheld the grey dawn. The mountains began to give forth their forms from out the darkness, and the East came rushing toward us with arms full of joy for all our sorrows. Then it was for him to be glad exceedingly that had sorrowed immeasurably. Peace could bring to no other heart such joy, such rest, such honor, such trust, such gratitude. He but looked upon it as Moses looked upon the promised land. Then the wail of a nation proclaimed that he had gone from among us. Not thine the sorrow, but ours. Sainted soul, thou hast indeed entered the promised rest, while we are yet on the march. To us remains the rocking of the deep, the storm upon the land, days of duty and nights of watching; but thou art sphered high above all darkness and fear, beyond all sorrow or weariness. Rest, oh weary heart! Rejoice exceedingly, thou that hast enough suffered. Thou hast beheld Him who invariably led thee in this great wilderness. Thou standest among the elect; around thee are the royal men that have ennobled human life in every age; kingly art thou, with glory on thy brow as a diadem, and joy is upon thee for evermore!

"Over all this land, over all the little cloud of years that now from thine infinite horizon waver back from thee as a spark, thou art lifted up as high as the star is above the clouds that hide us, but never reach it. In the goodly company of Mount Zion thou shall find that rest which so many have sought in vain, and thy name, an everlasting name in heaven, shall flourish in fragrance and beanty as long as men shall last upon the earth, or hearts remain to revere truth, fidelity and goodness. Never did two such orbs of experience meet in one hemisphere as the joy and sorrow of the same week in this land. The joy was as sudden as if no man had expected it, and as entrancing as if it had fallen from heaven. It rose up over sobriety, and swept business from its moorings, and ran down through the land in irresistible course. Men wept and embraced each other; they sang or prayed, or, deeper yet, could only think thanksgiving and weep gladness.

"That peace was sure, that Government was firmer than ever, the land was cleansed of plague, that ages were opening to our footsteps and we were to begin a march of blessings, that blood was staunched and scowling enmities sinking like spent storms beneath the horizon; that the dear fatherland, nothing lost, much gained, was to rise up in unexampled honor among the nations of the earth—these thoughts, and that undistinguishable throng of fancies, and hopes, and desires, and yearnings, that filled the soul with tremblings like the heated air of midsummer days—all these kindled up such a surge of joy as no words may describe. In an hour, joy lay without a pulse, without a gleam, or breath. A sorrow came that swept through the land, as huge storms sweep through the forest and field, rolling thunder along the skies, disheveling the flames and daunting every singer in the thicket or forest, and pouring blackness and darkness across the land and up the mountains. Did ever so many hearts in so brief a time touch two such boundless feelings? It was the uttermost of joy and the uttermost of sorrow—noon and midnight, without space between.

"The blow brought not a sharp pang. It was so terrible that at first it stunned sensibility. Citizens were like men awakened at midnight by an earthquake, and bewildered to find every thing that they were accustomed to trust wavering and falling. The very earth was no longer solid. The first feeling was the least. Men waited to get strength to feel. They wandered in the street as if groping after some impending dread or unde veloped sorrow. They met each other as if each would ask the other, 'Am I awake, or do I dream?' There was a piteous helplessness. Strong men bowed down and wept. Other and common griefs belong to some one in chief, they are private property; but this was each man's and every man's. Every virtuous household in the land felt as if its first-born were gone. Men took it home. They were bereaved, and walked for days as if a corpse lay unburied in their dwellings. There was nothing else to think of; they could speak of nothing but that, and yet of that they could speak only falteringly. All business was laid aside, pleasure forgot to smile.

"The city for nearly a week ceased to roar, and the great Leviathan laid down and was still. Even Avarice stood still, and Greed was strangely moved to generous sympathy with universal sorrow. Rear to his name monuments, found charitable institutions, and with his name above their heights, but no monument will ever equal the universal, spontaneous and sublime sorrow that in a moment swept down lines and parties, and covered up animosities, and in an hour brought a divided people with unity of grief and indivisible fellowship of anguish! For myself, I cannot yet command that quietness of spirit needed for a just and temperate delineation of a man whom goodness has made great. I pass, then, to some considerations aside from the martyr President's character. And, first, let us not mourn that his departure was so sudden, nor fill our imagination with horror at its method. When good men pray for deliverance from hidden death, it is only that they may not be plunged, without preparation and all disrobed, into the presence of the Judge.

"Men long eluding and evading sorrow, when suddenly overtaken, seem enchanted to make it great to the uttermost—a habit which is not Christian, although it is doubtless natural. When one is ready to depart, suddenness is a blessing. It is a painful sight to see a tree overthrown by a tornado, wrenched from its foundations and broken down like a reed; but it is yet more painful to see a vast and venerable tree lingering with vain strife, when age and infirmity have marked it for destruction. The process of decay is a spectacle humiliating and painful; but it seems good and grand for one to go from duty done with pulse high, with strength full and nerve strong, terminating a noble life in a fitting manner. Nor are we without Scripture warrant for these thoughts: 'Let your loins be girded about. * * * Blessed are those servants whom the Lord, when He cometh, shall find watching.' * * * Not those who die in a stupor are blessed, but they who go with all their powers about them, and wide awake, as to a wedding. He died watching. He died with armor on. In the midst of hours of labor, in the very heart of patriotic consultations, just returned from camps and council, he was stricken down.

"No fever dried his blood, no slow waste consumed him. All at once, in full strength and manhood, with his girdle tight about him, he departed, and walks with God. Nor was the manner of his death more shocking, if we will surround it with higher associations. Have not thousands of soldiers fallen on the field of battle by the bullets of an enemy, and did not he? All soldiers that fall ask to depart in the hour of victory, and at such an hour he fell. There was not a poor drummer boy in all this war, that has fallen, for whom the great heart of Lincoln would not have bled; there is not one private soldier without note or name slain among thousands, and hid in the pit among hundreds, without even the memorial of a separate burial, for whom the President would not have wept. He was a man from and of the people, and now that he who might not bear the march, the toil and battle, with these humble citizens, has been called to die by the bullet, as they were, do you not feel that there is a peculiar fitness to his nature and life, that he should in death be joined with them in a final common experience? For myself, when any event is susceptible of a nobler garnishing, I cannot understand the nature or character of those who seek rather to drag it down, degrading and debasing, rather than ennobling and sanctifying it.

"*Secondly:* This blow was but the expiring rebellion; and as a miniature gives all the form and features of its subject, so, epitomized in this foul act, we find the whole nature and disposition of slavery. It begins in a wanton destruction of all human rights, and in the desecration of all the sanctities of heart and home. It can be maintained only at the sacrifice of every right moral feeling in its abettors and upholders. It is a two-edged sword, cutting both ways, desolating alike the oppressed and the oppressor, and violently destroying manhood in the victim, it insidiously destroys manhood in the master. No man born and bred under the influence of the accursed thing can possibly maintain his manhood, and I would as soon look for a saint in the darkness of perdition, as for a man of honor in this hot-bed of iniquity. The problem is solved, its demonstration is complete. Slavery wastes its victims, it wastes estates. It destroys public morality, it corrupts manhood in its centre. Communities in which it exists are not to be trusted. Its products are rotten. No timber grown in its cursed soil is fit for the ribs of our ship of State or for our household homes.

"The people are selfish in their patriotism, and brittle; whoever leans on them for support is pierced in his hand. Their honor is not honor, but a bastard quality which disgraces the name of honor, and for all time the honor of the supporters of slavery will be throughout the earth a by-word and a hissing. Their whole moral nature is death-smitten. The needless rebellion, the treachery of its leaders to oaths and trusts, their violations of the commonest principles of fidelity, sitting in

Senates, Councils and places of trust, only to betray them; the long, general and unparalleled cruelty to prisoners, without provocation or excuse; their unreasoning malignity and fierceness, all mark the symptoms of the disease of slavery, that is a deadly poison to soul and body. There may be exceptions, of course, but as a rule, malignity is the nature and the essence. Slavery is itself barbarous, and the nation which upholds and protects it is likewise barbarous. It is fit that its expiring blow should be made to take away from men the last forbearance, the last pity, and fire the soul with invincible determination that the breeding ground of such mischiefs and monsters shall be utterly and forever destroyed.

"It needed not that the assassin should put on paper his belief in slavery. He was but the sting of the monster slavery which has struck this blow, and as long as this nation lasts, it will not be forgotten that we have had our 'Martyr President,' nor while Heaven holds high court or Hell rots beneath, will it be forgotten that slavery murdered him.

"*Third:* This blow was aimed at the life of government and of the nation. Lincoln was slain, but America was meant. The man was cast down, but the Government was smitten at. The President was killed, but national life-breathing freedom and benignity was sought. He of Illinois, as a private man, might have been detested, but it was because he represented the cause of just government, liberty and kindness, he was slain. It was a crime against universal government, and was aimed at all. Not more was it at us than at England or France or any well compacted government. It was aimed at mankind. The whole world will repudiate it, and stigmatize it as a deed without a redeeming feature. It was not the deed of the oppressed, stung to madness by the cruelty of the oppressor; it was not the avenging hand against the heart of a despot; it was the exponent of a venomous hatred of liberty, and the avowed advocacy of slavery.

[Mr. Beecher illustrated the point by a report of the interview between Governor Pickens and Lieutenant Talbot, a few days prior to the attack on Fort Sumter, wherein Pickens admitted that the South had really no cause of complaint; but that the leaders, hoping to deceive the people, had manufactured the necessary indignation at Northern insults, and were determined to separate, even though confessedly without good grounds.]

"*Fourth.* But the blow has signally failed. The cause is not stricken, but strengthened; men hate slavery the more, and love liberty better. The nation is dissolved, but only in tears, and stands more square and solid to-day than any pyramid in Egypt. The Government is not weakened, it is strengthed. How readily and easily the ranks closed up. We shall be more true to every instinct of liberty, to the Constitution, and to the principles of universal freedom. Where, in any other community—the crowned head being stricken by the hand of an assassin—would the funds have stood firm, as did ours, not wavering the half of one per cent?

"After four years of drastic war, of heavy drafts upon the people, on top of all, the very head of the nation is stricken down, and the funds never quivered, but stand as firm as the granite ribs in the mountains. Republican institutions have been vindicated in this very evidence. God has said, by the voice of his Providence, that republican liberty, based upon universal freedom, shall be as firm as the foundation of the globe.

"*Fifth.* Even he, who now sleeps, has by this event been clothed with new influence. Dead, he speaks to men who now willingly hear what before they shout their ears to. Like the words of Washington, will his simple, mighty words be pondered on by your children, and children's children. Men will receive a new accession to their love of patriotism, and will, for his sake, guard with more zeal the welfare of the whole country. On the altar of this martyred patriot I swear you to be more faithful to your country. They will, as they follow his hearse, swear a new hatred to that slavery which has made him a martyr. By this solemn spectacle. I swear you to renewed hostility to slavery, and to a never-ending pursuit of it to its grave. They will admire and imitate his firmness in justice, his inflexible conscience for the right, his gentleness and moderation of spirit, and I swear you to a faithful copy of his justice, his mercy, and his gentleness.

"You I can comfort, but how can I speak to the twilight millions, who revere his name as the name of God. Oh, there will be wailing for him, in hamlet and cottage, in woods and in wilds, and the fields of the South. Her dusky children looked on him, as on a Moses come to lead them out from the land of bondage. To whom can we direct them but to the Shepherd of Israel, and to his care commit them, for help, for comfort, and protection. And now, the Martyr is moving in triumphal march mightier than when alive. The nation rises up at his coming. Cities and States are his pall-bearers, and cannon beat the hours with solemn procession. Dead—dead—dead—he yet speaketh! Is Washington dead? Is Hampden dead? Is David dead? Now, disenthralled of flesh, and risen to the unobstructed sphere where passion never comes, he begins his illimitable work. His life is grafted upon the Infinite, and will be fruitful now as no earthly life can be.

"Pass on, thou that hast overcome! Your sorrows, oh people, are his pæan! Your bells, and bands, and muffled drums, sound in his ear a triumph. You wail and weep here—God makes it triumph there. Four years ago, oh Illinois, we took him from your midst, an untried man from among the people. Behold, we return him, a mighty Conqueror! Not thine, but the Nation's--not ours, but the world's. Give him place, ye Prairies! In the midst of this great continent, his dust shall rest, a sacred treasure to myriads who shall pilgrim to that shrine to kindle anew their zeal and patrioism. Ye winds, that move over the mighty spaces of the West, chant his requiem! Ye people, behold a martyr whose blood, as articulate words, pleads for fidelity, for law, for liberty."

At the conclusion of the discourse, during which many of the congregation were affected to tears, Mr. Beecher offered another Prayer—a Hymn of Victory was sung—and the services closed with a Benediction.

ADDRESS BY GENERAL HIRAM WALBRIDGE.

At a large meeting of the congregation connected with Dr. Dowling's church, New York, General Walbridge was introduced, and delivered the following noble address on the death of the President:

GENERAL WALBRIDGE'S SPEECH.

"The history of a nation is nothing more or less than the biography of its distinguished sons. Whenever, therefore, a citizen of any community has attained such a position as to concentrate within his own person the affections of his countrymen, whatever affects him, for the time being, affects the State. And whenever such an individual is transferred to that list which makes up the record of the distinguished dead, just in proportion to the extent of his influence while living will be the respect paid his memory by those who shall come after him. The just appreciation by posterity of those who have rendered eminent services either in the Cabinet or in the field, is one of the strongest incentives to virtue and moral worth—an obligation which it is the highest duty of society to protect and cherish. Thus impressed, the American people since the assassination of their lamented President, with hearts overflowing with sadness, have gathered in their primary assemblages in every section of the Union, to pay appropriate tributes to the memory of the great and good man who, springing from the loins of the people, without adventitious aid, by the force of his eminent virtues, his patriotic services, his strict adherence to principle, and the fidelity with which he pursued his convictions on all questions affecting the interests of the State and influencing the destiny of the people, rose to the highest dignity recognized in the land. The peaceful death by the ordinary course of nature of a citizen occupying such an exalted position, and invested with such honors, would at any time awaken the sensibilities of the people. It is not strange, then, that the national emotion is stirred from its innermost depths at the brutal and cowardly act of the murderous assassin, under circumstances so peculiar as those which surrounded the recent death of the President of the United States. But mysterious are the ways of Providence. Called without solicitation on his part to discharge the high duties incident to the Presidential office at a period of unexampled bitterness in our political history, just as he comprehended the period had arrived when he might tender forgiveness to the great body of the people who had been induced to engage in the rebellion—reserving for subsequent consideration whatever action the Government would feel called upon to take in reference to the leaders of this foul conspiracy—for purposes unknown to us the Great Infinite, at such a moment, suffered the hand of the assassin to take the life of the Chief Magistrate. But who is there that will say it has thereby taken the life of the nation? For all realize at this moment, even amid this unbroken lamentation, and before the mortal remains of our illustrious President are confined to their final resting-place, that this last dispensation of Providence has only the more thoroughly strengthened the fixed determination of the American people to preserve intact their liberties and perpetuate their government to those into whose keeping in the future is to be confided the control of Constitutional government. Upon two former occasions in our political history, the second officer in the Government has been called upon to discharge the duties of Chief Magistrate. How widely different the circumstances that have attended the death of the late President, who by this wicked rebellion had been prevented from exercising his legitimate functions as President over a large number of States that were in revolt? Yet at the moment when the murderous blow was struck, he stood within sight of the promised land. He realized, doubtless, that if Providence was to continue his existence, the latter portion of his second Administration was to be marked by the recognition of his authority over all the States as they existed antecedent to the rebellion. It is true, that when he departed from Washington to visit the headquarters of his most illustrious commander, just previous to that wonderful series of events which terminated not only in the surrender of the rebel capital, but the capitulation of the vetern army of the so-called Confederacy, many anxious prayers were offered to heaven that, in his journey in the confines of a district so recently infected with treason, that his life might be spared, and that no murderous blow might be inflicted, which, robbing him of life, should deprive the people of their legitimate representative. When consequently he returned from his late mission, to be himself the bearer of the good tidings of the complete overthrow of the rebellion, and to give to the nation assurances that peace was not so far distant, his return to the Capital was hailed throughout the Nation with notes of acclamation and praise. Had we not reason to believe that our great and good President, protected by Providence, bore a charmed life, not simply for himself, but as the representative of twenty millions of people, engaged in the benificent mission of commending to the world the benefits of free republican institutions. Man proposes, but God disposes. That was the instant which Providence had selected to terminate his earthly existence. May we not reasonably conclude that the measure of his greatness was complete, and that no lengthened years—no subsequent exertion—no additional labors, could add to the dignity and the greatness of a life so pregnant with usefulness and renown? Such a legacy for the unborn millions that hereafter shall speak his name and bear his praises, as the representative of the American people, who finally guaranteed Republican institutions to the Western Hemisphere? Washington severed the colonies from Great Britain—he aided to lay broad and deep the foundations of the Republic. But the civilization of that age was not adequate to found institutions of government which should meet all the requirements of that higher civilization which should come when human slavery was to be everywhere regarded an element hostile to the true interests of a great, free, and Christian people. Where the labors of Washington terminated, the labors of Lincoln began. Washington formed a Republic which assumed to recognize political equality. But while it declared that all men were free and equal, it recognized within its limits an institution of human bondage. Washington was permitted to expire, surrounded by mourning relatives, in the tranquil shades of Mount Vernon, conscious by his own reflection that the hour of his mortal existence had been attained. How unlike the death of our illustrious President. In the enjoyment of perfect health, seeking that relaxation essential for the strength of his faculties, after the arduous labors in which he had been engaged, without a moment's note of preparation, in the twinkling of an eye the bullet of the assassin pierced that majestic brain, whose workings had wrought out the permanent prosperity of this great people; and whose judicious counsels had borne us triumphantly through the most gigantic rebellion recorded in history.

"It is true a single arm directed the accursed bullet, but the murderous purpose which could conceive such an atrocity could only result from the stifled enmity of that barbaric institution, which for centuries had enslaved millions of the human race, and had inaugurated within the boundaries of the Republic of the United States an oligarchy of crime which fattened on the sweat and toil and blood of the victims over which it exercised such material power. But no single death can expiate this great crime. Our beloved President was the representative of freedom and of free Government. He will live in history as the exponent of American Republican Constitutional Government. His murderous assassin was the Representative of that accursed Rebellion, and his name will live in immortal execration, as the exponent of the conspiracy which had for its object the overthrow of the Government of the United States, in order that another government might be formed in this Christian age resting on the basis of human Slavery. Lincoln shall live with Washington in immortal renown, while Booth and Davis shall forever stand in the same record of infamy to provoke the indignation of the virtuous and good. Each were the representatives of their respective civilizations. Washington and Lincoln illustrated the genius of free institutions—of a Government which recognized individual political equality—which had for its object the recognition of the rights of man—which made labor dignified—which secured for all men equal privileges, and which founded a government which permitted the humblest individual, by the exercise of virtue, sobriety, industry, and integrity to attain the highest dignities of the Republic. Davis and Booth represent that false civilization which has for its object the institution of a Government which divided society into classes—which made the interests of the many subordinate to the interest of the few, and which, while claiming to be a Government of freedom, was the most grinding, odious, military despotism on earth—a Government whose power was employed to enslave a dependent race—which degraded labor in order that a favored few, discarding the Divine injunction that by the sweat of his brow man should earn his bread—placed itself in conflict with our Divine religion, and in conflict with all the elements on which the prosperity, peace and welfare of the State can safely rest; a semi-barbarous civilization, incompatible with the fundamental principles on which the republic is based; a civilization which caused Davis to attempt the overthrow of his country, with the utopian idea that he could rear another government which, claiming to be free, was to retain within its limits that refractory element which had cursed the Republic of the United States from the day of its origin to the day when the illustrious deceased by his verdict declared that within the limits of the United States, slavery should no more exist forever; a civilization which stimulated this wicked and murderous assassin to fondly imagine that by the death of the great and good President of the United States he might thereby aid the falling fortunes of the so-called Confederacy—if, indeed, he was not stimulated by the ignoble purpose of living forever in history by connection with Mr. Lincoln's death, as Judas lives in infamy in conjunction with the Prince of Peace, whom he betrayed. It is impossible to conceive what test our institutions should be subjected to in order to prove their ability to meet any emergency that may arise. Twice involved in foreign war, the

Government of the United States have indicated the strength and power of institutions based upon the intelligence, virtue, integrity, and power of the people. The question, however, still remained—was such a Government as adequate to suppress domestic treason as to resist foreign aggression? The Government of the United States, led by its noble, kind-hearted President, proved itself adequate to this emergency, and henceforward Republican institutions will be regarded as capable of suppressing domestic treason as any form of government recognized among men. And yet it seems to be the will of heaven that when this was accomplished, and the grave responsibilities that cluster around the punishment of the bold, wicked, unscrupulous conspirators who have inaugurated this gigantic treason had arrived, another was to be selected to determine the measure of justice which should be meted out to them. One whose whole life has been familiar with the machinations by which the conspirators organized a public sentiment, having for its object the overthrow of the Government of the United States. Let us rejoice that that selection has fallen upon one who brings to the discharge of his high office a long and arduous career of unbroken fidelity to the interests of the masses, to the amelioration of whose condition he has devoted the best energies of his existence. Thoroughly familiar with the demoralizing effects of that institution whose continued existence was a wrong to the industrial classes of the whole nation, to him may be well awarded the high prerogative of inaugurating those great reforms essential to the continued prosperity of the people as they emerge from the desolating influence of the terrible internecine war through which we have so recently passed. But we must not forget that even this strong arm is powerful only as it is invigorated with the strength and confidence of the people. Thus sustained, who shall measure the greatness and renown which awaits the administration of the Government upon which we are about to enter. Called to exercise power under circumstances so grave and unexpected, enough has already transpired to assure the public confidence that the interests of the people and the honor of the republic will be safe in the hands of the present Executive. Indicating his future policy, as he points to his past illustrious and persistent record, foreign Governments may learn that hereafter the policy of this nation is to be that early inaugurated by Washington, which sought to advance its own great interests without any entangling alliances abroad: and equally assuring them there must be incorporated upon this continent no institutions unfriendly to the continued advancement of the Government of the United States; while the masses abroad can equally appreciate that the President of the United States will be glad to welcome here all those who desire to change their material condition and advance their material prosperity by availing themselves of the benefits of that beneficent legislation, which secures to each man a home—a measure which owes its success to the sagacity and foresight of President Johnson more than to that of any other living man. He early comprehended that through the agency of the 'Homestead Bill,' if it could once be established, he might make an inroad upon the oligarchy of the South, who recognized slavery, and by its agency fomented the treason which ultimately struck for the overthrow of the Government. The people of the United States themselves are to be assured that justice, though tempered with mercy, will, nevertheless, be executed upon all who have sought to take the life of the nation, and that treason must be regarded the most odious crime recognized in our social and political system."

As a fitting close to this volume, we append the following powerful article, on ABRAHAM LINCOLN, written by Henry Ward Beecher, for the New York Ledger, and published in that paper of May 20th, 1865. We think it is the best utterance on the great topic of the day which has yet seen the light of publicity. In addition to its power and eloquence, and splendid philosophical analysis, it contains some startling facts which will be new to most people.

ABRAHAM LINCOLN.—BY HENRY WARD BEECHER.

The last act of the sublime drama has at length been finished, and the most wonderful spectacle of the age, or perhaps of time, has been completed!

Mr. LINCOLN'S assassination is not a single act, but the last of a series, of which it forms the consummate whole. It is seldom that history of itself falls into such natural and dramatic periods as may be marked in the wonderful tragedy of five years! It will be seen, too, that the excitement of feeling, at each step seeming to have reached its bounds, still rose, until in the last grand catastrophe it surpasses all that man conceived possible or endurable. And among the many other things demonstrated by this civil revolution, is the capacity of communities to endure profound excitements prolonged through wide periods of time. The excitement of the Kansas struggle was only a preface to the higher glow of the Presidential canvass of 1860. But that was itself inferior to the profound anxiety and feeling of the period between November, 1860, and March, 1861, during which Secessionism developed into civil war. When, in April, 1861, Fort Sumter was assaulted, all feeling before seemed tame, compared with that fire of patriotism which swept the land. That feeling consolidated into a determination which the various defeats and victories of four years had no power to change. The flame-like character of popular feeling was changed, but only as wood that blazes, at length grows even hotter yet when it becomes coals.

In this last year of the war, as victory upon victory, East, West and South, foretokened the glorious consummation, the nation grew more joyful, until, on the fall of Richmond and the surrender of Lee, it seemed as if the people had expended no vital force in former emotions, but burst with all the freshness of unwasted hearts into the luxuriance of tropical joy. Was it possible that human nature could bear another and greater strain? No one would believe it who had not seen the grief, horror and indignation of the weeks following Mr. LINCOLN'S death. The sorrow was like the rolling in of an ocean tide. It quenched the exultation of victory, and the joy of anticipated peace, as completely as a brand is quenched when thrown into the sea. Men forgot that they had been glad. The banners and decorations of victory were left to mingle with exhibitions of mourning, and one could not tell whether the vast pageantry said, "Victory is swallowed up in Death," or "*Death is swallowed up in Victory.*"

No voluntary sign of sorrow was half so striking as the unconscious silence of that ever-roaring city of New

York! A half million people thronged the city on Monday and Tuesday, and filled the streets to suffocation. Yet the presence of the MIGHTY DEAD kept all so still and gentle, that a bird flying over would be unscared by noise, as if it were midnight, or a Sabbath day.

A martyred President was the city's king. His pulseless hand stretched out a sceptre, which awed all men to silence!—Before that Hearse enmities died, jealousies and rivalries coiled and hid, pleasure forgot its rules, avarice its toils, and for more than a week, the imperial city that disdained always before to be subdued to any common sentiment, now silently and humbly watched and waited, in all its streets, to offer homage and affection to him, when dead, for whom alive it would never give a vote!

As a private citizen, Mr. LINCOLN would have lived respected, and died lamented as a kind, faithful and honest man, and slept with hundreds of others, in a few years undistinguishable. He had no such gifts of power as would have raised him, in spite of circumstances, to eminence. His was not a brain that dominated. His will was firm, but not executive nor despotic. His mind was broad and strong, but slow and laborious in its methods. Truths did not break upon him with flash and instant revelation. He saw them far off, obscurely, as nebula, and like an astronomer, he resolved them only by patient observation. Thus, he suspected things to be true long before he was sure, and he was sure long before he had made out the whole matter with distinct accuracy. He travailed with truth in long gestation, but when once it was his he loved it with intense parental instinct. His wisdom was moral wisdom. His power and success sprung from moral qualities. It was not intellect but manhood that ennobled him.

Mr. LINCOLN is, perhaps, the most eminent instance since the days of Washington of a man made great by the inherent wisdom of true goodness. And such a nature can scarcely be delineated apart and separate from the events of that history which called out his virtues. This is particularly true of Mr. LINCOLN for two reasons: First, because his excellence did not assume the form of a few bold qualities, but was the sum of many simpler qualities maintained under great trial and provocation. And secondly, because we are now but just beginning to see the moral character of those bad men against whom he acted.

That so soon in our history the dark crimes which stained the later periods of Roman and mediæval European history should have taken possession of the leading Southern conspirators, could scarcely be imagined by those who have been accustomed to study the effects of slavery upon the masters, in the light of servile apologists, rather than under the guidance of great principles of human nature.

It is now known that a separation of the South from the North was resolved upon as a matter simply of political ambition, without any reference to supposed grievances; that the allegations of injury, of fears for the future, of political injustice, were deliberately framed by Southern leaders as a means of exciting and uniting the common people of the South, while their authors, among themselves, never pretended to believe in the truth of their own representations.

There is, also, the gravest reason to believe that all moral restrictions were yielded, and that crimes the most infamous were deliberately employed as the means of promoting the bad ends of these conspirators. Those who know most of the interior of affairs, scarcely doubt that Harrison was poisoned, that Tyler might fulfil Southern plans of war with Mexico. With even stronger conviction is it affirmed that Taylor was poisoned that a less stern successor might give a suppler instrument to Southern managers. Who doubts, now, that it was attempted to poison Buchanan at the National Hotel, and leave Breckinridge in his room? It is a matter of verified history that efforts were made to take off Mr. LINCOLN before he should be inaugurated. And now, the whole world is astounded by the hideous crime by which he has been removed from life.

This perspective is needed to reveal the characters of the chief men in this superlative infamy of secession. We do not believe that the Southern *people* were privy to such crimes, or that all who became conspicuous in the Southern councils and armies knew of such things, but that the real leaders were men steeped in crime, and capable of the utmost infamy, we have not a doubt.

To misguided millions, unconsciously inspired and led by men of such a spirit, Mr. LINCOLN addressed the policy of kindness and conciliation for nearly two years. It was as if a Christian martyr had appealed to the reason and kindness of lions and tigers in a Roman amphitheatre!

But, though now known to have been misplaced, we must study Mr. LINCOLN's forbearance and gentleness, from his own point of view. Never was man less disturbed by passion, by party heats, by anger or rashness. In the wild excitements which raged on every side, amidst treacheries, defeats, and gloom, amid lukewarm patriots, imbecile generals and divided counsellors, he maintained on the whole, a straightforward and elevated course.

After Mr. LINCOLN with long and painful hesitation determined to issue his *proclamation* of Liberty, a change took place, not only in the general policy of Government, but in the success of his administration.

He relinquished the impractical hope of conciliating the South; he boldly assumed the reserved powers of Government. He called to his aid men of nerve in the field, and, freed from the toils of a doubtful expediency, and of nice practical management, he fell back upon broad moral grounds. There his true nature had full scope; and every hour after he conformed his policy to moral reason rather than to precedent, and political device, and hackneyed expedients, Mr. LINCOLN grew strong and successful. Then began those victories which in spite of reverses eat into the Southern power, and consumed its strength. Then Mr. LINCOLN took his place in the estimation of eminent men in all the world, as a true and great statesman. Then, for the first time in two-score years, America had a President that embodied and really represented the principles of her history and her institutions!

Mr. LINCOLN'S re-election, in the midst of a civil war, by a people burdened with taxation, smarting with bereavements, assailed by factious partisans infected by the poison of Southern sympathy, is one of the remarkable events of history! Even more than the sublime homage of universal grief which waits upon his death, it is a monument of honor to his name. The unerring judgment of an intelligent common people passing by the dangerous glitter of military renown, with singular discretion put the State again into the hands of a citizen proved to be honest, discreet, patient, wise and thoroughly good.

The tragedy of Mr. LINCOLN'S death gives to his name a heroic renown which his plain and unassuming manners might have missed. He has taken his place among the few great men of history. Not a stain of cruelty rests upon it. It is all luminous with unquestioned gentleness and lenity. Not one act of his administration can be censured as inspirated by Vanity, Self-interest or Pride. Amidst the disturbances of civil war and the confusion of a vast revolution, he is seen standing always temperate, calm, and wise. All his messages, letters and addresses may now be searched for a line or a word whose spirit can be rebuked, now, in the elevation and solemnity of these hours which follow his death!

We write another name in the Calendar of Great Men. We place new trust in institutions and principles which breed such men among the common people!

His form has fallen but his name abides forever. The bad men who have filled our times with infinite mischiefs are passing away to eternal infamy. The Patriot and Christian Statesman, in bright apposition, shall rise to shine forever, like the stars in the firmanent.

THE END.

www.ingramcontent.com/pod-product-compliance
Lightning Source LLC
LaVergne TN
LVHW010216110826
845151LV00004B/1099

9781425527891